THE
VOICE
OF
TERROR

Figure 1.   Johann Most, 1886
Kean Archives, Philadelphia

THE
VOICE
OF
TERROR

A Biography
of Johann Most

Frederic Trautmann

Contributions in Political Science, Number 42

GP

GREENWOOD PRESS
Westport, Connecticut • London, England

Library of Congress Cataloging in Publication Data

Trautmann, Frederic.
  The voice of terror.

  (Contributions in political science, no. 42
ISSN 0147-1066)
  Bibliography: p.
  Includes index.
  1. Most, Johann Joseph, 1846-1906. 2. Anar-
chism and anarchists—Germany—Biography. 3. Anar-
chism and anarchists—United States—Biography.
  1. Title.   II. Series.
HX898.M67T7   335'.83'0924 [B]   79-8279
ISBN 0-313-22053-0

Library of Congress Catalog Card Number: 79-8279
ISBN: 0-313-22053-0
ISSN: 0147-1066

First published in 1980

Greenwood Press
A division of Congressional Information Service, Inc.
88 Post Road West, Westport, Connecticut 06881

Printed in the United States of America

10 9 8 7 6 5 4 3 2 1

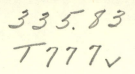
To
Elizabeth Delano Whiteman
and
Maxwell Whiteman

The history of terrorist tactics in America largely centers about the career of Johann Most.

Robert Hunter, *Violence and the Labour Movement*

CONTENTS

Contents

ILLUSTRATIONS

PREFACE

Johann Most—anarchist, libertarian, communist—is easy to like and easy to hate, for he did nothing halfway. When he wanted to drink, he got drunk; when he sought change, he urged revolution; and when he wanted an official removed, he demanded murder. Drink, urge revolution, and demand murder in private? He preferred the street, the platform, and the press. According to your bias for or against radical politics, agitation, and personal excess, you can call him a hero or brand him a villain; many have done both. I have viewed him in his time, described him, set forth his beliefs, told what he did, and showed what he suffered—all, I hope, with proportion. In the interests of proportion, and to be fair, I let him speak often for himself: the voice of terror was also the voice of honesty; he spoke without equivocation or scruple. Letting him speak for himself, I have translated those of his words that appear here, and nearly all appear for the first time in English. Having heard him out, after studying him in his time, balancing hero against villain, I should award him Robert Louis Stevenson's "Here lies one who meant well, tried a little, failed much:—surely that may be his epitaph, of which he need not be ashamed."

Frederic Trautmann

Glenside, Pennsylvania
June 6, 1979

ACKNOWLEDGMENTS

Thanks:

To Beth Trautmann for perceptive reading and insightful comment. Again and again, with honesty to scholarship and sensitivity to style, she returned chapters: "No, Frederic—I want your *best.*" And I rewrote them again and again.

To Maxwell Whiteman, polymath. He suggested that the biography of Most should be written and that I might write it. His superb collection of books and trenchant criticism proved invaluable.

To Temple University Library's capable and congenial Marie Adams. What should I have done without her?

To the Library's Jeanne Sohn and Wayne Maxson. They worked wonders.

To David Bartlett and Kenneth Arnold of Temple University. They said the right things the right way at the right time.

To J. Richard Abell, Arlow W. Anderson, Paul Avrich, Samuel Blitz, Fred Buchstein, David T. Burbank, Arthur Calabrese, Andrew R. Carlson, Richard Drinnon, Will Durant, E. Ivy Fischer, Harold M. Green, Ernst K. Herlitzka, James Joll, Walter Laqueur, David M. Neigher, David Porter, William O. Reichert, Gerald Runkle, Edward C. Weber, Mark Weber, Stanley B. Winters, George Woodcock, and Howard Zinn—for information, advice, and encouragement.

Not to have finished this book would have betrayed them; they helped write it. May it repay their trust and fulfill their expectations!

AUTHOR'S NOTE

The organization of this book is both chronological and topical. Parts I, II, and III cover the major periods of Most's life: 1846-1882, 1882-1892, and 1893-1906. Within a part, each chapter treats a chief aspect of Most's life during the respective years. Thus, Chapter 1 recounts personal life, 1846-1882; Chapter 2, political beliefs, 1846-1882; and so on. For detailed chronology of Most's life straight from beginning to end, see Appendix A.

INTRODUCTION

Herr Johann Most of New York, famous the world over as an Anarchist.   The Boston *Globe*, March 30, 1891

His particular contribution was to introduce and spread the doctrines of anarchism in America at a time when labor dissatisfaction was at its highest.

Cecyle Neidle, "Johann Most," in *Great Immigrants*

Johann Most was called "The Wild Beast." To the St. Louis *Post-Dispatch* he looked like a bulldog ready to bite anybody who crossed him. Two emperors, the Iron Chancellor, a queen and her prime ministers, five presidents, and the London and the New York *Times* loathed and dreaded him. He said, "Tyrants and the bourgeoisie hate me. I hate tyrants and the bourgeoisie. Our mutual hatred is my pride and joy."

He attacked church, state, custom, privilege, convention, and law. He fought authority with the ultimate strategy of the one and the weak against the many and the strong: terrorism. Break rules, he taught, until you can make your own—or perish; and the golden rule shall be, "No rules!" He said, "I was in rebellion before I was out of diapers."

Max Nomad classified him an apostle of revolution and named him "The Preacher," a "terrorist of the word." For, though Most spent forty years urging propaganda-by-the-deed, he was a propagandist-of-the-word: editor, publisher, pamphleteer, and orator. He accepted Marx's first duty of a revolutionary leader: show the masses their destiny and teach them their task. When he was not lecturing twice a week about anything from assassination to Zwingli, he was on agitation-tours of hundreds (if not thousands) of miles, giving speeches, cajoling, twisting arms, buttonholing, and exhorting—and writing much of his weekly *Freiheit* meanwhile. "His greatest exploits," said the St. Joseph, Missouri, *Gazette*, "have been those of the tongue."

He did not originate ideas. As a thinker he was a cipher, a shadow of Marx and a burlesque of Kropotkin. Marx and Kropotkin were first-class thinkers; Most, a first-class agitator. He vivified their ideas and put them across. To him, words made revolutions: "Change minds to change society." He devoted his life, and lost it, to changing minds. He was the *voice* of terror.

Nothing but prison and illness muffled him. Prison muffled him often; police dragged him from the platform. Illness muffled him seldom; he refused to admit illness. Death silenced him in the middle of an agitation-tour, and the career that began in a Vienna coffeehouse ended in a Cincinnati crematorium.

He started with labor agitation in Austria, continued in socialist politics in Germany, advanced to party leadership and a seat in parliament, and fled the Anti-Socialist Law into exile in London. He struck back with terrorism. His machinations informed *The Princess Casamassima* and *The Secret Agent*. James and Conrad laid these novels in the London underground and gave them characters like him. "Assassination is a concomitant of revolution," he said, "if you choose to call the forcible removal of insufferable oppression, assassination." Britain could stand such a mouth no more than Austria and Germany had stood it. Austria and Germany had jailed him, and Britain jailed him. All three declared him destructive of security at home and dangerous to stability abroad. When released, he picked up the pieces Scotland Yard left of *Freiheit* and sailed to America.

He toured the country, united the Left, and set it on the road to Haymarket Square. He revived the Black International, convened its congress, and drafted its manifesto. He wrote *The Science of Revolutionary Warfare*, the classic manual of terrorism. His battle cries—"Hail Anarchy!" and "Long live the Revolution!"—landed him three more times in prison. Then death took him from behind while he looked ahead. Between 1882 and 1906 the New York *Times* had published over 100 articles about him. Hundreds of newspapers published his obituary; many cheered the end of this "foulest of creatures."

In hostile newspapers he is red-mouthed, unwashed, wild-eyed— the snarling fiend who aims a pistol with one hand while hurling a bomb with the other. Between his teeth he grips an arsonist's torch, burning, ready to set fire to a church or a bank. From his pockets daggers and hypodermics protrude; from his hatband, recipes for poisons. He rejoices at groans of the magistrate stabbed, gloats over the policeman axed, beams at the child maimed, and kicks the face of the clergyman castrated. He savors burned gunpowder, delights in flaming buildings, drools for blood, craves to claw flesh, longs to gouge eyes, and hatches dynamite plots. He dreams of capitalist corpses stacked like cordwood. Gleefully he fixes a target, a maternity ward full of mothers and infants, and hisses: "As you suckle, so shall you suffer." He shrieks: "Down with law, down with society, down with peace, decorum, and order! Up with ANARCHY!"

What anti-anarchists believed, anthropologist Cesare Lombroso confirmed: Most's physiognomy, displaying "acrocephaly and facial asymmetry," was of the criminal type. Most was therefore criminal anarchy incarnate.

Yet he went to prison never for what he did, always for what he said. He was not the practitioner, only the voice of terror. He never did anything more violent than swat flies. He said, "To hell with America" and "Love has enslaved the world—hatred shall liberate it." Samuel Gompers said that Most talked violence but practiced prudence.

To Emma Goldman, a miserable childhood, frustrated ambitions, and a scarred face made Most harsh and inexorable. He was not to blame for his defects and shortcomings; he could not help what he had to be. She would excuse his faults, therefore, and emphasize his virtues; ignore his failings and celebrate his accomplishments.

Others did not agree. He proclaimed himself a revolutionary (they said), yet he resisted change in his own habits; he was no better than the reactionaries he despised and vilified. He was so wishy-washy that he called anarchism madness, then became an anarchist. He said, "So soon will the future belong to the proletariat that optimism today may seem pessimism tomorrow," and thereby spoke contrary to a flood of evidence. His speeches accordingly were mindless harangues and dizzy diatribes, amounting to the braying of an ass. After nearly a quarter-century in America, he could not accept the fact that he was the aging leader of a dying movement in a country hostile to him and inimical to his ideas. He deserved to be likened to one deluded borer attacking a field of alien corn. With him, Irving Howe said, "fervor counted at least as much as sense." Marx and Engels, angered by his opposition to their ideas, said he was not a revolutionary but a huckster of revolutionary phrases. August Bebel said, and James Huneker underlined, that he drank too much and could not hold it; he put his hopes on a glass of beer and blew them away with the foam. The Lord Chief Justice of England, saying he incited others to crime but was too craven to commit the crimes himself, sentenced him to sixteen months at hard labor. The New York *Times* said he had no dignity, no nobility, and no charity; he was the epitome of envy and malice, craft and cowardice, and vacillation and venom; regulated minds rejoiced to see this enemy of society in the dock. George Woodcock said he provoked hysteria and perpetrated bloodshed "with the sinister enthusiasm of a malevolent and irresponsible child."

But his partisans said he was kind to animals, generous, a loyal friend, compassionate and dedicated. Thousands cheered him, thousands mourned him. Like Carl Sandburg's dynamiter, he ate steak and onions in a German saloon, and laughed and told of wife and children and the cause of the working class; in many newspapers a national enemy, yet a lover of life, of free laughter, red hearts, and red blood everywhere. Rudolf Rocker said he was the herald of social revolution; his example, a huge flaming beacon, would guide the oppressed along the thorny path to a better future; he earned a place in the people's pantheon of heroes.

Karl Kautsky, once Most's partisan, later his opponent, called him intelligent, adroit of tongue and deft of pen, enterprising, industrious, and well-read, yet superficial, tactless, arrogant, sensation-seeking, short on discipline, and irresponsible: a farrago of contradictions and an enigma at once respectable and despicable.

Yet nearly everyone has forgotten him. His sole previous biography, in German, appeared in 1924.

Hero or villain, he does not deserve to be forgotten. In Morris Hillquit's judgment, the modern revolutionary movement produced few as picturesque. Indeed, "Most, the picturesque" was the phrase of a dozen newspapers. To Emma Goldman he was "the famous Johann Most, the leader of the masses." The London *Times* put him "in the front rank of American anarchists." James Joll advanced him to first in that rank.

Most himself said, "No anarchist forces his views on another; that's authoritarian." Here he would say, "Reader, read for yourself and make up your own mind—authority be damned!"

PART I

On the Rise: Europe, 1846-1882

1

PERSONAL AND PRIVATE

1831: Weavers rebel in Lyons, France.

1833: The first German-speaking workers' educational association is founded at Biel, Switzerland.

1836: Fourierists are active in France and Belgium. Icarian communism and Buchez's cooperative movement begin.

1848: Louis Blanc presents the proletariat in the provisional government after the February revolution in Paris. They are crushed in street fights four months later.

1848: Revolution shakes the German states. Communists agitate in the Rhine district. Peasants are liberated in Austria.

1850: Revolutions fail. Reaction sets in throughout Europe. Reaction in Germany, shaped and directed by Bismarck, perseveres until 1918.

1858: Workers' educational associations federate in Switzerland.

1864: The first German section of the International is founded.

1867: The first Swiss section of the International is founded.

1868: Swiss workers' educational associations join the International.

Children put through a crucible usually perish. The child
who survives, though marked, has been hardened to bear
the worst. I survived, marked and hardened. Most, *Memoirs*

An untended childhood accident which caused his facial disfigurement, a scorned and lonely youth spent wandering
from place to place, sometimes starving, sometimes finding
odd jobs, was natural food for an animus against society. In
Most it sprouted with the energy of a weed.

Barbara W. Tuchman, *The Proud Tower*

Johann Most's mother, a governess, left work when the children
pointed at her belly and snickered. Johann Most's father, a clerk,
spent more than he earned. City Hall refused them a license, because applicants had to prove solvency. Later, when people said,
"What you want is against the law, Jack," Johann Most said, "I
was born against the law."[1]

Cholera killed his mother. His stepmother made him polish
boots, carry water, wash clothes, build fires, clean lamps, and run
errands—before breakfast. She fed him enough to sharpen appetite but not enough to blunt hunger. Famished, he begged and stole.
She beat him. Terrified, he ran away, but returned, crying. She beat
him. The harder he cried, the harder she beat. When he sulked, she
beat. When he did nothing she could fault, she beat on principle.[2]

One night in the depth of winter, when he was sick, she sent him
to bed in an unheated room. His cheek froze. For five years, on the
left side of his face, abscesses suppurated, flesh rotted, and bone
corroded. Quacks prescribed nostrums. He wore hot and cold
poultices, swallowed oils, drank teas, sipped broths, and gulped
liquors. He was redolent of a sickroom and stank like a morgue.
Physicians gave pills, dusted and smeared his cheek, pulled his
teeth, and gave up. Professors of medicine read more books, shook
their heads, and concluded: "Cancer. Incurable. *Incurable*." Finally
a surgeon opened the cheek from temple to mouth, scraped, chiseled,
and pounded, and sewed the wound shut as if it were a rip in last

year's dungarees, administering five doses of chloroform meanwhile. The operation lasted an hour and a half; the effects, a lifetime.

From that face—cheek twisted and mouth pulled into a wrinkled, malformed, lurid knot—people turned in revulsion and recoiled in disgust. In that face doors to jobs, hearts, and dreams slammed. He had to show it to an intolerant world until his beard covered it. Even then his left side was his dark side; and he turned it from all eyes, especially the eye of the camera. Later, American jailers shaved him and displayed their "ugly, little, mad anarchist" like Barnum's latest freak.[3]

As cruel as the stepmother and as vicious as the jailers was the teacher who loved to make pupils smart. This potentate of the classroom kept canes, straps, switches, whips, sticks, and clubs behind the desk and chose one to inflict the pain to fit the offense. For each error in arithmetic, four lashes of a whip; and pupils who could not add or subtract learned to multiply. With each lash he intoned, "Evil lurks deep in the breast of the child, but the whip drives it out." He was soon committed to an asylum.

Although in school Most won prizes for scholarship, real education began at home, where his natural mother had started to teach him to read and write and to love learning. He taught himself thereafter. Contemptuous of frivolous pastimes, he spent evenings reading history, science, and the classics of literature. To live was to study, and he studied until he died. Books lined his room from floor to ceiling, row on row. Of newspapers he could not get enough. Acute and learned in the history of socialism, anarchism, and the labor movement, he was a keen and diligent observer of their progress. How to pass time was never a problem, not even in prison; he spent it reading, studying, and writing. For them, time was ever short. Always he ordered himself to "make more time for study!" Always he asked jailers for "a bigger table, please; more space to study, thank you!" Offered extra pay to work longer at binding books, he said he wanted, not to bind books, but to read them. Called lazy for not earning more money, he said he wanted, not to be rich, but to be human.[4]

Religion was taught at school, and he learned to hate it. He dodged confession and persuaded others to do the same, and teachers and priests flogged him. To the end of life a militant atheist with the zeal of a religious fanatic, he knew more Scripture than many clergymen knew—the better to confound them with contradictory passages. To him, religion was "The God-Pestilence." His essay by that title has been continuously in print in several languages since its publication in 1887.

His attack on religion did not stop at the theoretical. He persuaded friends in Hermannsburg, a pious community, to forget church and spend Sundays in taverns. Stories of how they caroused multiplied until tavern keepers refused to serve them. He retaliated. On the evening of sermons on the missions, a big evening, with farmers coming from miles around, he drugged the watchman and sounded the fire alarm. His friends planted in the congregation screamed: "Fire!" The congregation dispersed. Next morning the watchman was still asleep, under a tree, with the alarm-horn fastened to his head and pointing up like the horn of a rhinoceros.[5]

In secondary school he excelled in subjects he liked and quarreled with the teachers of those he disliked. He was beaten and locked up. In revenge he spread snuff. Teachers coughed and sneezed. He was beaten and locked up again. Then, like Roderick Random, he formed cabals. He organized a strike when the teacher of French laid punitive work on a cabal, and was expelled.

For two weeks he pretended to continue, going out mornings with books under his arm, worried. His stepmother learned the truth from a classmate. Cane in hand she confronted him. His father stepped in. After a quarrel she decreed that the good-for-nothing leave home. His father, white and shaking, called him into the bedroom and said, "I turn your fate over to you. Choose a trade, then go learn it. And may your rebelliousness be pounded out of you."

"How about bookbinding? It will do until I become an actor."

His father sneered and pointed to the mirror. "Look at yourself. That *face* on the stage? Don't make me laugh."

Bitterness tinged the few words they exchanged henceforth. Johann left home soon, to learn bookbinding, and never returned. When a journeyman, he passed through his home town but avoided his father. Years later, when Johann ran for parliament, his father gave speeches for the opponent.

Johann became a bookbinder but wanted to be an actor. He read about acting, studied plays, memorized roles, watched actors, recited poems, and declaimed in public. When people listened, he took heart. In his mind's eye he saw himself on the stages of the world and imagined crowds rising to their feet, dazzled, applauding him. So he dreamed for years, and over and over he said to himself, "Someday, when my face is right. . . ."[6]

But facts obtruded. For a life on the boards he was too ugly, and his face would never be right. An actor? A star? You? People scoffed. "If a pregnant woman saw you, the child would be born a monster," and "You belong in an institution." He told Emma Goldman: "The cruelty of it, the bitter cruelty! To think that I could have been in Possart's [the German actor's] place, perhaps even greater than he, but for my dreadful face." She, remembering his superb rendition of Baumert in Hauptmann's *Weavers*, said: "How different his life might have been had he been able to satisfy that craving! Recognition and glory instead of hatred, persecution, and prison."[7]

Apprenticed to a bookbinder named Weber, he had to bind from 5:00 in the morning until sunset in summers and until 10:00 at night in winters. "Slavery," he called it. He and Weber quarreled again and again, because he refused to attend church and sneaked away to see plays instead. When Weber, smoldering about impiety and truancy, found a defective brush in a glue pot, Weber threw the pot at him, called him "criminal," and released him six weeks early. Weber became Most's archetypal capitalist, a brute worthy of every rage workingmen could vent on him.

Most left Augsburg, a journeyman in the craft that attracted a race of itinerant revolutionists. Seventeen years old and weighing seventy-five pounds, but proud to be a journeyman and happy to be away from the tyrants of his youth, he felt ageless and grand. The thought of freedom made him shout and sing, and the sky seemed to smile at him—until he got a job.

The workday was fourteen hours long. Rooming in an attic, he shared the bed with another journeyman and many bugs. The event of every sixth week was the changing of the sheets. A pounding on the door routed him out at 5:30 A.M. Breakfast was one-seventh of a loaf of bread and a cup of black coffee. At noon: thin soup, scanty vegetables, and a scrap of overcooked meat. Overcooked to kill the maggots, he said. For dinner: three slices of sausage and a few potatoes. An evening out? Unthinkable. At best, a week's thrift let him splurge on Sunday with three or four hours in a coffeehouse, sipping coffee he wanted to gulp, nibbling the roll he wanted to bolt, and reading every newspaper from front to back.[8]

Dissatisfied, he moved to Prussia. But Prussia went to war with Austria, and he joined thousands thrown out of work. Horrified, he watched Prussia hoist flags, beat drums, roll out cannon, and sound bugles. Disgusted, he saw Prussians, even those idled by war, march along singing the national anthem. Enraged, he called the king a cannon-fodder princeling and Bismarck a gangster. A band of Prussians heard him, chased him over hill and dale, like hounds after a fox, and might have killed him had he not eluded them. A few days later he barely escaped arrest for lese majesty.

He went from job to job in fifty cities in six countries. Life among the international lowly nourished and matured an idea that serving under Weber had planted, the idea that distress was the lot (unjustly) and meaningless were the lives (unnecessarily) of the working class, his class. War must stop, and he wanted to stop it. Poverty must end, and he determined to help end it.

In Vienna, fired and blacklisted for staging a strike, he was unemployable. A friend loaned him tools to make hatboxes and matchboxes, notebooks, and cigar cases, which he hawked evenings and Sundays, until the police stopped him because he had no license. He refused to get one, and they ordered him off the street.[9]

Thus he ended his years as a craftsman in the way he had begun his years as an apprentice: in rebellion. Since childhood he had learned to hate authority in all forms and to despise prevailing social conditions, and he hated and despised them until death.

He also hated and despised women. He wanted relations with them, but they looked at him and flinched. Answering whispers that he was having an affair, he compared himself to the husband of the lady in question: "He's a strapping fellow; I'm a weakling. He's handsome; I'm ugly. How can a ghoul be a Don Juan?"[10]

Taking refuge in misogyny, he remembered his stepmother as bigoted, avaricious, cruel—a bitch. In Vienna he spoke unkindly of only one fellow socialist, Marie Podany. He said she was an ignorant chatterbox, a camp follower, who stuck a grubby finger into every pie, provoked jealousy, caused rows, and raised stinks. The problem was, she was a woman. His expletive for people who irritated him, regardless of their age or sex, was "toothless old women!" The females in the American anarchist movement he called "sexual opportunists," who wanted to catch men. The problem was, they were women first and anarchists last. To him, wine was poetic; love, prosaic. Love left a bad taste. "To women my heart is nailed shut."[11]

His beard transformed him. Women took front seats at his speeches. After one speech, a tall young woman with purple flowers in her hat crowded closest to him. "All during his outpourings, she had watched him with a devotional look. She evidently thought him a prophet."[12]

He put misogyny aside and married Klara Hänsch, the beautiful daughter of a gendarme in Chemnitz. Theirs was a misalliance that soured him again and for years on women. During his imprisonments she had affairs with other leaders of the Saxon labor movement. Quarrels erupted over "Who will sleep with Klara tonight?" The community gossiped, and he was the pitied cuckold. The Mosts' children died young, followed by Klara herself, after seven years away from him.[13]

Another marriage and some liaisons were attempts at love that begot hate. His affiliation with Emma Goldman was platonic, then sexual, then platonic again. "Love, love—it's all sentimental nonsense," Emma heard him say; "there is only sex!"[14] She rejected him, they resumed relations, he broke with her, and she horsewhipped him.

In his forties, having come to want a mate to admire him, bear children, keep house, and dote on him, he married Helen Minkin, an immigrant working girl he had lived with for years. She gave him two sons. Strong, warm, and in love with him, she changed his ideas on marriage and family. He loved her and his sons. She became his good right arm, helping run *Freiheit* and writing articles as blistering as any he aimed at the worst of enemies. On his deathbed he called for her. When he died, her grief was profound. She sustained *Freiheit*, in memory of him, for three years.

Still, to him, home and family were secondary to the Cause. With Fred Hoff of *The 42nd Parallel* he believed the revolutionist

"oughtn't to have any wife or children, not till after the revolution." He cared nothing for his brothers and sisters. He valued
friendship less than the Cause; anything contrary to the Cause he
condemned even in a friend. He told friends, "If you're not for It,
you're against me."[15]

In coming to love the Cause, he typified radicals of his time.
Many had been intelligent, sensitive children whom hardship, neglect, scorn, or brutality had imbued with hatred that drove them
to aberrance. Often they were neglected, scorned, or brutalized
because they were deformed. This deformity, or something else
beyond their control, had usually shattered an ambition. Shattered
ambition, deferred hope, and unfulfilled opportunity made anarchists of some of the cleverest men Terence Powderly ever knew.[16]

Of those who influenced Most's ideological development, Victor
Dave (rumored to be the natural son of the president of the Belgian
revenue board) spoke little of childhood, giving the impression it
was painful. August Reinsdorf was the academically gifted boy who
became a sullen typesetter and an angry anarchist. Wilhelm Hasselmann's father deserted Hasselmann and after his mother died
he grew up in the family of a rich uncle, who treated him as a
poor relation.[17]

Nascent radicals, frequently impoverished, became more resentful when, after they saw and felt disparity between rich and poor,
propaganda told them poverty was unnecessary and wrong. Because
they rejected religion or had never known it, and groped for meaning and sought faith elsewhere, they followed leaders who seemed
to have answers; they saw God in Karl Marx. But not even Marx
had answers for the pathologically embittered: they often killed
themselves.[18]

Most contemplated killing himself. Had he not adopted principles he could live for, he might have been buried nameless in a
potter's field, dead by his own hand.

The final juncture of a career toward leftist radicalism was a
crisis of belief that pushed to the brink of despair. Were despair
not bypassed, suicide followed. Those who bypassed despair often
did so with the help of an apt and timely propaganda that explained
what produced the crisis and told how to turn from despair to hope.

Most, in crisis, pondered hopelessness and injustice. The working class, his class, was exploited. *Why?* Something should be done. *What?* Wrongs should be righted. *How?* Somebody was at fault. *Who?* There had to be remedies. *Where?* Things might improve. *When?* He felt problems but could not articulate them, sensed abuses but did not understand them, and asked questions but failed to answer them. Where to turn?

At the brink of despair he groped for meaning, craved direction, and sought faith. The quest had neither far to go nor long to last, for he was in the Jura region of Switzerland. Known as much for its radicals as for its watches, the Jura produced more socialists and anarchists per capita than anywhere else in the world. Passini in *A Farwell to Arms*, speaking like the watchmakers of the Jura, says: "We think. We read. We are not peasants." Amid a blooming buzzing profusion of radical ideas, Most was soon poring over Lassalle and cogitating on Marx. He attended a workers' festival in La Chaux-de-Fonds, the home of a local of the International; its orators preaching the gospel of the *Communist Manifesto* made sense to him. They saw what was the matter and knew what should be done and persuaded him to their position. His crisis was over.

He joined. The newest of the local's seventeen members, he was also the hardest-working. He recruited more members himself than the rest of the local recruited together. He was elected secretary.

"For the first time, and from then on, I was human," he said. "The private Me shriveled, and the Philistine in me dried up. The cause of mankind was my cause. Mankind's every stride filled me with joy. Every setback, caused by reaction, roused my hatred of reactionaries and their institutions. . . . I acted, thought, spoke, and wrote according to my feelings, I found satisfaction, and I was delighted to be alive."[19]

So profoundly had the Cause seized him, so far did leftist ideals carry him, that forty years as a partisan of labor and a champion of the Left brought him self-doubt but once. Driven by abuse and repression to the alien shores of Britain, which looked as problematic to him as to Julius Caesar, he pondered the course and the goal of his life. He was a stranger in a strange land, without money, friends, or employment; he didn't even speak the language. Not merely had he no home, he had no homeland. Germany had locked him out forever.

The pessimism of the Devil grabbed me [he said], and the Devil tried with pointed horns to show me the path one must take when one wants to get ahead, ahead to a comfortable fireside, ahead to enjoyment, ahead to a life without danger, struggle, feuds, and betrayal by "friends."

Get ahead, get ahead—that would have been a reasonable urge, had I been willing to entertain it. Three times—in Chemnitz, Mainz, and Berlin—after I pitched a tent, hailstorms of political battles broke overhead and smashed the tent. And then the hurricanes of my public life drove me from place to place, a pauper. One can get one's fill of such an existence; thousands have.

Imprisonment in Vienna and Suben, in Chemnitz and Zwickau, in Berlin and Plötzensee—not to mention sojourns in other dungeons—in short, six years behind bars, eating at stingy tables, could grind down a stronger man than I. (My weight: 105 pounds.) And then exile!

Enough surely to prompt second thoughts about the direction of my career. But I held firm. I wanted neither to reach "the good life" nor to earn a livelihood in the usual sense. I had to do what I did because in my brain an obsession pounded: *The Revolution must happen!*[20]

Converted to new ideals, which had given him reason to live and delight to be alive, he wanted to dedicate in gratitude the life thus regained and devote the life thus enriched to advancing those ideals. He wanted to agitate the Revolution. As events in Austria told him Austria was the likeliest place, he went to Austria.

NOTES

1. *Freiheit*, 20 June 1896. *See also* Johann Most, *Memoiren* 1:9-10.
2. Most, *Memoiren* 1:16-17. Most, *Acht Jahre hinter Schloss und Riegel*, p. 8.
3. Most. *Memoiren* 1:13-15. "Ugly little mad anarchist" is a composite of words that American jailers used to describe Most.
4. Ibid. 1:39-40. Emma Goldman, *Living My Life*, pp. 29 and 66.
5. Most, *Memoiren* 1:43-46.
6. Ibid. 1:18-20. *Acht Jahre*, pp. 8-9.
7. Goldman, *Living*, p. 380. *See also* Goldman, "Johann Most," p. 159.

8. Most, *Memoiren* 1:21-31.
9. Ibid. 1:38-63.
10. Ibid. 1:56.
11. Ibid. 2:63. *See also* Goldman, *Living*, pp. 33-34.
12. *New York Times*, 18 April 1887, p. 1. *See also Pittsburgh Post*, 19 November 1894.
13. Most, *Memoiren* 3:27-28. Most, *Die Bastille am Plötzensee*, p. 5. Ernst Heilmann, *Geschichte der Arbeiterbewegung in Chemnitz und dem Erzgebirge*, p. 84.
14. Goldman, *Living*, p. 72.
15. *Freiheit*, 20 August 1896.
16. Terence Powderly, *The Path I Trod*, pp. 200-201.
17. Karl Schneidt, "Vom jungen Anarchismus," pp. 622, 672, 718.
18. Ulrich Linse, *Organisierter Anarchismus im deutschen Kaiserreich von 1871*, pp. 22-24.
19. Most, *Memoiren* 1:52-53, 55.
20. *Freiheit*, 20 June 1896. *See also* 20 July 1896 and 7 January 1899.

2
POSITIONS AND PERSUASIONS

1750: The Industrial Revolution begins. It regiments society into antagonistic classes. Workers destroy machines and factories. New laws protect machines and factories.

1784: Fever in Manchester cotton mills prompts the recommendation that children not work at night or over ten hours a day.

1838: Chartism starts its pro-labor agitation.

1844: Weavers rise in Silesia. Hauptmann and Heine later immortalize the weavers' plight.

1848: Marx and Engels, in the *Communist Manifesto,* proclaim the revolutionary role and predict the indubitable triumph of the working class.

1849: Schulze-Delitzsch founds associations of shoemakers and joiners, the first of his cooperative movement.

1863: Lassalle begins the General German Workers' League, in opposition to Schulze-Delitzsch's Liberal party.

1864: Marx assumes leadership of the International. Lassalle dies in a duel.

1867: Marx publishes *Capital.*

The house of socialism has many rooms, and many different
ideas have, at one time or another, sheltered under its roof.
Sidney Pollard, *The Idea of Progress*

I am a socialist. I shall be a socialist, to the best of my ability, so long as I live, no matter what. I shall hold high the
banner of socialism forever.
Most, at the trial for high treason: Vienna, 1870

The revolutionary spirit is mighty convenient in this, that it
frees one from all scruples as regards ideas.
Joseph Conrad, *A Personal Record*

SOCIALIST

"A feeling very generally exists," wrote Carlyle, "that the condition of the Working Classes is a rather ominous matter at present;
that something ought to be said, something ought to be done about
it."[1] Labor, like a sleeping lion pricked by the goad "of social infamy, of heinous laws," was "breathing shorter and beginning to
stretch its limbs and stiffen its claws."[2] Marx and Engels' specter
was haunting Europe—the specter of Communism. Hermann
Schulze-Delitzsch feared the worst unless labor's radical tone
modulated. He said and did something: he sponsored workers'
educational associations.

Most joined one. It displayed Schulze-Delitzsch's portrait, kept
a library of insipid books, taught capitalism, and sponsored lectures
on freedom through unity, the virtue of saving, the value of hard
work, and liberty through education. The portrait irritated Most
(*ugly*, he thought), the library annoyed him, and the lectures put
him to sleep—to be awakened by patriotic, sentimental, and nos-
talgic singing and a game of questions and answers.

The singers crooned about a beloved home where a spring
bubbled at the door, or belted out stanzas in praise of fatherland,
or warbled over the love of God and the sanctity of His holy name.
The game posed questions on the origin of the crab louse, the ex-

traction of the eyes of chickens, the significance of the Paris World's Fair, and the distillation of cleaning fluids. A disgusted Most said "Nonsense," and stamped out in a huff.[3]

Meanwhile, handsome, dark-eyed, intense Ferdinand Lassalle was organizing the first German workers' party and accelerating the German labor movement. Lassalle was a scholar, an agitator, and a swashbuckler—a supreme example of each. Bertrand Russell estimated him: "No one has ever understood the power of agitation and organization better . . . no one has ever possessed in a greater degree the power of flogging men's minds into enthusiastic activity."[4] Money had talked for Schulze-Delitzsch, a wealthy industrialist, but Lassalle broke him; labor took eloquence and magnetism as legal tender now. Scornful hands turned Schulze-Delitzsch's portrait to the wall ("Away with that counterfeit!"), and he died in obscurity. Fully Lassallean only a short while, Most held years longer to Lassalle's idea of a powerful state and of the iron law of wages. Lassalle's flamboyant agitation he imitated for life.

Lassalle began while Marx was hardly known. When Marx's ideas circulated at last, they were half-heartedly received, for Lassalle was flashy, Marx jejune. So the *Communist Manifesto* languished, *Capital* seemed doomed to antiquarian interest, and Marx appeared destined to go down as the busiest dry-as-dust in the history of the British Museum. He turned pages in silence while crowds across the Channel adulated, "Lassalle! Lassalle! Lassalle!"

Actually, Marx was ahead of Lassalle. Marx was laying down theory that would endure as doctrine, and respect for his doctrine proved stronger than adulation for Lassalle. Respect gained and authority established, Marx assumed leadership of the International Working Men's Association—agency for the overthrow of capitalism and instrument for the propagation of Marxian socialism. His emissary Wilhelm Liebknecht established locals and won affiliates in Germany and Austria. Where few had known of Marx, the International made him famous; his ideas, pent-up for years, burst forth with a vengeance. Lassalle died the same year; and since Lassalle's personality had been a main attraction, with Lassalle died the reason many belonged to the General German Workers' League, and the damage to the League could not be repaired. After

Lassalle crumpled into a pool of his own blood, nothing stood in the way of the International's progress.

Locals of the International burgeoned. Agitators, by oratory, pamphleteering, and word of mouth, saturated audiences with Marxist doctrine. True to the vigor of the *Communist Manifesto*, the agitators framed the doctrine in impelling style.[5] Marxist orators moved Most to Marxism.

As Lassalle's socialism differed importantly from Marx's only in how to effect the state and how long to retain it, so Most and comrades changed from Lassalleans to Marxists as easily as they changed to new shoes.[6] To Most, Lassalle was the model agitator and Marx the preeminent theorist. Most admired, not Lassalle less, but Marx more. Most the Marxist edited a popular version of *Capital*, and Most the social revolutionary and anarchist kept much of his Marxism for life.

He helped organize a Marxist social-democratic party in Austria, which endorsed this program:

1. A philosophy of labor:

• Since labor produces all wealth and all culture, while society makes productive labor possible, the fruits of labor belong to society, which shall distribute them to labor according to need and in the interests of the commonweal.
• The dependency of the working class, caused by capitalist monopoly of the means of production, results in misery and oppression.
• The emancipation of labor requires that the means of production become the property of society and that labor be cooperatively regulated.
• The emancipation of labor must be the task of the working class, for all other classes are reactionary.

2. The ideal government is a free people's state. To Most, this meant a republic or a constitutional monarchy, in which the citizens were social, political, and legal equals and in control of their own affairs.

3. The principles to effect the ideal government:

• Opposition to present political and social regulations, unjust to the highest degree.

• Abolition of class distinctions.

• Destruction of the present means of production (the wage system), organization of cooperative societies, and payment to every worker the value of his work, to eliminate wage slavery.

• Letting a democratic state guide economic emancipation, thus answering the social question by answering the political question first.

• Making the Social-Democratic Workers' party a solid front, and letting each member exercise his influence for the good of the whole.

• Affiliating with the International, to acknowledge that loyalty must be to the proletariat.

4. The policies to guide the ideal government:

• Universal, equal, direct suffrage, by secret ballot, to all men over twenty years of age, in all elections.

• Popular participation through petition, referendum, and recall.

• No more discrimination by class, property, birth, or religion.

• A militia instead of a regular army.

• Separation of church from state and school.

• Education compulsory in primary school and free at all levels of education, in public educational institutions.

• Independent courts, public trials, trial by jury, and judicature without cost to the adjudicated.

• Freedom of press, association, and assembly.

• A normal workday, limited work by women, and no child labor.

• No more direct taxes, but a single progressive income and inheritance tax.

• State support of cooperative trading systems and state loans for manufacturing cooperatives, democratically administered.[7]

Most agitated that program until agitating it got him imprisoned for high treason.

SOCIAL DEMOCRAT

Most believed that Social Democracy was the blueprint for a free and happy society, peacefully, honestly, and honorably arrived at; the party's egalitarian orientation and Marxist principles guaranteed it. He believed that Social Democracy could come to power and turn the blueprint into policy; the party's recent successes and immediate potential assured it. True to his belief, from the death of Lassalle to the passage of the Anti-Socialist Law, Social Democracy consolidated and assimilated the gains of the past, organized and compromised to solve the problems of the present, and planned and acted to secure the promise of the future. To those ends congresses were held, elections won, newspapers founded, and propaganda distributed. In those enterprises he was a leader— the chief Social Democrat, after Wilhelm Liebknecht and August Bebel, and in some ways surpassing even them.

He was the party's unofficial publicist, and what many Germans knew of the party and its program they knew from him. He said, let us begin by accepting as facts that socialism and the labor movement are healthy growing partners, and that the socialist idea is so widespread that its winning of adherents cannot be stopped.[8] This vigor has forced socialism's enemies to retreat to specious arguments and invidious questions.

Enemies argued that egoism prevents a socialist state; people— selfish, greedy, individualistic—are out for themselves alone. In truth, he retorted, people are and always have been cooperative and communal, socialistic. Individualism, never the way of mankind, is an aberration of certain men.

Enemies asked how socialism can pretend to be a philosophy of viable government when a socialist state has never existed. A socialist state, he answered, has been neither possible nor necessary until now. Obeying the economic laws of history, socialism is emerging from capitalism, just as agricultural society emerged from nomadic, and capitalist from agricultural. Capitalistic organization of industry recedes before socialistic mobilization of the proletariat: so history has decreed.[9]

He fumed that his enemies were lying, saying that Social Democrats want to share and share alike, down to the last pair of shoestrings, and intend to abolish marriage, destroy the family, institute matriarchy, betray the fatherland, extirpate religion, annihilate art, and ignore science—after fomenting a revolution, the bloodier the better.[10]

To dispel lies and erase misconceptions, he said, let us tell the truth!

Lies are possible and misconceptions arise because Social De-

mocracy little resembles socialisms of the past and has nothing to
learn from archaic social thinkers. Absurd, if not arcane, were the
notions of St. Simon, Owen, Fourier, and Cabet. Worse were those
of Proudhon, because they were more confused. Unfortunately,
people's attention fastened to Proudhon's sticky language like a
fly to flypaper. Proudhon's slogan, "Property is theft," and his
name for his madness, *anarchy*, though meaningless, were catchy;
and they caught a lot of people. Proudhon, Blanqui, and the conspiratorial clubs of France in the 1830s and 1840s caused people to
think socialism a theory of violent revolution. Blanqui tried to
proclaim the Republic with 300 armed men in Paris in 1839—the
lunatic! And that nonsense endures. Truth is, Social Democracy
seeks power peacefully and legally—rationally—through the established political process.

Accordingly, Social Democracy is not warmed-over mush. This
legitimate socialism originated recently and derives from Blanc,
Lassalle, Marx, and Dühring. Blanc suggested that the state must
institute socialism, Lassalle popularized the workers' manufacturing
cooperative, Marx defined the class struggle, and Dühring realized
that democracy must precede socialism.

Especially, Social Democracy cannot be accused of any "share-
and-share-alike" philosophy; that crotchet was peculiar to communal and utopian socialists. Legitimate socialism espouses neither
division nor sharing but concentration and centralization. Socialism
wants to increase the power created by capitalism, mass it in the
democratic state, wield it over the means of production, shape with
it every facet of society, and thereby improve the lot of humanity.
Of course, concentration and centralization are drastic changes not
to be effected overnight.[11]

Meanwhile, reforms must be sought. Chief among them is a
shorter workday. True, it is not a cure but a palliative; for in capitalism an iron law dictates that wages cannot in the long run amount
to more or less than subsistence. But in the short run a reduced
workday will lessen supply, increase demand, and thereby raise
wages temporarily. Before they lapse, Social Democracy will come
to power and change things for the better, permanently. If employers resist demands for a shorter workday, workers must stand
together, stand firm, stand up, and fight.[12]

And after reform, revolution: realization of the egalitarian ideal, gradually and peacefully, by democratic processes, including elections. Government will become an instrument of the people and hold the means of production; industrial managers as well as political leaders will be elected. Equality will extend to all spheres—economic, military, civil, judicial, educational, administrative, and social. Disparity of income will be abolished. The principle that takes from each according to ability and gives to each according to need will justly equalize income.

Consumption, too, will be socialized. Anyone will get as many of the good things as everyone else. Physicians, clinics, hospitals, schools, libraries, and museums will be free, comparable in quality, and equal in access to all. The theater, made educational, will become a power to cleanse the spirit, improve taste, and sharpen the critical faculty; and it will be free and without discriminatory seating.[13]

Enemies interrupt, he said, by whining, "How is this debauchery to be paid for?" He answered that at first it would be by taxes, perhaps higher than now. But before you bemoan socialism's taxes and their humanitarian use, remember the ten billion marks of capitalism's taxes spent on the Franco-Prussian War. Furthermore, waste will be eliminated. Militia are cheaper than a standing army. Bloodsucking by religion will be stopped, courts and bureaucracy streamlined, and high salaries and expensive privileges and costly prerequisites eliminated. But taxes are only for the transition. When socialism is complete, the government will withhold what it needs before distributing the good life to all.

In other words, moderate sacrifice will produce substantial reward. Indeed, after socialism takes society in hand—that is, puts the means of production under state control, rationalizes employment, and changes the allocation of resources from selfish to humane needs—working life will be reduced, perhaps to ten years, lasting from, say the age of eighteen to twenty-eight, followed by creative and fulfilled retirement.

Enemies continue whining, he said, and raise the specter of overpopulation. Create the socialist utopia and population will outrun food; war, famine, and disease are necessary to keep population tolerable. Nonsense! The world has not begun to produce what it

can produce. Let mankind cooperate, adapt areas of the earth each
to its potential, and create systems of distribution; and not until
centuries hence might people have to worry about how to feed and
where to put offspring. If those problems do arise, socialism will
solve them.

So much for economics. On the social side, the status of women
is the important issue. The relation of men to women determines
man's humanity and fixes the level of cultural development. Men
degrade humanity (hence themselves) by preying on and subju-
gating half the human race. Women must therefore be emancipated.
"A woman's place is in the home" and "She is happiest there" are
false and pernicious ideas rife among men. "Emancipation means
the woman smokes cigars, wears trousers, leaves her family, and
does not work"—false and pernicious again. Rather, socialist equality, the product of logic and investigation (and therefore scientific),
dictates that she be free to do what a man does and be similarly
treated and equally paid. She, too, is "man" in the word *mankind*.
Justice demands that a new genealogy be traced from mothers and
that children take their mothers' names, because paternity is never
certain. Lest woman be relegated to nursing and rearing, to laundering, scrubbing, mending, and cooking—drudgery too long considered "hers"—so-called woman's work will be socialized in laun-
dries, child-care centers, and dining halls; and traveling crews will
clean houses. If a woman in trousers chooses to smoke a cigar, that
will be her affair, and so will her liaison. Manhood suffrage in the
Social Democratic program is temporary. When women, under-
developed intellectually and stunted emotionally because of centuries of bondage, are ready for the vote, they will get it.

Socialism destroy marriage and wreck the family? Remember
that marriage and the family result from historical experience; they
take diverse forms under manifold influences in different places at
various times. Neither any reasonable socialist nor anything in socialist doctrine wants to abolish or retain them arbitrarily. True,
the family in Western society, the model for the State, is the State
in miniature and the source of the State's evils and perversities.
But what changes will be made in the family, especially after women
get their tardy emancipation, remain for men *and* women of the
future to decide.

Enemies, lips sealed by cruelty, say nothing of capitalist barbarity and socialist benevolence. Capitalism tells those who can swim, *swim*; those who can't, *drown*. It exists to oppress and punish; citizens give their substance and sacrifice their lives and get back oppression and punishment. Socialism will not set adrift on the sea of indifference pregnant women, the elderly, the ill, and the crippled; it will provide sanitariums, give professional care, and supply necessary paraphernalia; and it will salary those capitalism calls undesirable. Socialism can do no less; its maxim is equality. Socialism will be the engine of humanitarianism.[14]

The worst of the lies calls the Social Democrats killers and spoilers, *anarchists*! The liars cite the ravings and ragings of Blanqui, proof, they say, of socialism's destructive nature. In truth, Blanqui was a madman who belongs as much to socialism as heaven to hell. Socialism embodies constructive change and inspires creative improvement. Violence and disorder characterize capitalism, not socialism. Look around. Society is capitalist, and violence and disorder abound. Even if socialists want violence, they cannot succeed by violence, as long as they are in the minority. When they become the majority, as is inevitable, violence will be superfluous, for what the majority wants, the majority gets; nothing prevails against the majority. Accordingly, the Social Democrats neither preach nor foment revolution, but underscore the truth and spread the news of socialism. "Therefore," Most said, "I want, not your fists, but your minds! I ask, not for violence, but for knowledge! Only think: the idea shall triumph!"[15]

Yet, ten years later, he wrote *The Science of Revolutionary Warfare*, to teach how to destroy and kill.

RADICAL SOCIAL DEMOCRAT

Newly arrived in London, Most said: "Make no mistake: I was, I am, I shall be a Social Democrat." He began *Freiheit* (Freedom), subtitled it "The Organ of Social Democracy," and in it proclaimed, "Long live Social Democracy!" In early issues it announced, "We intend to display the standard of Social Democracy *fully*" and "We reprint the program of Social Democracy; it is also the program of this paper."[16]

Pages 24 and 25 are in reverse order.

other leaders of Social Democracy, who were changing in the opposite direction. Inchmeal, he was moving toward revolution, they toward accommodation. Therefore they called him *radical*.

They read with horror the first *Freiheit* denunciation of "traitors to the fatherland, the shame of Germany, in the uniforms of the soldier and the priest, who daily manacle the people anew with heavier chains while doing nothing to ease the burdens they heap hourly on the people's shoulders." If not enough paper existed to catalogue the atrocities, their monstrousness could be documented in hunger, legalized crime, hypocrisy, and unconscionable taxes. The article ended with a blast at Bismarck.

Social Democratic leaders read the promise of more of the same, forthcoming in the next issue, and wished Most dead before the next issue. They had decided to obey the Anti-Socialist Law, chart a moderate course, cooperate with the government, and work within the system. He had expatriated himself to escape the Law and was steering an impetuous course, denouncing the government and repudiating the system. While they tried to curry favor with the government, he attacked the government. As he claimed to speak for Social Democracy, his attack roused the government's wrath against Social Democracy, which roused Social Democracy's wrath against him. How Social Democrats wished he would shut up!

A month later, though continuing criticism of the government, he again dissociated himself and the Social Democrats from *Putsches* and *coups de main*. "We are not militants, we are not conspirators, and we do not believe in violence." He agreed with Gladstone that a minority, however able, cannot defeat the majority and that the majority can assume power without violence. "We are revolutionaries, but we want a revolution of the spirit."[18]

Next week he stormed that both government and party condemned him. He supposed Bismarck cursed him once before retiring and three times on arising. He imagined Liebknecht and Bebel threw darts at his photograph, while Bernstein and Hasenclever kept *Freiheit* at commode for reasons other than reading. He began to use the words "violence" and "revolution" as if they denoted right action.

In another month, no longer urging assumption of power through the political process, he advocated incendiary propaganda and sug-

Wanting *Freiheit* to be Social Democracy's official organ, he opened it to Social Democrats. "You want a place to criticize the German police state? Here it is!" He used the party's roll as *Freiheit*'s mailing list. He promised to report the news and interpret it from the Social Democratic point of view. He claimed that *Freiheit* met the criteria for excellence in a party organ through its concentration—everything important in a few pages; proportion—enough space to theoretical and critical articles; viewpoint—bitter and ruthless against enemies of Social Democracy; and goals—freedom and justice for the oppressed. He enumerated what *Freiheit* stood for: "*justice*—and we oppose injustice; *freedom of work* —and we oppose wage slavery; *education for all*—and we oppose ignorance and barbarism; *peace and tranquility*—and we oppose genocide, class war, and anarchy; and *a socialist people's state*— and we oppose the despotic class state."[17] Social Democrats should have agreed with those criteria and accepted that enumeration; they had appeared in Social Democratic newspapers before the Anti-Socialist Law.

Social Democrats should also have agreed with some 100 theoretical and philosophical articles in which he stressed cooperation to replace competition as the hallmark of society, called for recognition of the eminence and mission of labor, and urged concentration of power—political, economic, and social—in the government of a democratic state. He called these goals expedient, just, and obedient to laws of history that decreed socialism for the society of the future.

Thus he declared himself still a Social Democrat, he founded *Freiheit* to serve Social Democracy, and he promulgated Social Democratic doctrine.

What, then, was different? How had what he once believed altered? Why call him radical?

Impatient, impetuous, and impulsive, he fretted at the prospect of evolution. Wait decades or generations, he fumed, for the answer to the social question, which millions deserved *now*? Expect an answer from a parliament that gave Bismarck his Anti-Socialist Law and cowered whenever Bismarck barked? The oftener he phrased such queries, the more his idea of how Social Democratic goals were to be reached changed. Step by step, he differed from

gested violent revolution. He now believed that the masses, to fulfill their destiny, had to act—in ways other than hearing speeches,
reading newspapers, and casting votes.

At the same time, other Social Democratic leaders wanted
nothing but conciliation with the government. While he was beg-
ging, arguing, demanding, and assuming to associate as a leader
with them, they were dissociating themselves from him. "He speak
for us? That twerp? Presumption, sheer presumption: arrogance,
pure arrogance!" Liebknecht, Bebel, Hochberg, and Bernstein—
"the chief trumpeters of retreat," according to a supporter of Most's
in Leipzig—led oral and written campaigns against him.[19] Social
Democracy was not a revolutionary party, they claimed, and therefore Most could not presume to speak revolution in its name.
Liebknecht gave a speech to that effect in parliament itself.[20]

Most argued that Social Democracy was a revolutionary party.
He cited hundreds of articles and speeches. His favorite was Liebknecht's speech of May 31, 1869, in Berlin, asserting, "Socialism
cannot be realized within the present state. Socialism must overturn
the state." Therefore Liebknecht and followers were betraying their
heritage, while he was loyal to it. They might call him radical; he
called himself old guard. Moreover, he said, they in their craven
narrowness could see but two alternatives, conciliation or revolution. They chose the first and fastened on him the outrage of the
second. In truth (he prided himself on speaking Truth), he in his
acute broadmindedness argued for a middle way of propaganda to
unify the masses and prepare them for right action as soon as right
action could be determined.[21]

Away he went then from the other leaders of the party. In March
he spoke of dispatching troops to the social revolution, and in June
of fanning the fires of revolution. *Radical*, a harsh word, was not
the harshest he had with the other leaders now. They called him a
traitor and a troublemaker. He called them dictators and stool
pigeons. In London and a score of places on the Continent, his
followers came to blows with their followers.[22]

Yet the quarrel signified that he saw himself as the Social Democrat with right ideas, trying to prevail against oafs who had some-
how got control. He agreed enough to want to dispute differences.
When he stopped disputing, he had become a social revolutionary.

NOTES

1. Thomas Carlyle, "Chartism," p. 118.
2. Henry James, *The Princess Casamassima*, pp. 232-33.
3. Most, *Memoiren* 1:50-51.
4. Bertrand Russell, *German Social Democracy*, p. 42.
5. Ibid., pp. 46, 54-57, 79-80. William Harbutt Dawson, *German Socialism and Ferdinand Lassalle*, pp. 135-37.
6. Most *Memoiren* 1:51-53.
7. Ibid. 2:36-42. Wilhelm Schröder, ed., *Handbuch der sozialdemokratischen Parteitage*, pp. 464-65.
8. Most, *Der Kleinbürger und die Socialdemokratie*, pp. 1-18. Most, "Utopien," p. 37.
9. Most, "Utopien," pp. 36, 39-40. Most, *Die Lösung der socialen Frage*, pp. 6-12.
10. Most, *Kleinbürger*, pp. 29-34.
11. Most, *Lösung*, pp. 13-26.
12. Most, *Betrachtungen über den Normal-Arbeitstag*, pp. 1-16.
13. Most, *Zum Genossenschaftswesen*, pp. 1-18; and "Die Scheune," pp. 65-66.
14. Most, *Lösung*, pp. 27-42.
15. Ibid., p. 43. *See also* Most, "Utopien," p. 41, and *Kleinbürger*, p. 57.
16. *Freiheit*, 4 January 1879. *See also* Karl-Alexander Hellfaier, *Die deutsche Sozialdemokratie während des Sozialistengesetzes*, p. 47.
17. *Freiheit*, 21 June 1879.
18. Ibid., 8 February 1879.
19. Ibid., 7 June 1879.
20. Kurt Brandis, *Die deutsche Sozialdemokratie bis zum Fall des Sozialistengesetzes*, pp. 58-60.
21. *Freiheit*, 3 May and 19 July 1879. Most, *"Taktik" contra "Freiheit,"* p. 11.
22. *Freiheit*, 19 July 1879.

3

PUBLIC AND POLEMICAL

1840: The Communist Workers' Educational Association begins in London.

1866: Prussia defeats Austria seven years after France defeated Austria; and Austria, fearing internal dislocation, institutes reform.

1869: Wilhelm Liebknecht and August Bebel found the German Social-Democratic Workers' party at Eisenach.

1870: The Austrian government disbands unions.

1871: Prussia defeats France. Germany becomes an empire. The Commune is crushed.

1875: Lassalleans and Eisenachers unite into the Social Democratic party at Gotha.

1877: German socialists win 500,000 votes and a dozen seats in parliament.

1878: Max Hödel (May 11) and Carl Eduard Nobeling (June 3) try to assassinate the German emperor. The Anti-Socialist Law passes in October. Berlin orders Social Democratic undesirables out. Refugees flee to Britain and America.

1879, September: *Sozialdemokrat* begins in Zurich.

1880: The World Congress of Social Revolutionaries convenes in London.

1881, March 13: Assassins kill Alexander II in St. Petersburg.

It was Social Democracy's wildest time. The favorite of the
masses was Johann Most.

Walter Frank, *Hofprediger Adolf Stoecker*

So, on the 26th of December 1878, at ten in the evening, I
decided to hurl a thunderbolt at that miserable state of
affairs. I founded *Freiheit*.   Most, *Freiheit*, June 20, 1896

AUSTRIA

Two lost wars shook Austria to its rotten foundations. National
unity tottered. To ease discontent, reduce strife, and promote cohesion, the emperor ordered reform. Labor, granted freedoms of
association and assembly, organized. Thousands of workers at their
first rally cheered a call to fight for freedom. The first labor newspaper took as a motto: "Proletarians of all countries, unite!" Soon
in Austria, as in all Europe, clocks would strike the hour of Karl
Marx; and Marx's proletariat would strike the factories and workshops of capitalism.

Marx's emissary Wilhelm Liebknecht formed locals of the International in Vienna. When Most heard of Liebknecht's success and
read about the strength of the Austrian movement, he went to
Vienna, saying, "That is the place for an agitator."[1]

Preparation for the stage had equipped Most for the agitator's
role. He had wanted to be a great actor; now he wanted to be a
great agitator. Believing that a great agitator must be a consummate
orator, he enlarged and refined talents needed for the platform—
talents he had in abundance. Reading the playwrights he learned
how and when to be direct or subtle, ironic or sarcastic, funny or
serious and to wield the power of the well-turned phrase, exert the
vigor of the right word perfectly placed, and loose the force of a
vivid figure of speech. Observing actors, he mastered the appropriate movement, the well-timed gesture, the impelling tone, and
the striking glance. He trained himself to fit expression to an audience's mood and to gesture to match the spirit of the speech. Therefore, when the voice of terror boomed, a reservoir of power, a

lifetime of observation, decades of learning, and years of rehearsal were behind it; and it stirred audiences.

In Switzerland at workers' meetings he had debated all comers on any question. In Vienna, attending a meeting every evening and two or three each Sunday, he took part in discussions and rose on the floor to contest speakers. His reputation for rejoinder spread, and his notoriety for invective grew. Eyes widened and jaws dropped when he repeated an opponent's speech sentence by sentence from memory and refuted each. Rivals who feared and envied him complained, "Don't cross Most. He knows the issues backwards and forwards, he throws words like darts, and he hits the bull's-eye every time."[2]

Soon he was giving speeches. He addressed topics foursquare and to each brought something fresh and interesting. Clichés never passed his lips.

"He's big—burly, husky, brawny—a tiger," said reporters after a speech.[3] At five feet three and a hundred pounds, he was big the way Napoleon was big—in presence, in force of character, in passion for a cause, in fierceness of will, in dash. With Most, size was a matter not of dimension and physique, but of mind and spirit. When he spoke, people heard a giant.

Power of address made him popular, as did knowledgeable discussion and skillful debating, faithful attendance at meetings, and concern for issues. Playwrighting helped, too. He wrote for a workers' festival a play satirizing bourgeois society, and it was a hit.[4] Within days he was a candidate for leadership; within months, a leader. His name went up on big red posters, down in little black books, and around in government memoranda.

The government worried. Labor's hotheads met every evening— and on Sundays from morning until night; radical ideas swirled about like snow in a blizzard; and orators spoke more boldly and leaders grew cockier—especially the rabble-rouser Most. Thousands turned out for meetings, voiced unanimity for principles, and stood in concert behind policies. Factionalism there was none. Leaders set and orators proclaimed goals: "Destroy capitalism!" "Make society over new!" The government wondered, "Did our liberality create a monster?" The government stopped wondering when 10,000 workers demonstrated in Vienna.

Most's words rang out the loudest. "Liberalism is a swindle. The clergy are traitors, the bourgeoisie cut the workers' throats, the police and the military stand guard over this mess, and the government says everything is in order."[5] The following morning, newspapers called him insolent and demanded the arrest of the impudent bookbinder. He was arrested for disturbing the peace, summarily tried, and sentenced to a month's close confinement. Defiantly he counted the days until he could speak again.

Meanwhile, labor meetings were forbidden. If they occurred, police broke them up. Artisans, allowed to assemble on matters of craft, were watched—and stopped if discussion became political. Most, a day out of jail, spoke to fellow bookbinders on glue. Police, hearing innuendoes about the government in his words ("a sticky mess"), broke up the meeting and shook their fists in his face.[6]

For six months he and other leaders obeyed the law, avoided the clutches of the police, and planned a demonstration that would prove that labor meant what labor said. At 9:00 A.M. on the day parliament was to open, workers streamed through the streets to the rendezvous, formed a column, and marched toward parliament —50,000 to 60,000 strong, according to rumors that terrorized the city. The police made ready, and the army awaited orders; but both could not have stopped this outburst, short of carnage. The demonstrators intended to drive their point home. Parliament postponed opening.

Massing at parliament anyway, the demonstrators surged around it like the sea around a raft, until they threatened to topple statues, upset monuments, and bring flagpoles crashing to the ground. Disrespectful to locked doors and undaunted by cocked pistols, a delegation handed Count Eduard Taafe, head of the cabinet, a petition for more freedom to organize.

Meanwhile, leaders—Most among them—addressed the demonstrators. His figure caught their attention; his voice fell compellingly on their ears; his words brightened their eyes; and his sentences, in staccato bursts, enflamed their minds.

The delegation reported back that Taafe took the petition but called it unconstitutional. The demonstrators left parliament and marched up and down the streets, singing, shouting, and stamping their feet until the pavement shook and the buildings resounded.

All night, police patrolled and firemen stood by and the army kept watch, while the city cowered behind locked doors. Nobody had seen anything like it.

Most and thirteen others, for their parts in the demonstration, were tried for high treason. Believing the agitator should seize every chance to agitate, he spoke as if the witness stand were a tribune; and he addressed not so much the court as the world outside, and posterity. He played to the gallery, the only audience he would recognize. The prosecutors were able men, Austria's finest; but against him in the art of expression they were amateurs. He punned, coined phrases, and turned the prosecutors' questions into jokes on the prosecutors. The gallery loved it.

"Yes, I gave speeches. Yes, I am a loyal socialist. But if I was a threat to the state, I was a friend to freedom. If I was an enemy of law and order, I was an ally of liberty and progress. If you judge such constructive criminality and such justifiable malefaction and such reasonable transgression wrong, punish me."[7]

He got five years in prison.

From the witness stand he had addressed the world outside, and now it answered. Newspapers editorialized, and people spoke in his behalf. Workers all over Austria erupted in such demonstrations that the government declared workers' associations of every kind illegal. A general strike gripped Vienna. The police, unable to keep order, called in the army. Its display of weapons, including cannon, was in vain. Common soldiers favored the strike, and their officers had to drive them against unarmed strikers as if against the elite of Prussia. Strikers scattered before half-hearted bayonet attacks, re-formed, and continued demonstrating. After three days the government poured on the troubled waters an oil of promises: Most would be released. Demonstrations ebbed, strikers returned to work, but the tides of public opinion flowed as strong as ever for Most.[8]

When he was released, a throng welcomed him. At the train station two burly bricklayers lifted him above the turbulence of waving hands and carried him to a rostrum. He shaded with a comrade's hat his eyes from the sun and looked at the sea of faces. It was calm now, expectant, deferential. It waited, willingly, for his eloquence to ruffle it. His voice rang with new authority, for he had won a proletarian rebel's proudest credentials: conviction of high treason. He thanked the comrades for the reception and urged war against tyranny and exploitation. The comrades cheered.

Newspapers called him brazen and ungrateful, a foreigner, a rascal, and a boor: set free, he insulted people he should have thanked; he was an incubus on Austrian life, a stain defiling the national character, and a maggot feeding on the country's moral fiber.

He throve on these attacks. The fiercer they became, the more he agitated. He outgrew Vienna. Touring the country, he accelerated the movement. In every city from Vienna to Trieste, crowds roared approval, took literature, and subscribed to the party newspaper.

To oratory he added poetry. He had composed it in prison, and comrades had spirited it out on scraps of paper tucked into unlikely and uncomfortable places. One poem, *"Arbeitsmänner"* (Workingmen), set to music, caught on with German-speaking socialists in Europe and America. When he became an anarchist, they disowned him but kept his song, publishing it without the author's name, and sang it until he died, and after.

Comrades were helping him smuggle into Austria poems sent to Leipzig for printing, when a gendarme stopped the smugglers and eyed their luggage. They invited him to the next inn, where he could better examine the luggage. After a drink he found thousands of copies of *"Arbeitsmänner."* He insisted on singing it. They linked arms, lifted glasses, drank, and sang until his head sank to the table. Soon the poems were circulating throughout Austria, and stricter measures were enforced against socialists and smugglers.[9]

In response, Most and comrades agitated more. They proclaimed themselves Jacobins who would exterminate mankind's enemies. In Jacobinian fashion, they wore distinctive caps, blouses, and pins; and they publicly exchanged revolutionary slogans. They called one another "Citizen." The revolution, they said, was imminent.

The government, having seen more than enough of such behavior and heard too much of that kind of talk, classified Most undesirable. When he returned to Vienna from a speaking tour—"Proletarians of the world, unite!" had been his slogan—the commisioner of police sent for him.

"You agitate," said the commissioner. "You preach communism, violence, and revolution. You repay amnesty with ingratitude. Therefore you shall be deported forever."

"Forever?"

"Yes."

"That's big talk. Who thinks Austria will last forever?"

The commissioner's brow darkened and veins in his neck swelled.

"Most, you have five days to get out of the country. Forever."[10]

Most made the rounds of workers' meetings, saying goodbye at each. Thousands cheered him to the railway station. He leaned out of the train, the train started, he waved, and they waved. Their cheers widened and deepened. He looked back as the train drew away—back at bright faces, hands waving, hats lifted, and handkerchiefs fluttering. As years passed, he looked back again and again at the Austrian workers united in a cause, innocent in faith, and convinced of triumph. For ahead lay Germany, Britain, and America; and there, among comrades, ambition and disagreement bred fighting and caused division, and spelled sadness for him.

GERMANY

When Bismarck created the German empire, he mangled the German socialists. They lost thousands to death on the battlefield, lost leaders to imprisonment for opposing the war, lost respect for contesting the formation of the empire, and lost all seats in parliament but one. Dissension split what few socialists remained, and the factions hated each other. In the whole of Bavaria, Most found about a hundred of former thousands. Hatred grew while numbers dwindled. They had not met for months.

"We must rebuild," he said, and took up the Cause with energy that roused the lackadaisical and with vigor that excited the indifferent. He organized meetings, called conferences, and gave speeches across Bavaria. Morale and membership increased, hatred subsided.[11]

But in the flush of postwar patriotism, anyone dared call anything treason. "Treason!" said conservatives, of his speeches in praise of the Commune. "Treason!" agreed the authorities. They broke up his meetings, closed his places of meeting, and drove him out of Bavaria.

He went to Saxony, where there was more freedom of expression, and joined socialist leaders Wilhelm Liebknecht and August Bebel.

A week later, workers demonstrated in Chemnitz against parliament's rejection of the 10-hour day. He gave a speech. "Forget petitions, comrades. Form to fight!"

Local socialists liked it so much they offered him editorship of their *Freie Presse*, the former editor having been jailed. He accepted.

In Leipzig the authorities hated the speech so much they forbade his speaking in Leipzig. When he came to town to test the ban, they ordered him out.

Workers across Saxony, sure that anyone banned in Leipzig must be a hit, asked him to speak. But Saxony's climate of free expression turned frigid. A point at which liberty became license was established, and he passed that point. Libertarians could be tolerated; revolutionaries had to be stopped.

Stopping him was hard. The city of Glauchau, which prohibited any gathering where he was to speak, permitted a rally featuring Hans Meister. When Meister turned out to be Most, the audience cheered while the police pouted. In Meerane, gendarmes surrounded a restaurant and prepared to arrest him; but he was in Crimitzschau, speaking to a packed house. In Reichenbach the police let him speak, intending to arrest him afterward; but he disappeared into the crowd. Searches of every hotel and watches on every exit of the city produced only a forger and three prostitutes.

Meanwhile, *Freie Presse*'s equipment creaked and he labored in a barn redolent of manure. Employees, advertisers, and subscribers there were none. Circulation amounted to what the editor could beg, persuade, or bully; occasionally it reached 200. Debts were rife.

He plugged his nose, published the paper, and gave speeches. Strong phrases attracted advertisers, and broad humor won subscribers. He added a satirical supplement, *Nutcracker*, which attracted more advertisers, won additional subscribers, and further irritated the authorities. Liebknecht objected: "Such language, Most!" Most retorted that he did what he had to do. "You agitate your way and I'll agitate my way." He would get out an issue, ride a train, give a speech, dodge police, nap on someone's sofa, ride a train back, and get out the next issue. "Work more, sleep less, and don't waste a second," he said. In six weeks the *Presse* had 1,200

subscribers; in a year, 3,000. He moved it to a different building:
no more odor of manure.[12]

"His capacity for work and power of agitation breathed a new,
incomparably strong, and energetic life into the party."[13] Infused
with the new life and aroused by his agitation, metal workers struck
in Chemnitz, in the first industrywide strike in Chemnitz's history.
The 8,000 strikers wanted a ten-hour day without reduction of
wages—a bold position, an emphatic request, sure to be resisted
despite the strikers' numbers and pugnacity. At the head of the
strike and behind the demands, Most counseled not to strike until
payday, to have money to stay out as long as possible. Employers
hired scabs and deployed arms. He dispatched leaflets to workers
all over Europe: "Stop scabs. Send contributions." Employers
hired more scabs and circulated anti-strike leaflets. He prodded
strikers with speeches and pasquinades. Police dispersed rallies,
guarded scabs, and arrested pickets. He could not collect enough
money to sustain the strike, and strikers went back to work with
hunger in their bellies and anger in their eyes. He had impelled,
organized, and directed—but lost—one of the important strikes of
the German labor movement.[14]

Undaunted, indeed encouraged by the strikers' sustained anger,
he wrote and spoke to fan discord and renew the strike. In a year,
employers filed forty-three indictments against him; he went to
court nearly every day. Litigation took time and sapped energy,
both dearer to him than money, but all indictments were dismissed
and he went free. Not only did he win his cases, but also, as he
retained no attorney, his forensic eloquence enhanced his reputation in the party.[15]

Soon, when Liebknecht and Bebel went to prison, he became the
party's administrator in addition to being chief agitator. He organized a congress and gave the principal speech, in defiance of police
harrassment. He left Chemnitz and the *Freie Presse* for Mainz and
the *Volkstimme*, and did the work two had done before. Elected to
parliament, he commuted between Berlin and Mainz: MP by day,
editor by night. He gave speeches on tour. He published a collection of songs that circulated with favor in the party. Often he would
not sleep for three days straight. Yet he and his newspaper neither
flagged nor failed. His editorials were peppery, his speeches salty.

If he took on the labors of Hercules, he mustered the power of Hercules to accomplish them. Such was his strength, such his passion, that prison had not sapped his vitality or corroded his mind. "By gymnastics and mental exercise evading degradation," he left prison "in full vigor, and immediately took his place on the platform and in the editor's office."[16]

He was at his best during the celebration of the anniversary of Sedan in Chemnitz.[17] In the morning, patriots festooned their houses with streamers. Protesters, at his instigation, draped theirs with tax receipts. Before noon, on the front page of a *Celebration Extra*, from his pen and press, a parody of "that idiotic Wi-Wa-Watch on the Rhine" denounced patriotism. On the back page the "Song of the Soldier" began: "I'm a soldier but I don't like it." At noon, in a concert of patriotic music, the *Extra*'s rustling irritated the conductor. In the afternoon, colporteurs darted with bundles of it into the front doors of taverns and shot empty-handed out the back. Behind them, patriots and protesters roared and howled as they read it with rage and delight. In the evening, protesters marched through the city, carrying banners and singing from Most's *Proletarian Songbook*. Swarming into the patriots' meeting they booed the orator into silence and hissed him off the platform. Then they cheered Most's oration. Most had turned Sedan Day into Most's day as an agitator.

Thereafter he missed no chance to address mass meetings, and he arranged many himself. He gave rousing speeches, debated (and humiliated) prominent anti-socialists, and attracted national attention. He glorified the Commune. His eulogies turned funerals of Social Democrats into demonstrations for Social Democracy and increased the size of the party. "Low and dastardly elements follow him," his enemies sneered; but in fact, intelligent and upstanding natures joined him, especially as repression worsened.[18] He led a leave-the-churches movement that emboldened atheists and terrified the pious, and 2,000 left the churches.[19] The Emperor himself, exclaiming over "this certain Most," declared that religion must be maintained and Most punished.

But in parliament, neither the majority nor his own party let him speak. The majority so dreaded his eloquence and so hated his invective that majority speakers would not yield to him and the chair refused to recognize him. His party, fearing he would rile the majority and enrage Bismarck, begged restraint and threatened, "Hold your tongue!" Fulminating at being muzzled, he took the floor out of order. The sergeant-at-arms ejected him.[20]

Disagreeing, voters reelected him by more votes than the first time. He edited the Berlin *Freie Presse*, second in importance among party dailies; and subscriptions increased until it rivaled the leader. He wrote for magazines, published pamphlets, and made agitation-tours that took him as far as Switzerland. Shirking duties as an MP, he increased work as an agitator tenfold. Parliament was silly now: "I care nothing for that puppet show."[21]

By 1878 he had agitated workers, stirred coals of resentment, poked embers of discontent, and fanned the resulting anger until Germany grew hot with unrest. The authorities feared his power; after systematic, ferocious, and officially sanctioned repression, he polled 10,000 of 24,000 votes cast for five candidates in the Chemnitz district. Supporters dared appear at a meeting of Empire Loyalists, brave violence, and shout: "Three cheers for Most!"[22] Therefore when Bismarck set out to destroy the Social Democrats, he went after Most.

To Bismarck the Social Democrats were republican, internationalist, anti-Junker, and atheist: against everything he stood for, enemies of his Prussianized Germany. How could he forget that they had opposed his war and put socialist ideals above German glory? Even with the war won and Germany unified into an empire of world power, they fought him. Traitors to Germany, they championed the international proletariat. They rejected his state socialism. In this time of depression they appealed with growing strength to the unemployed; and by blaming him for economic woes they put him in bad repute with the middle class. The cock of the socialist walk seemed to be Most, strutting and crowing and preening—and ready for the imperial axe.[23]

Fed up, Bismarck took against Social Democrats all legal action; homes were searched, meetings stopped, and people detained. But all legal action fell short; it merely harrassed, only maimed; he wanted to kill. Because his government, a coalition, would not agree to extermination of the Social Democrats, nothing less than a national emergency could empower him to smash them. Adept at fabricating a national emergency, he had neither to wait long nor look hard for an Ems telegram.

Max Hödel's three shots missed the Emperor, but the police got Hödel. In his pockets they claimed they found cards naming him a member of the Social Democrat and Christian Socialist parties, a Social Democratic magazine, a subscription list to a Social Democratic newspaper, and photographs of Social Democratic leaders, including Most. Three weeks later, Carl Eduard Nobeling's shotgun blasted twenty-eight pieces of lead into the Emperor's arms, shoulders, neck, head, and face. Bismarck had his Ems telegram. Word circulated that the would-be assassins were socialists. A storm of indignation, like the storm that swept Prussia to war against France, swept Bismarck's Anti-Socialist Law through parliament.

Immediately 150 periodicals were suppressed and 1,200 other titles (including Most's works) banned.[24] Besides choking off the party line, action against the Social Democrats' forty-one papers and fourteen presses threw many leaders out of work. New employment, unemployment, exile, or becoming a police spy—each had its takers; and Social Democratic leadership dispersed. Berlin went under martial law. Bismarck stationed troops on Berlin's Templehof field, to strike down uprisings. Arrests numbered 1,500. The American ambassador warned Americans visiting Germany not to talk politics. Get out of Berlin in twenty-four hours, the police told Most, whose name crowded the top of a list of undesirables.[25]

"Help me," he said to comrades. They turned a cold shoulder, chilled by fear of guilt by association.[26] They did not want to be seen with a man convicted of crimes including high treason; scarcely out of jail, he was again under the eyes of the police. Struggling for survival as Social Democrats, comrades compromised their militancy and strained to keep within the law. They declared the party disbanded. (He snorted: "Disband the party in order to save it? How's that for logic!") They wanted to tiptoe patiently and restore legally, not plunge (his way) headlong into provocation and repression. He was therefore odious, a pariah. He applied for work, looked for friends, asked for help, but heard, "We don't want your big mouth bringing the police down on us. Shut up and get out!"

Government and party and associates and friends against him, unable to find work or peace of mind—what to do but leave the country?

Sailing for London, the haven of exiles, he began his journey westward: via London to New York, via new ideas to new beliefs, westward to social revolution and anarchism.

BRITAIN

Andreas Scheu, Austrian socialist, remembered, "London. There I was at last! Escaping the police of one of Europe's slave states and arriving in one of Europe's freest—I cannot describe my happiness."[27]

British freedom drew refugees from the Continent for decades. Marx and Engels and the Communards preceded Scheu. Then Germany's Anti-Socialist Law drove others, including Most, to London. Frank Kitz, British socialist, recalled, "Crowded with refugees, our hall at times resembled a railway station, with groups of men, women, and children sitting disconsolately amidst piles of luggage."[28]

Defeated in fact, these lonely strangers retreated into talk. Nightly, in their clubs, they maintained

> the cause
> Of truth, in word mightier than they in arms.

The more the refugees talked, the more eloquent they became; practice made perfect. They printed their eloquence and sent it as propaganda to their homelands. From the Continent, into the narrow crowded streets of Soho, had poured hundreds of refugees babbling in foreign tongues; and out of the same streets poured thousands of tracts in the same tongues, bound for the Continent. The Berlin Political Police declared: "The whole of European revolutionary agitation is directed from London."[29]

One club, the Communist Workers' Educational Association, once militant, but lackadaisical when Most joined, was without leadership, insipid, drifting: a card party and a coffee klatsch. He invigorated it and set it on course—hard left. He edited its publications and spoke for it at rallies, and his editorials and speeches were the talk of radical London. Six months after his first speech the Berlin Political Police felt the club's renewed power among London's "monstrous engines of subversion."[30]

Most, chief engineer, ordered full speed ahead. He helped convene the World Congress of Social Revolutionaries. He laid plans and roused enthusiasm for the International Anarchist Congress, and he instigated and directed its pourparler. Pleased by the results, as the IAC endorsed violence as an act of social revolution, he published its proceedings, then worked to convene more congresses.

But his newspaper was his prime concern. Told, "You'll need six months to raise money for the first issue; the comrades have none," he labored around the clock and raised it in three days. He filled the Hall of Science with comrades and, in a voice hoarsened by three days of talking, said he was founding *Freiheit*. "Help me, help me now, help me, please—help me!" They roared *yes* and pledged 600 subscriptions.[31]

He wrote, edited, and set type at home, and distributed from there. The parlor, castellated with bundles of newspapers, was the dispatch office. In the bedroom he corrected galleys and kept records. The kitchen served equally the needs of cookery and typesetting. In any room he and associates might plan an editorial on the castration of the Pope. When police impounded everything pertaining to *Freiheit*, they had to sort ink bottles from beer bottles and separate manuscripts from cheese.

Banned on the Continent, *Freiheit* infiltrated first through the mails. To throw postal inspectors off the track, and every week to force police to get a new warrant to confiscate, he gave the first forty-four issues each a different title. But in the mails *Freiheit* met censorship perfected by long practice and priding itself on thoroughness. When Bismarck threatened to open every letter entering Germany, *Freiheit* had to be smuggled. Up to 4,500 copies of each issue, as well as articles reprinted as pamphlets, were sneaked past customs—in mattresses, until a sharp-eyed inspector heard a crackle. Then the smugglers crammed *Freiheit* into boxes and cans that looked like merchandise and food. Soon, smuggling the paper itself got too tough; and the printing plates were smuggled instead.

Aimed at Germany, Austria, and Switzerland, *Freiheit* also hit

France, Belgium, Italy, Hungary, the Balkans, Poland, and wherever else German was read. Supply could not meet demand. Claiming it passed from hand to hand and was read to pieces, Most held up samples that were creased, smudged, and tattered—read to pieces. Socialists of Pest took it. Radicals of Bohemia read it and looked to him for leadership. Belgian radicals gathered used copies and smuggled them into Germany. Chemnitz police raided the office of *Freie Presse* three months after *Freiheit* began, and seized every issue of *Freiheit*'s initial quarter, including the first, already a collector's item and damaged by eager hands. The Berlin Political Police, hearing *Freiheit* beat the drum of revolution, predicted trouble from this paper that loomed as a force in European subversion.

Freiheit sounded Most's cry to rally the Social Democrats: "Long live the Revolution!" He defined Social Democracy as revolutionary socialism and called himself its spokesman. The old leaders (he said), those lukewarm socialists and bourgeois democrats, were subverting the party's principle of revolution. Many of the rank and file, disappointed with the other leaders and angered by persecution, liked his advocacy of assassination and dynamite. In Berlin a majority of Social Democrats took his side.[32] As Bakunin had sown discord and reaped a schism in the International, so Most was sowing discord and reaping a schism in Social Democracy.

Meanwhile, the other leaders, trying to revive the party and close the schism, scheduled a congress in Rohrschach, Switzerland. Planning to confront them and strike for leadership, he left London secretly, traveled through France incognito, and surprised them. Liebknecht and Bebel, afraid to debate him, cancelled the congress.[33]

He stayed to lecture. Thousands cheered him in Zurich, Basel, St. Gallen, Bern, Freiburg, Vevey, and Geneva. Hundreds swore allegiance to revolutionary socialism.

Liebknecht and Bebel hit back. They called him a burning limb. "Cut him off the trunk of the party!" They denounced *Freiheit* and belittled him. Do not read *Freiheit* (they told the rank and file) but help the police suppress it. Liebknecht scolded, "In asylum across the Channel, behind a pint of porter, you can preach revolution as if it were a game. Such rashness could be overlooked if it did not land the innocent in jail and help extend the siege against us." Change (they told him) or be expelled from the party.

Soon, whispers called him General BoomBoom, signifying he wanted to shoot his way to the Revolution. The whispers became rumors, insinuating that BoomBoom thinks too little and drinks too much. He slinks around London in a red scarf, one hand on a dagger, the other on a pistol. Aping Marat he edits *Freiheit* in a damp cellar. He is an agent of the police. At Plötzensee he tried to kill himself twice; hence *Freiheit* is the product of a sick mind. He loves a Salvation Army officer and for such love will sacrifice himself and forsake the Cause. He has sold *Freiheit*'s mailing list to the police. And that officer is not female.[34]

He believed that Social Democrats originated the whispers. The wilder the whispers, the more he assailed Social Democrats and the more fiercely he oppugned their policies.

To contradict him and to squelch *Freiheit*'s clamor Social Democrats began their own newspaper. *Sozialdemokrat*'s first issues stirred the party and spread hesitation among many who had been for him. What *Freiheit* said, it refuted. It spelled out a Social Democracy to appeal to Germanic ideals—firm, organized, brisk, sober, energetic, disciplined—a doctrine of hard work and self-denial within the law, to renew and restore. Compromise, moderation, and gradualism; reform instead of revolution; the possible rather than the optimum: those were the party's watchwords now. He took *Sozialdemokrat* like a slap in the face.[35]

Finally, in congress at Wyden Castle in Switzerland, the resurging Social Democrats expelled him. He had sneered at such pronouncements before. "What toothless snarls the party emits, like an old cur wheezing its last!" But in this one there were teeth; not only out of the party, he was also to be ostracized. The delegates, who had come to Wyden confused and irresolute, went home clear-sighted and purposeful and rejuvenated the party, bringing back many who had joined him.

Wyden concluded Social Democratic actions against him, all potent. He could neither pretend to represent nor hope to lead Social Democracy now. By Wyden made "more reckless" (he said), "more waspish" than when driven to London, he turned left to social revolution.[36]

He urged terror and expounded propaganda-by-the-deed. "Shoot, burn, stab, poison, and bomb." "Sweep away what would block the social revolution." "Revolutionaries with the courage of your convictions and the sense to assassinate: ready, aim, FIRE!"[37]

Britain, freest country in Europe, let him write with impunity and speak unchecked. But on the Continent, terrorism brought reprisal. Police raised barriers against *Freiheit*. Distributors were tracked down and locked up. Readers were punished. Police incinerators burned hot with hundreds of copies, week in and week out.

In turn he directed emissaries on the Continent—Wilhelm Hasselmann, Victor Dave, John Neve, and others—to band together "the best comrades of a place" into cells. In Vienna, Prague, Berlin, and cities between them and London, cells raised money, gave speeches, circulated pamphlets, put up posters, won converts, and distributed *Freiheit*. To the effectiveness of this network the Social Democrats paid tribute by organizing an imitation, Postal Service Red.[38]

As Most became more militant, more cells formed and grew more violent. They reinforced printing presses and augmented disappearing ink with knives, rifles, pistols, codes, sulphuric acid, strychnine, petrochemicals, and dynamite. Soon, enough cells would be armed and inspired, enough comrades ready to step out to assassinate as easily as they sat down to breakfast, and they would overthrow the governments of Europe. So Most believed. Hasselmann agreed; directly, 4,000 cells in Berlin and 100,000 armed men in the rest of Germany would be set to fight for freedom.[39]

But police saw the peril. Spies infiltrated Most's organization: newcomers and strangers entered unquestioned; investigation was the way of authority, and social revolutionaries hated authority. Moreover, Social Democrats, otherwise at odds with police, cooperated in spying on Most. He drove one spy out of the office with a club, but the rest went undetected.

Then on the Continent a crackdown began. Shipments of *Freiheit* were seized and smugglers jailed. Two girl friends of an emissary, arrested, gave up letters by Most. Wilhelm Ludwig Fleuron, an emissary, led police from *Freiheit*'s office to cells in Paris, Geneva, Zurich, Vienna, Pest, Prague, Breslau, Dresden, and Leipzig—and generated evidence to incriminate half of Most's organization and send Most to the block. Karl Ludwig Klein, an unemployed shoemaker spending money like a sheik, let slip in Brussels that he was going to Germany to assassinate, but never slipped again. Frankfurt police seized explosives and poisons. Berlin police caught August Reinsdorf carrying a dagger near the home of the chief of police. Six months after the crackdown began, police drew in a complex of nets and shoals of evidence and arrested Dave and forty associates, Most's finest. Most's organization was smashed.[40]

Anger drove Most's pen and hatred informed his oratory as never before. He cheered the assassination of the Czar. "Sterling propaganda-by-the-deed!" He thundered, "Let more monarchs be killed!" A rally adopted his resolution that assassination continue "until the last tyrant, the last plutocrat, and the last priest are dead." *Freiheit* celebrated the assassination with a column framed in red, headlined: "AT LAST," and shouting: "Triumph! Triumph!" Justice had dispatched the vilest of beasts; but the carcass of one Romanoff, even if blown to bits, represented merely a moral victory. A monarch a month must be killed until nobody wanted to play monarch anymore.[41]

British authorities did not long ponder this outburst. Liberal and radical newspapers, while opposing prosecution, admitted that what Most said was shockingly unprecedented. The Russian ambassador told the British prime minister that Russia wanted Most silenced. Against Most the German ambassador used his offices, with a vengeance. Most went to the House of Correction at Clerkenwell, saying, "The government respects freedom of the press only as much, and tolerates it but as long, as the ruling class approves it."[42]

A few years later he expressed the same thought, in another courtroom, in greater anger, in a different country: America.

NOTES

1. Most, *Memoiren* 1:57. *See also* Most, *Acht Jahre hinter Schloss und Riegel*, p. 13.
2. *Freiheit*, 25 July 1896.
3. Ibid., 1 August 1896. *See also Arbeiterzeitung* (Vienna), 20 March 1906.

4. Herbert Steiner, *Die Arbeiterbewegung Österreichs*, p. 17.

5. Most, *Memoiren* 1:59-60.

6. Ibid. 1:64-67.

7. Ibid. 2:51-53. *See also* Heinrich Scheu, *Der Wiener Hochverrats-prozess*, pp. 286-87.

8. Most, *Memoiren* 2:56-63. Steiner, *Arbeiterbewegung*, pp. 59-61.

9. Most, *Memoiren* 2:66-67. Leo Stern, *Der Kampf der deutschen Sozialdemokratie in der Zeit des Sozialistengesetzes*, p. 670.

10. Most, *Memoiren* 2:61.

11. Ibid. 3:6-8. Dieter Kühn, *Johann Most*, p. 76.

12. Most, *Memoiren* 3:12, 43-44. *See also Freiheit*, 29 March 1879. Ernst Heilmann, *Geschichte der Arbeiterbewegung in Chemnitz und dem Erzgebirge*, pp. 79 and 92.

13. Heilmann, *Arbeiterbewegung*, p. 63.

14. Rudolf Strauss and Kurt Finsterbusch, *Die Chemnitzer Arbeiterbewegung unter dem Sozialistengesetz*, pp. 19-22.

15. Most, *Memoiren* 3:14-16, 69-70.

16. Max Nettlau, "John Most," p. 13.

17. Most, *Memoiren* 3:16-20.

18. Karl-Alexander Hellfaier, *Die deutsche Sozialdemokratie während des Sozialistengesetzes*, p. 49.

19. Walter Frank, *Hofprediger Adolf Stoecker*, p. 422. *See also* Eduard Bernstein, *Die Geschichte der Berliner Arbeiterbewegung*, p. 353.

20. Kühn, *Most*, pp. 95-96. Ulrich Linse, *Organisierter Anarchismus im deutschen Kaiserreich von 1871*, p. 42.

21. Most, *Memoiren* 3:68.

22. Strauss and Finsterbusch, *Arbeiterbewegung*, pp. 29-30. Ernst Drahn, *Johann Most*, p. 9.

23. Otto von Bismarck, *Politische Reden* 9:22. *Freiheit*, 18 July 1896.

24. Koppel S. Pinson, *Modern Germany*, p. 207. William Harbutt Dawson, *German Socialism and Ferdinand Lassalle*, p. 291.

25. Most, *"Taktik" contra "Freiheit,"* p. 2. Rudolf Rocker, *Johann Most*, p. 61. Karl Schneidt, "Vom jungen Anarchismus," p. 585.

26. Hans-Josef Steinberg, *Sozialismus und Sozialdemokratie*, p. 115.

27. Andreas Scheu, *Umsturzkeime* 3:5.

28. Frank Kitz, "Recollections and Reflections," p. 18.

29. Reinhard Höhn, *Die vaterlandslosen Gesellen*, p. 106.

30. Ibid., pp. 124-25. *See also Freiheit*, 11 January 1879. Schneidt, "Anarchismus," p. 586.

31. *Freiheit,* 27 June 1896 and 7 January 1899. *See also* Kühn, *Most,* p. 127.

32. Hellfaier, *Sozialdemokratie,* p. 111.

33. Schneidt, "Anarchismus," pp. 668-70. Most *"Taktik" contra "Freiheit,"* p. 43. *Freiheit,* 7 January 1899.

34. Most, *"Taktik" contra "Freiheit,"* pp. 15-16. *Freiheit,* 24 May 1879.

35. Eduard Bernstein, *Sozialdemokratische Lehrjahre,* pp. 108-13. *Sozialdemokrat* (Zurich), 5 and 12 September 1880. August Bebel, *Aus meinem Leben* 3:44, 121, 128.

36. *Freiheit,* 4 July 1896 and 7 January 1899.

37. Ibid., 1881: 11 June and 23 July. *See also* Ludwig Brügel, *Geschichte der österreichischen Sozialdemokratie,* 3: 112-13. Max Nettlau, *Anarchisten und Sozialrevolutionäre,* p. 154.

38. Joseph Belli, *Die rote Feldpost,* pp. 69-70.

39. Andrew R. Carlson, *Anarchism in Germany,* pp. 214 and 227. Steiner, *Arbeiterbewegung,* p. 190. Albert Weidner, *Aus den Tiefen der Berliner Arbeiterbewegung,* pp. 54-57.

40. Höhn, *Gesellen,* pp. 43-44, 62-65. Staatsarchiv Potsdam, Rep. 30, Berlin C, Polizeipräsidium, Nos. 8720, 8721, 9892. Gunther Bers, *Wilhelm Hasselmann,* p. 55. *Freiheit,* 7 May 1881.

41. *Freiheit,* 19 March 1881.

42. *Freiheit,* 7 January 1899. *See also* Linse, *Anarchismus,* p. 132. Brügel, *Arbeiterbewegung* 3:163-64. Friedrich Engels to August Bebel, 30 March 1881, Karl Marx and Friedrich Engels, *Werke* 35:174-75.

4
PENALTY AND PUNISHMENT

1849: The Saxons imprison "the dangerous alien radical Bakunin" for a year, sentence him to death, reprieve him, and pass him to the Austrians. They chain him to a wall for a year, sentence him to death, reprieve him, and pass him to the Russians. They put him away without trial for six years. He gets scurvy, his belly bloats, and his teeth fall out.

1870: Austria convicts labor leaders and leftist agitators of high treason.

1871: Liebknecht and Bebel do time for opposing war loans in 1870.

1872: Convicted of new crimes, they are jailed again.

1873: Prussia, completing the penitentiary at Plötzensee, prides itself on the latest in penology and the finest in prison architecture.

1874: Kropotkin is clapped into the Peter and Paul fortress in St. Petersburg.

1879: Louis Auguste Blanqui (1805-1881), released again, has spent nearly half his life in prison.

1880: As anti-leftist opinion runs high, Bismarck wins renewal of the Anti-Socialist Law. A second round of seizures, investigations, censorship, and arrests begins.

Every editor of a socialist paper, and every agitator, knew it
was part and parcel of his calling to go to prison from time
to time.   August Bebel, *Aus meinem Leben*

As he had studied the social conditions of different countries
in his earlier years as a wandering artisan, so he explored
their jails in later life as a traveling agitator.
Morris Hillquit, of Most, in *Loose Leaves from a Busy Life*

In prison and out—that sums up the career of Johann Most.
Cincinnati *Enquirer*, March 18, 1906

OFFICIALS AND POLICE

On September 26, 1872, in a coffeehouse in Coburg, Most opened
the Chemnitz *Tageblatt* beside a cup of coffee. The coffee grew
cold as he read the news that Johann Most, a fugitive from justice,
had gone into hiding.

Fled? Gone into hiding?

Arrest, trial, and incarceration were occupational hazards—as
normal to the terrorist as burns to the baker or cave-ins to the
miner. The peasant listens for the cock at dawn, the terrorist for
the knock at midnight. Handcuffs, truncheons, police wagons, detention centers, courtrooms, jails, prisons—Most knew them all.
Detectives shadowed him, spies searched his quarters, informers
squealed on him, constables rifled his belongings, gendarmes leveled
pistols at him, jailers frisked him, inspectors questioned him, judges
rebuked him, guards prodded him, curiosity-seekers leered at him,
and criminals laughed at him. Still, if he were wanted, he would
go; he kept no revolver at bedside.

He pushed aside the coffee, took out pen and paper, and wrote,
"Bring on the officials and police, conduct hearings, try me, and
lock me up. I'm ready. Just let me finish my speeches first!"[1]

Officials and police intended to let him do nothing of the sort.
No longer could he and the rest of Germany's socialists cover with
the tiniest of constitutional fig leaves a growing nakedness to har-

rassment. Meetings were prohibited or dispersed. Club-swinging police dispersed one because the speaker called religion a leash. Most was denied a permit to speak on "Assassination and Social Democracy" and forbidden to report publicly on the last session of parliament.

Officials and police supported, even aided, the goon squads organized by employers and conservative political parties. "Empire Loyalists," the squads called themselves. They disrupted socialist meetings and terrorized socialist leaders—at which outrages police closed their eyes, officials winked, or officials and police lent a hand. When trespassing socialists at a meeting of Empire Loyalists proposed three cheers for Most, Loyalists knocked down and tied up the socialists, with help from the police commissioner, who prided himself on knots learned in the navy.

Worse for socialists, employers before elections vowed dismissal of any employee who was a socialist, read a socialist newspaper, or voted socialist. Sunrise on election day, 1878, beamed on Chemnitz plastered with posters: "Most is dead!" How many eyes descried, between the block print of "is" and "dead," the tiny "morally"? Despite systematic and legally condoned suppression, Most got 9,899 votes to his opponent's 13,842.[2]

Worse for Most, at 5:00 in the morning after Nobeling fired on the Emperor, sixteen policemen raided his apartment, arrested him, ransacked it, and took away every scrap of paper plus the ashes from the stove. The police took him away too, but handled the ashes more gently. Unable to establish that he was a co-conspirator of Nobeling's, the police released him. The looks on their faces suggested they had eaten the ashes.[3]

Shortly thereafter, 2,000 people jammed the assembly room of Berlin's Hotel London. Most was in good voice and high spirits. Nothing excited this frustrated actor and pleased this militant orator more than a big expectant audience. The police were there, the chief himself at their head, sitting where he could see and be seen. His boots, helmet, and insignia proclaimed that His Majesty expected loyalty and decorum. Having been able only to wangle a permit on the topic of the Imperial Commission of Health, Most dilated on the Commission's report of poor sanitation. The chief fidgeted, for the speech was racing toward lese majesty and might rush past it into treason. Most said that anti-socialists stressed Hödel's possession of Most's photograph—proof, they claimed, of where responsibility lay. "Now," said Most, "if the report of poor sanitation had been in Hödel's pocket, where would responsibility lie?"

The chief blanched, shot out of his chair as if it had turned into a cactus, and shouted: "Dissolved! Dissolved! This meeting is dissolved!"

A phalanx of uniforms packed Most off to six weeks in jail. He wanted to appeal and be released until the appeal was heard.

"Appeal you may," snapped the magistrate, "but be released you may not. The time has come to put an end to your machinations."

"I ask. You refuse. That is my story with officials."[4]

At Plötzensee he asked to be put, not to manual labor, but to writing or editing, the work he had been doing for years.

"I've seen too many of you characters who call yourselves authors and editors," said the warden.

Most said he did not deserve to be treated like a criminal. Was this any way to handle a member of parliament, a representative of the people?

"Don't deserve it? You socialist, you are worse than the worst criminal—below thugs, thieves, and hoodlums. You want to steal *all* property. And if you had your way, you'd set up a guillotine and cut off heads day and night."

Most wondered, "This is justice?"[5]

He went to London but did not escape Continental justice. Spies watched him. Whenever he crossed the Channel, police were waiting for him.

He crossed to Brussels in 1879, eluded twenty detectives, gave a speech, saw spies in the audience, slipped out, evaded thirty detectives, and took a room. At 6:00 A.M. the next day, forty detectives "Book him for vagrancy," a red-faced lieutenant growled. But Most showed money and a ticket to London and was on the next arrested him in his pajamas. He could not be booked for addressing exiled Germans about politics in Germany; it was not a crime. train to London, without the money.[6]

Yet the more the Continental police harrassed him, the more the British police ignored him, until the killing of the Czar. Charles

Edward Marr, a teacher of German in London, read *Freiheit* on the killing. "One of the vilest tyrants," he read, "corroded through and through by corruption, is no more." The glorious bomb "fell at the despot's feet, shattered his legs, ripped open his belly, and inflicted many wounds. . . . Conveyed to his palace, and for an hour and a half in the greatest of suffering, the autocrat meditated on his guilt. Then he died as he deserved to die—like a dog."[7] Disgusted, Marr sent the article to Lord Hamilton in Parliament and asked whether proceedings would be taken. Hamilton called for an interpellation.[8]

Answering the interpellation, Home Secretary Harcourt said that the article broke the law and ordered Most arrested. The story was in the newspapers when Inspectors Hagan and Von Tornow, four constables, and two wagons appeared at 101 Titchfield and found Most reading about himself. A typesetter came from the back room, waved a copy of the same newspaper, and said they had no right to arrest anybody. The constables threw him out.

Into one wagon they put everything of Most's, "everything not nailed down," Most said, "except the furniture"—watch, letters, money, notebooks, postage stamps, documents, and much of the forthcoming *Freiheit*. Into the other they shoved him. Hands manacled, unable to hold on, he knocked back and forth during the ride, like the clapper of a vigorously pulled bell. After several miles and many bruises, he landed in what he called "a hole blacker than a continental European could guess existed in England."[9]

The magistrate looked at him askance. "Too dangerous to be at large. Bail denied."

His trial was one of London's biggest that year.

HEARINGS AND TRIALS

In Central Criminal Court, in London, Most stood accused: "A malicious and evilly disposed person," in a "scandalous wicked malicious and immoral" libel, "unlawfully maliciously and wickedly" attempted in defiance of morality and good government to encourage and justify assassination and murder, especially of the emperors of Germany and Russia. Against "the peace of Our said Lady the Queen Her Crown and Dignity" he created potential "discord between Our said Lady the Queen and the said Sovereigns and Rulers of Europe." The Lord Chief Justice of England presided.[10]

Kautsky and Engels believed that Most would go free.[11] No twelve men in Britain would agree to convict; freedom of expression was too dear. Besides, Most was the first charged in twenty years under the Offences Against the Person Act; so long unused, the Act was nearly forgotten. Moreover, how could the vague and impotent Act apply to verbal offenses, especially newspaper invective, when the Act had been aimed at conspiracy? In the sole precedent, Simon Barnard had been acquitted for publishing against Napoleon.[12]

Still, Engels admitted, to convict Most there were reasons above objective interpretation and grounds beyond appropriate application of the law. For if acquitted, Most would become a hero and a model to radicals, and in the government's view a champion of an irresponsible press. Convicting him would set an example that might curb radicals and discourage use of the press to urge terror. His was more than the case of a foreigner who spoke out of turn.

He came from Newgate underground to the Court, in handcuffs. The Lord Mayor of London, the Lord Chief Justice, other lords, the other judges, and the attorneys awaited him. They wore cowls, Geneva bands, silk stockings, buckle shoes, capes, and powdered wigs. He thought himself bewitched into a bygone century.

Ticket-holding spectators only were admitted, to control the crowds. Some comrades helped cram the gallery; and others, without tickets, filled the street outside. Police superintended the gallery, because at the arraignment a comrade interrupted a reading of Most's description of the assassination, shouting: "Hear! Hear!"

Entering the dock at 10:00 A.M., Europe's chief terrorist was on trial and on view, in the uniform of a prisoner in Newgate. A murmur ran through the crowd. Somebody said, "That's Most? That runt? Why's his face all puckered up?"[13]

Most was not called as a witness, and he did not request nor was he asked to speak in his own behalf. His English was barbarous, no translator was provided, and prosecution and defense saw, in the light of his confession, no reason to hear him. Not talking, never moving except for a twitch of his beard, he watched with flashing eyes two of Britain's finest: Sir Henry James, Attorney General of

England, heading the prosecution; and A. M. Sullivan, M. P., Britain's outstanding libel attorney, leading the defense.

Frank Kitz had engaged Sullivan, who hesitated (he disagreed with Most) but consented. "This man is being persecuted, and I will do what I can for him," because England's treatment of him was "Russian rather than English."[14]

Kitz got contributions especially from Joseph Cowan, M.P. for Newcastle, and from other M.P.s. These sums, plus the defense fund in the Communist Workers' Educational Association and such contributions by sympathizers as $200 from socialists in New York, paid Sullivan's fee.

Since the article in question was unsigned, and Most not listed as *Freiheit*'s editor, Sullivan wanted to argue the strong position that Most's authorship had to be proved. Most refused. He would use every occasion, any outlet, even the courtroom, as a forum. Therefore he confessed authorship and publication. "I wrote those words. I meant them. Freedom of the press says they are lawful. The rights of man say they are justified."[15] Consequently, guilt or innocence turned on whether the article was legal.

Sullivan argued:

• To convict would damage freedom of the press, especially as the Offences Against the Person Act should not be construed to cover newspaper invective.[16]

• There was precedent for acquittal.

• Authors—Shakespeare, Milton, and Byron, to name but three— had written with honor the equivalent of what Most was on trial for; and statesmen—Disraeli and Gladstone, to name but two—had with honor urged regicide.

• Most's article did little harm in Britain; its being written in German meant few Britons saw or heard of it.

The prosecution argued in behalf of what the Attorney General called decency, morality, order, and national security:

• What betrays these ideals is immoral, breaks the common law, and violates the Offences Against the Person Act.

• Publications betraying these ideals have been silenced without harm to freedom of the press.

• Were the accused guilty of mere general invective, he should go free; but he did not simply celebrate murder and call for more. He named the victim (the old Czar) and specified others to be killed (the new Czar and the Kaiser).[17]

The jury, favoring public morality and national security over freedom of the press, said, "Guilty."

Appeal failed. The Chief Justice passed sentence. A grave offense and cowardly, he said, "that a man, himself safe under the shield of a great and free people, sitting at home at ease, may excite others to run into fearful dangers, which he himself shrinks from attempting. . . . I pass upon you a sentence which I believe, indeed which I know, to be a sentence very hard to bear—imprisonment, with the addition of hard labour, for sixteen calendar months."[18] The sentence was in fact eighteen months, for Most had already been detained two.

William Morris, British poet and socialist, said it was "dastardly"; the Chief Justice exemplified the mixture of tyranny and hypocrisy that govern the world.[19]

Tyranny and hypocrisy had governed Most's trial in Vienna years before, according to Most. The prosecution asserted the international character of the labor movement and called the program of the Social Democratic party (as a logical but repugnant consequence of the labor movement) evidence of labor's subversive internationalism. Most, a Social Democrat, was therefore a subversive internationalist. This internationalism, plus his intent to incite seditious violence, threatened the government and endangered the empire. Proof consisted of newspapers and pamphlets, speeches by him and others, and descriptions of demonstrations, strikes, rallies, and marches. Most was therefore guilty of high treason, as charged.[20]

Fearing demonstrations against this trial of the popular Most, the government alerted a regiment of the army, guarded the court with all available police, and limited spectators to sixty, thirty of whom could be friends of the accused. Presiding judge and associates, in military uniforms heavy with braid and carefully brushed, sat with the prosecutor behind a table on which lay bundles of documents. Whenever an oath was sworn, the clerk lighted two candles that flanked a crucifix. Another table served the press. The fourteen accused, in two rows of chairs behind their attorneys, faced prosecutor and judges.

Tageblatt reported Most in a simple gray summer suit, face twisted—at first glance a comic figure. "But when you look at him closer, at the way he listens with glittering eyes to questions, and when you hear his adroit answers, you must remember the French Revolution. Then you must admit, this seeming nonentity is to be taken seriously." Calm, intense, determined, apt, and ready, he reminded *Tageblatt* of men who beheaded a king and shook the world.[21] The Austrian government wanted no royal heads rolling or world-shaking quakes originating in Vienna.

Questioning him, the prosecution tried to emphasize the international character of the labor movement, confirm his advocacy of violence, demonstrate his preaching of sedition, validate his agitation of treasonous ideas, and verify his masterminding of demonstrations. He boasted of membership in the labor movement and admitted participation in demonstrations, but he said both were legal. He had done nothing wrong. Questioning others, the prosecution adduced a tissue of generalities and speculations, vaguely anti-Most, but telling less than Most about Most's activity in the labor movement and doing less than Most to fix complicity in leading the demonstration in question. Witnesses against him were hard to find; many workers, artisans, and tradesmen favored him openly, and more supported him secretly.

Giving one speech in his own defense, he spoke not so much to the court as to the gallery and beyond, and less to contemporaries than to posterity. He claimed vindication in the court of world opinion and pled exoneration in the tribunal of history. "Socialism is an idea whose time has come." A government that wanted to stop the clock ignored history, served narrow self-interest, and suppressed freedom. "When you accuse me of high treason, you commit high treason." The judges' eyes widened.

"I confess, I am a socialist. I confess, I shall be a socialist always. I shall uphold socialism with all my power. I shall never let its noble flag dip.

"Condemn me if you can, if you will, if you must. If I have earned punishment, punish me. I can bear any verdict."[22]

He got five years in prison. The court ruled that being a member of the labor movement, a socialist, an advocate of sedition, and a leader of a demonstration amounted to high treason. The verdict astounded Hermann Greulich, the Swiss editor and publisher; given recent Austrian liberality and the facts of the case, Most should have gone free.[23]

At the same time in Germany, repression was harsher. Under the popular charge of lese majesty, a drunk in Potsdam got two and a half years for proclaiming, "The Emperor is dead, he lives no more," and a woman in Brandenburg eighteen months for, "Well, the Emperor's not poor, he can take care of himself." Later, Most, back in Germany after serving his sentence in Austria, was still expressing openly with caustic tongue his contempt for authority; and he assumed, whenever arrested, that it was for lese majesty. No surprise when police broke down his door, or surrounded him on the street, or manhandled him in a restaurant. He only wanted to know, "Whose majesty did I insult yesterday?"[24]

Therefore, when a telegram from Berlin to the local police ordered his arrest in April of 1874, he wondered: a telegram? Telegrams from Berlin ordered arrests for the gravest of crimes, never for lese majesty. Hearing the charge of inciting to violence in a speech on the Commune, he was astounded. That speech had been dull, his worst in years. Eduard Bernstein, who read the speech, agreed; it was like an academic lecture. Then Most learned who sent the telegram and ordered the arrest, which explained everything.[25]

It was Prussia's attorney general and an arch-Bismarckian, Hermann Tessendorf, who captained a systematic and ferocious attack on the Social Democrats. He wanted to be Bismarck's minister of justice; and because Bismarck hated Social Democrats, to prosecute them was to please him. Word was, Tessendorf had a Social Democrat every morning for breakfast. With a shudder, Social Democrats remembered the Tessendorf Era decades after it was over.

Until April of 1874, Most had escaped—a fact that seemed to goad Tessendorf. How could he become minister of justice while Most, the salient Social Democratic agitator, flouted justice? Tessendorf declared that he would put public-enemy Most away for keeps. When Tessendorf heard of Most's speech on the Commune, he ordered Most's arrest.

That month they squared off in court. (In Germany, Most never employed an attorney; he defended himself.) Tessendorf called him atheist, vagrant, and criminal and labeled his speech volatile and indecent. Most retorted that he was the editor of a newspaper and a member of parliament, who served his party with distinction, his country with honor, his time in prison manfully. He had paid his debt to society with interest. He raised his hand and looked from judge to judge. "My speech, your Honors, set forth facts and praised nothing undeservingly." The judges sent him to prison. Tessendorf kept a perfect record against Social Democrats.

Twice more they met in court. The first time, Most got two months for blasphemy. The second, he cleared himself of blasphemy but got three months for saying, "So as not to provoke charges of lese majesty, we refrain from comment"—a jibe stinking with lese majesty, said Tessendorf; and the court agreed. The sentences were suspended, to be carried out if Most did not behave. He did not behave.

By the early 1880s he was such a force for sedition that at every trial for treason in Germany and Austria a theme recurred, "Most is behind this crime." When Victor Dave and fourteen others stood trial in Leipzig, they were in the dock but Most was being tried.[26] They plotted this insurrection; he originated such plots. They smuggled and distributed *Freiheit*; he edited and published it. They collected and used poison and dynamite; he put the idea into their heads. They were traitors; he masterminded, informed, and propelled an incipient revolution. They got two and a half years; he would have been lucky to escape the gallows. As it was, he served seven years in European jails and prisons.

JAILS AND PRISONS

When he went to jail to await trial in Vienna in 1870, grim faces met him. The jailer, called The Shoemaker's Hammer for his short body and long nose, looked as if he had swallowed nails and would

spit them into the eyes of the first prisoner to cross him. He glared
at Most, as if ready to spit nails, then said to the guards:
"Here's the holy terror, the big-mouthed speechifier. Take care
of him."

They stripped Most, searched his clothes to the seams and body
to the last hole (including mouth), confiscated knife and notebook,
dressed him in uniform, and led him through iron doors and down
gloomy passages to cell 25.

Eight prisoners endured in space designed for three. Those here
longest slept on a platform; the rest, on the floor. They shivered
under scanty threadbare blankets infested with lice, on ragged mattresses crawling with fleas. For bathing, a pail. Visitors were restricted; books, newspapers, and writing materials forbidden. Most
complained to the Hammer that such treatment violated rights of
political prisoners.

As if ready to spit nails into Most's eyes, the Hammer replied:
"Rights? Listen, Jack: you get what rights we give you. No distinctions, no favorites, *here*. That's justice. Equality. What you socialists are always screaming for. So shut up, or we'll shut you up."

Most did not shut up. He would communicate, even at risk of
the Hammer's wrath. Using a cellmate who ran errands and met
others from different sections, he made their cell the center of a
prison-wide network and appointed himself head of a conspiracy
in communication. Conspirators braided fabric from mattresses into
ropes, attached socks weighted with stones, and every evening
when clocks struck eight, raised and lowered messages and goods
through windows. Every conspirator liked best to find Most's newspaper, "Nutcracker," in his sock. Publication was irregular, depend-
ing on supplies of paper and ink. Each handwritten issue passed
from conspirator to conspirator, through the network. At the trial
the prosecution exhibited "Nutcracker" and described the network
as evidence of Most's treasonous character.

Convicted, he went to Suben, on the Bavarian border near Passau.
Once a hunting lodge and later a monastery, the prison overlooked
the village of Suben and the valley of the River Inn. The 300
inmates comprised young offenders being humanely reformed,
"distinguished convicts" here for crimes like grand larceny, and

political prisoners. Common criminals there were none, which pleased Most. He hated being thrown in with common criminals; his socialism did not go that far.

Political prisoners lived apart from the rest, wore street clothes, and ate and drank what they wanted. Costs of food and drink they bore themselves, with the aid of an official allowance. They had to work not at all. Daily they took two hours' exercise in the rose garden. An orderly made their beds, cleaned their rooms, polished their boots, and served their meals. Books and newspapers were not restricted in kind or amount. Guards and officials were polite. With Johann Pabst, also convicted of high treason, Most shared a spacious bright room, furnished with two chairs, two beds, table, clothes rack, and stove. The window gave "the high treasoners" a view down the valley into Bavaria. At the table he did much of what he liked best, reading and writing. How different Suben from Plötzensee![27]

Plötzensee was a new prison near Berlin, where he served his next long term, from 1874 to 1876. He rode there in "the green wagon," hunched, for the ceiling forbade even a short man's standing erect. The guard took post in front of the window, the only source of light and air. Shoved in with seven common criminals, Most learned how slaves felt when transported. After an hour of jolts and stench the wagon stopped, in a yard with brick walls around it. Barred windows scowled. Iron doors clanged shut.

He went to solitary. Officials feared that the nation's chief agitator in regular confinement would make mutiny. He preferred solitary, for he detested coarseness, horseplay, and homosexual advances and loathed communal urinating and defecating, marching in phalanx to toilet at appointed times and evacuating in the way of Prussian drillmasters. In solitary he could read and write at peace, in private.[28]

To him, as to fellow leftists of proletarian origin, prisons were universities. He said: "I owe my mind to imprisonment." In the finest of classrooms, solitary confinement, he absorbed ideas, systematized opinions, and "stored in my head things I could use later. I sharpened many an arrow for use in future battles."[29] There he mastered Dühring's doctrines and made the digest of *Capital*.[30] For there were hours and days and months and years of solitude, precious to the student. Only the beating of his heart, the rustle of pages, and the scratching of his pen alloyed the golden silence; and they made it more a treasure as they made it *his*. Only shadows tiptoeing across the floor and a spider spinning in a corner ruffled exquisite quiescence. Introspection opened mental doors, contemplation stretched imagination, mastery of fear stiffened courage, and study nourished understanding. He built trains of thought he hoped would carry mankind to a better world.

Meanwhile his world was a whitewashed cell furnished with a collapsible bed; a stool; a shelf holding brush, soup bowl, and pitcher; and a cabinet containing cup, shoe polish, butter dish, and knife and spoon. The soup bowl, generous enough to serve a family, was for soup and bathing. A commode, with running water, improved on pots, pans, and pails. Broom and dustpan flanked the cabinet. A notice ordered no burning of the gas after 8:30. Other notices:

> INMATES ARE TO RISE AT THE SIGNAL
> OF THE APPOINTED HOUR
>
> IF INMATES MISBEHAVE
> THEY MAY BE RESTRAINED
> WITH CHAINS
>
> WHEN IN THE PRESENCE OF AN OFFICIAL,
> INMATES ARE TO REMOVE THEIR CAPS
>
> GUARDS MAY SHOOT INMATES
> WHO RESIST AUTHORITY
> OR ATTEMPT ESCAPE

At any time, anyone could look in through a peephole in the door. Always the question gnawed his mind or haunted his dreams, "Is somebody watching?"

The day began when clocks struck 6:00 and orderlies banged pots and rattled pans and rolled barrels. An orderly offered a bucket, and Most filled the pitcher for the day's drinking and bathing.

Breakfast appeared through a hole in the wall, like feeding at the zoo. The gruel looked like glue and tasted like rotten spinach.

He gagged on the first spoonful. After weeks of hunger he could choke down half of it. At noon the hole shot open and a voice barked, "Soup bowl!" His returned full of brownish-gray "soup" called Rumfortsch: peas, barley, potatoes, crusts of bread, beans (all leftovers, long left over), spices, and salt in what smelled like dishwater. At noon, irregularly, beans, peas, lentils, rice, sauerkraut, potatoes, and turnips replaced Rumfortsch. At noon holidays, half a pound of beef with a glass of watery beer. Evenings, two pieces of bread.

Hunger resulted. The gruel that once sickened him he wolfed in seconds. Weeks of hunger. His weight dipped to ninety pounds. Disgust returned. For a while he could eat nothing of prison fare. Smuggling kept him alive. Eduard Bernstein visited every four or five weeks, leaving illicit salami, ham, chocolate, and cognac.[31] Still, Most grew thinner, paler, and weaker, for he was allowed one visitor every fourteen days. At last he came to terms with prison fare. The terms: eat it or die.

Daily after breakfast he washed bowl and spoon, made the bed, swept and tidied the cell, and polished his boots. Every second Saturday he scrubbed cell and furniture, hurling anger and hatred into washing, sweeping, polishing, and dusting with vigor that amazed guards.

Then the day's work—not the editing and writing he expected and would have liked, but bookbinding. "You may read and write when your binding is done," the supervisor told him; but he could not finish the binding expected in the time allotted. Sneering at a salary of six cents a day, he named himself Six-Penny Coolie.

He was allowed to send one letter every four weeks. He handed it to the section chief, who left it lying about for anyone to read. Then the chief read it and turned it over to his supervisor, who read it. He gave it to the head supervisor, who read it. By now, unless it had been burned for its seditiousness or edited out of comprehensibility, it was a circular; but it had not passed yet. After the police inspector read it, it went to the warden's office for the definitive reading at last. Three clerks, or four in hard cases, said to be cryptologists manqué, decided to confiscate, reject, or dispatch. A letter incoming took the same route in reverse. Some of Most's, written to fool censors but convey rebellion, passed. Others disappeared or returned marked "unacceptable," "dangerous," "subversive," or "traitorous."

As everyone who read letters talked about them (having little else to talk about) and talked in the presence of inmates, nothing in letters was secret. Two inmates employed as messengers got all over the prison, and the first thing they talked about was the latest in the mail. Anything Most wrote his wife might return to Most as a dirty joke on the lips of a guard or an inmate.

Pencils and paper were rationed. He used much of his for what became *The Bastille at Plötzensee: Pages Out of My Prison Diary.* Christmas 1874 he spent writing in the diary, after days without a pencil. A comrade had thrown one out a window to him, the best present he could have gotten.

Bastille, published soon after his release, told what he thought of the jewel of Prussian penology. Sketches of maltreatment, depictions of mismanagement, and indictments of abuse turned the jewel into paste. He boasted how he outwitted officials and finagled concessions. He claimed credit for a secret postal system and laughed at guards for never discovering it. Plötzensee's labor inspector told Bebel: "If we get our hands on Most again, he'll pay for this indignity."[32]

They got their hands on him again. When he went from Plötzensee back to agitation in 1876, he stayed free until the authorities carried out the two suspended sentences that Tessendorf had won against him. This term, five months in Plötzensee in 1878, he spent in confinement so solitary that he neither had a visitor nor saw another inmate. He had to wear a mask whenever anyone could see him, and few knew that under it was one of Germany's best-known faces.

In jail and prison in Britain three years later, practically anonymous without a mask, he helped make history nonetheless. Charged with seditious libel for his article on the assassination of the Czar, he appeared in the last hearing in historic Bow-Street Police Court, in April, 1881. Awaiting trial he was among the last wretches clapped into Newgate, the infamous old prison, soon to be closed. He drew no comfort from whatever honor accrued to the last sufferers in that sink of cruelty figuring since the twelfth century in British life and literature. Newgate's workaday atrocities exceeded

Newgate's historical and literary horrors. He heard the screams of
the condemned and shuddered. One of the world's ghastliest prisons, he called it, after serving in four countries' worst. "Wat Tyler,
the great fire, Moll Flanders, the Gordon riots, and Charles Dickens
be damned! I want humane treatment!"[33]

From there, in June, 1881, convicted of seditious libel, he went
to Coldbath Fields, the House of Correction at Clerkenwell. After
the customary interview with the newcomer, the chaplain marked
the door of Most's cell, "No religion! No church!"—as if to reverse
Passover and notify the angel of death that here was someone who
deserved a visit. "Hell would be too good for that infidel," the chaplain muttered.[34]

Judging by the food, Most was in hell. Half a pound of stale
bread morning, noon, and night; a dish of oatmeal, peppered with
mouse dung, morning and night; two or three cold potato-dumplings
at noon; a bowl of brown pea-soup three times a week; a serving of
stringy meat and moldy beans once a week; and half a pound of
rancid suet-pudding twice a week—served in metalware rusty and
unwashed. These were full rations, issued after four months. Before
that, twenty-five percent less.

He slept on boards every night the first month, twice a week the
second, and once a week thereafter. As long as he behaved, he
could send and receive one letter and have one visitor every three
months. A guard locked him and visitor into separate cages and
stood between them until the visit ended. Most smuggled, whatever
the prison; but under these conditions it was very hard; and the
guards here were difficult to bribe.

For infractions, a variety of punishments, from withdrawal of a
meal to flogging. The shrieks of the flogged told what awaited the
misbehaver.

He spent eighteen months in solitary, forbidden to speak to anyone but officials, and not until spoken to. He saw inmates at no
time but the half hour for exercise daily. In a gloomy yard, silent,
in single file, three paces apart, they circled the turnkey, who waved
as if cracking a whip. Now faster, now slower, they went on command, like thoroughbreds in training, except that thoroughbreds
are well fed, better groomed, and more spirited.

At first his was the infamous work of British prisons, picking oakum. After three months, fingers raw, he complained until he got to mend uniforms. For fifteen months he applied patches, sewed seams, and attached buttons. "Old women's work," he said. But old women chatter together; he talked to himself.

Forbidden to write anything but one letter every three months and refused implements of writing, he concocted ink of water and limestone, improvised pens of needles wrapped in thread, and wrote on toilet paper. Grayish-white ink showed vaguely on gray paper. To write was possible only between 5:00 P.M. and 8:00 P.M. And then, as guards wore soft-soled shoes and appeared presto at the peephole, he had to write lying against the door, listening. Thus he wrote many an article for *Freiheit*. Such copy tried typesetters' patience and produced ejaculations fit for toilet paper.

At Plötzensee, imprisonment had been harsh. At Clerkenwell it was harsher. The harshest was ahead, on New York's Blackwell's Island. Neither Plötzensee nor Clerkenwell but the Island tested his assertion, "Since childhood, life has been so vile I can bear anything."[35]

NOTES

1. Most, *Memoiren* 3:20. *See also Freiheit*, 20 July 1896.

2. Rudolf Strauss and Kurt Finsterbusch, *Die Chemnitzer Arbeiterbewegung unter dem Sozialistengesetz*, pp. 29-30.

3. Most, *Memoiren* 3:72-73.

4. Ibid. 3:76.

5. Most, *Die Bastille am Plötzensee*, pp. 16-17; *see also* pp. 7-9. Dieter Kühn, *Johann Most*, p. 101. Most, *Memoiren* 4:63-64.

6. *Freiheit*, 23 August 1879, 27 June 1896.

7. Ibid., 19 March 1881.

8. *Times* (London) 1881: 1 April, p. 4, 8 April, p. 8.

9. *Freiheit*, 11 July 1896; *see also* 2 April 1881. Baskette Court Case No. 593, pp. 17-23. *Times* (London), 1 April 1881, p. 4.

10. Baskette, pp. 1-4.

11. Karl Kautsky, *Aus der Frühzeit des Marxismus*, pp. 37-38. Engels to Eduard Bernstein, 14 April 1881, Marx-Engels *Werke* 35:183.

12. Baskette, pp. 28 and 31. *Times* (London), 6 May 1881, p. 12.

13. *Freiheit*, 11 July 1896. *See also* 2 April 1881, 23 April 1881.

14. Frank Kitz, "Recollections and Reflections," p. 18. *See also* p. 26.

15. *Freiheit*, 30 April 1881. *See also* Rudolf Rocker, *Johann Most*, pp. 121-22.

16. Baskette, pp. 30-34.

17. Ibid., pp. 41-46.

18. Ibid., p. 78. *See also Times* (London), 30 June 1881, p. 12.

19. William Morris, *The Letters of William Morris*, p. 149.

20. Most's account of the trial: *Memoiren* 2:5-51. *See also* Heinrich Scheu, *Der Wiener Hochverratsprozess.*

21. *Tageblatt* (Vienna), 6 July 1870.

22. Most, *Memoiren* 2:37-38.

23. Eduard Weckerle, *Hermann Greulich*, p. 143.

24. Most, *Memoiren* 4:21-24.

25. Ibid. 4:12-48. *See also* Most, *Die Pariser Commune vor den Berliner Gerichten*, p. 42 passim. August Bebel, *Aus meinem Leben* 2:256-57. Eduard Bernstein, *Die Geschichte der Berliner Arbeiterbewegung*, p. 295.

26. Johann Heinrich Künzel, *Der erste Hochverratsprozess*, p. 22.

27. Jail in Vienna and prison at Suben: Most, *Memoiren* 1:68-70; 2:53-57.

28. Prison at Plötzensee: Most, *Die Bastille am Plötzensee.*

29. Most, *Memoiren* 3:96-97.

30. Most, *Bastille*, p. 36. *See also* Hans Magnus Enzensberger, ed., Most, *Kapital und Arbeit*, p. 98. Digest of *Capital*: Most, *Kapital und Arbeit*, p. 93.

31. Eduard Bernstein, *Sozialdemokratische Lehrjahre*, p. 182.

32. Bebel, *Leben* 2:305. *See also* 268, 271, 297, 323.

33. *Freiheit*, 9 July and 4 September 1881; 27 June, 11 and 20 July 1896; 7 January 1899. *Times* (London), 4 April 1881, p. 8.

34. *Freiheit*, 11 July, 1896.

35. Bebel, *Leben* 2:281.

5

FROM EUROPE TO AMERICA

1867: Berezowski tries to shoot Czar Alexander II in Paris. The era of terrorism begins.

1867: Fenians sail the *Erin's Hope* to Ireland and try to land an armed force. Fenians lead risings in Ireland and England. Fenians attack a van carrying arrested Fenians and kill a policeman in Manchester. Fenians, trying to rescue a Fenian, dynamite a wall of Clerkenwell prison. Later, Most hails "the year of the Fenians" and calls them terrorists of the first water, revolutionaries nonpareil.

1868: The British execute Fenians for terrorism and murder.

1875: Charles Stewart Parnell begins obstructionism on behalf of Ireland. His filibusters keep Parliament in session nights through.

1880: The Social Revolutionary Club of New York, founded by Germans in November, offers aid to the Fenians.

1881: The British jail Parnell for opposing the land laws.

1882: In the German Reading Union in Brussels, after years of strife, fist fights break out between Most's supporters and Most's enemies.

They have more character over there, and their character is
essentially anarchistic. Fertile ground for us, the States—
very good ground. The Great Republic has the root of the
destructive matter in her.

The Professor to Mr. Ossipon, in *The Secret Agent,*
by Joseph Conrad

Revolution is the only lawful, equal, and effectual war.

Sergei Eisenstein, *The Battleship Potemkin*

On May 6, 1882, in Dublin, four men surrounded Lord Frederick
Cavendish and Thomas Henry Burke. Knives flashed. Blood-
drenched, stabbed eight times, Cavendish died in a pool of blood.
Blood bubbled from Burke's throat, and his last gasps gurgled
in blood.

The cry went up, "Murder!"

In St. Patrick's Cathedral a muffled bell tolled. The manager of
the Gaiety Theatre, fearing an uproar, shortened scenes and
quickened lines and emptied the house before it got the news. By
10:00 P.M., Dublin was in a swivet. Barrels of tar set afire could
not destroy the pall that settled as heavily as the overcast moonless
night itself.

The cry raced across Britain, "Murder!"

In London, Queen Victoria dispatched condolences to Lady
Cavendish and summoned the prime minister. He left dinner at
the Austrian embassy, chewing his last bite and wiping his mouth
while he ran for the carriage. He called on Lady Cavendish, then
met with the Queen. In churches, prayers went up; in public houses,
cries for revenge. Open meetings around the country, crowded and
tumultuous, expressed outrage at the crime, voiced sympathy for
the bereaved, and demanded vengeance.

The cry hurtled around the world, "Murder!"

Revulsion swept France. In Berlin, where extras announced the
birth of an heir to the German crown and described murder in
Dublin, horror prevailed over joy. America and India sent condolences.

The story filled eleven columns in the London *Times*,[1] and the atrocity went down in history as the Phoenix Park murders. Choosing officials of rank—Cavendish was Chief Secretary for Ireland, Burke the Under Secretary—Irish terrorists struck without warning and disappeared. Purposes: terrify the government, publicize discontent, and change policy. The atrocity was thus an act of propaganda-by-the-deed, of the kind Most taught, celebrated, and rejoiced in: daring, startling, horrifying, and foul.

The atrocity shook a Britain perturbed by events at home and agitated by circumstances abroad. Parnell, seeking rights for Ireland, was ruffling the Commons; and the Land League and the Fenian movement were rioting for reform in Ireland and murdering for separation of Ireland from Britain. Meanwhile, American agriculture seemed about to drive Russian agriculture off the international market, thereby to weaken the Russian government and visit chaos on Europe. Hence Most's article hailing the assassination of the Czar, deemed conducive to domestic terror and harmful to European stability, had brought reprisal: Most's trial for seditious libel in London the year before the Phoenix Park atrocity, and his sentence to sixteen months at hard labor in Clerkenwell.

His imprisonment had unified and inspired his followers. The United Socialists of London declared the attack on him an attack on them. The Social Revolutionaries of Bern said, "The imprisonment of Most, a blow struck to silence *Freiheit*, shall not silence *Freiheit*. We will fight to maintain it: our source of energy, our spring of brotherhood." Subscriptions to *Freiheit* and contributions to help Most came from London, the Continent, and America. The Communist Workers' Educational Association formed a defense committee, planned demonstrations, and appointed editors. At a shop in Foley Street, sales of *Freiheit* jumped from 3 to 100 per week.[2]

Freiheit then announced what the radicals of London thought of the nation that imprisoned Most. Brutal, oppressive, and barbaric, Britain mocked freedom of the press, caricatured equality before the law, and ridiculed trial by jury. British justice was a travesty, a hoax.

Now Britain prided herself on perhaps the world's and certainly Europe's freest press. Indeed, Most had published with impunity and without reprisal a series, "How Britain Stole India."[3] More-over, London received other countries' political and ideological lepers; colonies of these pariahs were honeycombing Soho. True to form, Britain tolerated castigation by *Freiheit*.

Then *Freiheit* rejoiced at the Phoenix Park atrocity. "A heroically bold act of popular justice," in a few exquisite thrusts of a dagger, murdered Cavendish and Burke and "splendidly annihilated the evil representatives of a malignant government based on brute force" and struck a magnificent blow for liberty. Cavendish was "only a poor simpleton," but the fact "in no way diminishes the significance of the admirable deed."[4]

Tolerant Britain, raw after centuries of friction with Ireland, was not tolerant enough to brook this celebration of Irish murder of Britons. Even British newspapers, disregarding a vested interest in free expression, sided with the government.

A raid missed *Freiheit*'s interim editors John Neve and Karl Schneidt. Neve especially was wanted, as he had taken charge of producing *Freiheit* in London and fomenting terrorism on the Con-tinent. Editing, corresponding, directing, bookkeeping, managing, planning, coordinating, he sustained the Cause when Most went to prison.

The raid took William Merten and much of the forthcoming *Freiheit*. In handcuffs, before an officer could clap a hand over his mouth, Merten shouted to his wife: "Go tell the others I'm taken on the same charge Most was." In court, Merten disclaimed re-sponsibility. "I'm only a typesetter." A typesetter named Louis Lang testified that Merten hired him and paid the rent on *Freiheit*'s offices. Convicted of "a scandalous wicked and seditious libel," Merten got three months in Clerkenwell.[5]

Neither the imprisonment of Most and Merten nor the seizure of an issue silenced *Freiheit*. Ten days after Merten's arrest *Frei-heit* called the arrest arbitrary, the police dastardly, and the gov-ernment scoundrelly. *Freiheit* praised the Phoenix Park assassins: "We side with the brave Irish rebels and tender them hearty brotherly compliments."

If *Freiheit* was raided for celebrating assassination, would less be done when *Freiheit* proclaimed brotherhood with assassins? Again the police hit *Freiheit*. Again they missed Neve and Schneidt.

But the police confiscated type, press, ink, tools, manuscripts, flyers, pamphlets, broadsides, handbills, and the file of *Freiheit* itself. Into the loaded van the police shoved Frederick Schwelm, handcuffed, protesting, "I'm only a typesetter."[6]

Charged with "a scandalous, wicked and seditious libel," he denied it. But German-speaking Inspector Hagan, leader of all raids on *Freiheit*, testified to Schwelm's arrest on the scene; and printer Henry Tusson proved entering into contract with Schwelm for 2,000 copies of the *Freiheit* in question. Schwelm appealed to the jury. "I'm only a typesetter." The jury returned, "Guilty." Schwelm pointed to the sword of justice hanging from the ceiling: "Take down that sham. There's no justice here." Less for libel than for flouting the court, he got seventeen months in Clerkenwell, fourteen more than the compliant Mertens and one less than Most himself. Schwelm pointed again to the sword and told the judge, "It ought to fall on you." A few months later it did fall, but on the sheriff, who had had nothing to do with Schwelm.

Freiheit continued.

The authorities wondered: "How? We seized its equipment and locked up its personnel." Angered, the authorities decreed that anyone caught writing, editing, printing, distributing, or selling it would be prosecuted.[7] Police staked out stores, newsstands, and print shops and shadowed the suspicious.

Freiheit faltered.

Although Most would contribute as long as he had toilet paper, although a few comrades dared write, although others made bold to edit, no printer would print, no distributor distribute, and no seller sell. They feared the police. John Bale and Sons, long printers to the Communist Workers' Educational Association, locked their doors to *Freiheit*. Then the police, hot after Neve, drove him to the Continent, never to return. Schneidt, feeling the closing of the ring, went to America. Among much of the CWEA, alarmed at Neve's fate and unnerved by Schneidt's retreat, brashness turned to fear, and support for Most changed to anger against him. "His bombast got us into this mess."[8]

Freiheit fled.

Some of the few members of the CWEA still loyal to Most, with help from anarchist Hermann Stellmacher, took the paper to

Schaffhausen, Switzerland. Then Switzerland, Europe's other exiles' haven, cracked down on terrorists. Swiss and Austrian police chased Stellmacher to the gallows in Vienna. *Freiheit* had to be produced in secret and its place of publication listed as London. Capable workmen could not be hired; they feared arrest. Incompetents edited, bunglers printed, and *Freiheit* looked like an apprentice's first handbill and read like a schoolboy's essay on last year's social problems. And the Swiss got tougher.

Freiheit failed.

Most left prison the same month, sounding ready for a fight. "I shall reestablish *Freiheit*."[9]

His letter to the Home Secretary, asking return of *Freiheit*'s equipment, brought surveillance. Shadowed day and night, he appealed to Irish MPs, friendly to him because he supported Ireland. They secured his right to property and privacy. The shadows were called off. He rented a horse and wagon, took Merten along as helper, and went to the police warehouse. The file of *Freiheit* was missing, never to be replaced; but among the welter of impounded goods he found his press (battered, perhaps beyond repair), newsprint, pamphlets, and flyers (torn, creased, smudged, and moldy), and type (shoveled into bags and thrown about like beans, and ruined). One look told him too much; without help, *Freiheit* was dead.[10]

There was no help. Comrades who published it in Switzerland, however loyal and well-meaning, had proved feckless. Scotland Yard jailed comrades, scared others to the Continent, and pushed many of the rest to America. Worse, his popularity sank. Comrades rejected him because he fouled with terrorism the purity of socialism. Comrades on the Continent, notably Karl Kautsky, sick of his lust for violence, returned to Social Democracy. In London, for the same reason, comrades shouted, "Down with *Freiheit*!" and "Away with Most!" The issue of whether he stay in the CWEA his friends and foes settled with knives and clubs. He stayed. But the CWEA, like the radical Continent and the rest of radical London, split; and he was the wedge that split them. *Freiheit* lost subscribers and contributors.[11]

Was *Freiheit* finished therefore? Was Most?

Seeking help everywhere, he even approached Marx and Engels, who disliked his part in the Dühring affair and detested his misrepresentation of their opinion of *Freiheit*.

Eugen Dühring was an economist at the University of Berlin and an able publicist. Publicizing his positivistic economics between 1874 and 1876, he won favor among Social Democrats even though he blasted Marx. Such leading Social Democrats and good Marxists as Bebel and Bernstein defected to Dühring. Marx and Engels fumed.[12] Then, in 1876, Most wrote an article extolling Dühring. It compelled an angry Engels to write *Anti-Dühring*, the seminal work in the interpretation and elaboration of Marxism. A stubborn Most kept *Anti-Dühring* from serialization in the party's chief newspaper and vexed Marx and Engels.

They were doubly vexed when Most announced that they favored his founding *Freiheit*. A lie, said Engels; they were reserved, hoping with little optimism that *Freiheit* would advance socialism; and they kept quiet meanwhile. When *Freiheit* turned social revolutionary, Engels repudiated it. With Marx, he said it had no revolutionary content, only revolutionary phrases. According to Engels, Most had told people that because Marx and Engels supported him (another lie), everybody else should too. Engels contemplated a declaration against Most.[13]

Then Most asked Marx and Engels for help, to restore *Freiheit*. Marx stroked his beard and told Most to see Engels, and Engels told Most off.[14]

"Not without talent," said Engels of Most, "but terribly vain, undisciplined, and ambitious."[15] Marx jeered "silly chatter, so foolish, so illogical, so dissolute that it finally dissolves into nothing, that is, into Johann Most's personal vanity."[16]

No help for *Freiheit* in Britain, then, and no help on the Continent. Worse, on the Continent subscribers deserted to *Sozialdemokrat*. In America, Social Democrat emissaries Louis Viereck and Friedrich Fritsche raised 30,000 marks for the party. Engels predicted that their success would dry up Most's American sources of money, the only ones left, and doom *Freiheit*.[17]

Then the Social Revolutionary Club of New York invited Most to America to lecture. Earlier he had advised comrades seeking safety, freedom, and a field for action to go to America; and now he took his own advice. There he could publish *Freiheit*. There railway workers fought pitched battles with militia. There social revolutionaries studied dynamite and tested time bombs and built infernal machines. There many Germans, especially newly arrived radicals, seemed ripe for agitation. America now, an agitator's paradise like Austria in 1869, was the place for Most.

A green young socialist with downy cheeks went to Austria then. Now a seasoned revolutionist, bearded, hardened by seven years behind bars, sailed for New York and leadership of the social-revolutionary movement in America.

NOTES

1. *Times* (London), 8 May 1882, pp. 7-8. *See also Freiheit*, 13 May 1882.

2. *Freiheit,* 18 June 1881. *See also* 2 April, 2 and 9 July 1881.

3. Ibid., 19 July to 23 August 1879.

4. Ibid., 13 May 1882. *See also Times* (London), 18 May 1882, p. 11.

5. *Times* (London), 18 May 1882, p. 11; *see also* 6 June 1882, p. 4. *Freiheit*, 20 May 1882.

6. Frank Kitz, "Recollections and Reflections," p. 26. *See also Times* (London), 6 June 1882, p. 4. *Sozialdemokrat* (Zurich), 10 August 1882.

7. Max Nettlau, "John Most," p. 13.

8. Josef Peukert, *Erinnerungen*, p. 197. *See also* Dieter Fricke, *Die deutsche Arbeiterbewegung*, p. 218.

9. *Freiheit*, 11 November 1882.

10. Ibid., 25 July and 1 August 1896; 7 January 1899. Rudolf Rocker, *Johann Most*, pp. 134-35.

11. *Freiheit*, 7 January 1899. Eduard Bernstein, *Sozialdemokratische Lehrjahre*, p. 84. Karl Schneidt, "Vom jungen Anarchismus," p. 626.

12. Richard Adamiak, "Marx, Engels and Duehring," pp. 98-112.

13. August Bebel, *Aus meinem Leben* 3:48 and 133. Marx-Engels, *Werke* 34:383.

14. *Freiheit*, 27 June 1896.

15. Marx-Engels, *Werke* 34:383.

16. Ibid. 34:474.

17. Reinhard Höhn, *Die vaterlandslosen Gesellen*, p. 94. Marx-Engels, *Werke* 35:170.

PART II

At the Peak: Europe and America, 1882-1892

6
PERSONAL AND PRIVATE

1820: Between 1820 and 1930, about 38,000,000 immigrate to the United States. The majority enter at New York. Many stay there.

1859: New York charters Cooper Union, built according to Peter Cooper's plans, with Cooper's money, and to be run according to Cooper's wishes to provide education for the working classes. Cooper, the nation's largest glue manufacturer, built the nation's first locomotive.

1863: Moneyed conscripts buy exemption. New Yorkers disapprove and riot.

1881: Wilhelm Hasselmann founds a society for the study of revolutionary science in New York City.

1886: Henry James publishes *The Princess Casamassima.*

1888: Alexander Berkman arrives in New York City, in steerage, from Russia via Hamburg.

1889, August 15: Emma Goldman arrives in New York City. She has little but youth, health, and an ideal. Terrified of the strange new world, she determines to meet it unflinchingly.

1890: Jacob A. Riis publishes *How the Other Half Lives.*

1895: Between now and 1901, yellow journalism hits anarchists hard.

1902: A throng follows the remains of Justus Schwab to the crematorium.

1907: Joseph Conrad publishes *The Secret Agent.*

The story of dynamite—the actual "stuff"—in the United States, as a weapon of the have-nots in their war against the haves, dates from Most's arrival in the country.

Louis Adamic, *Dynamite*

So great has been the dynamite rage, so deep-laid the plots, and so wide-spread the attempts, the reporter felt like asking Herr Most to touch the chair lightly as he seated himself. He might have been loaded.

The St. Joseph, Missouri, *Gazette*, May 15, 1883

Most made his bow to the audience amid cheers. He waved and silence reigned. The man who has been the cause of more than a score of double-leaded, sensational newspaper stories . . . pitched into his speech, and rattled away until perspiration fairly rolled down his brow and the red rose in his buttonhole fell in pieces to the floor. Again and again he roused his hearers to enthusiastic applause.

The Boston *Globe*, March 30, 1891

The steamship *Wisconsin*, sixteen days out of Liverpool, fifteen days not heard from, and four overdue, stood from nightfall until 2:00 A.M. off New York; from 2:00 until 8:00 A.M. she rode at anchor near Quarantine; and then on the flood of December 18th she limped to Pier 38 at the foot of King Street. Ashore came Johann Most. The *Wisconsin* had carried him through pounding waves, lashing winds, and pelting rain, snow, and sleet across the Atlantic. Then, with the *Wisconsin* in sight of land and nearly home, the bark *Ella* under full sail boomed out of a squall; and the *Wisconsin* and the *Ella* collided. Most shivered when he thought of the storms, and looked over his shoulder when he remembered the crash.

On the pier a score of men clustered, waiting. Each sported a scarlet ribbon in his lapel, and one waved a blood-red flag. Made eager by four days of expectation, they cheered, shouted greetings in German, surged to the gangplank, and surrounded a small man "of very fair complexion," with a sandy beard, blue eyes, a swollen cheek, and a prominent forehead. "Of very fair complexion" was how the New York *Times* described the effects of the noxious voyage.

The *Wisconsin* likely never carried anyone more famous than this outspoken editor, feisty member of parliament, vociferous agitator, brazen ex-convict, and notorious radical. Reporters, on the pier to cover the day's biggest story, opened notebooks, poised pencils, and asked his plans. He answered freely; it would be a few days until he saw reporters as henchmen of the capitalistic press.

"I shall, in this city and around this country, denounce the persecution of socialists and spread the truth of socialism."

How did he feel about going to prison in Britain, for his article on the assassination of the Czar?

"The Czar was a tyrant who trampled on the people. The British government was unfair to me. The abuse of me in Clerkenwell was more vicious than any in the dungeons of Austria and Germany."

Had Clerkenwell changed him?

"No. I outfoxed my keepers and published my beliefs. I'll continue to publish them. I'm more radical than ever."

His beliefs—what were they?

"Violence is justified against tyranny and tyrants. If society must be organized, communism is the way."

What did he mean by communism?

"A specialized, refined, advanced form of socialism."

What would communistic society be like?

"Everybody will own everything."[1]

The welcoming party pulled him away and, leaving the reporters scribbling furiously, took him to the East Side, to a meal, a bath, and a bed. He had suffered one of the severest storms in years on the Atlantic and had endured one of the harshest crossings in a decade. He was expected at a reception in the Germania Assembly Rooms later in the day; he would give a speech at Cooper Union in the evening; and in a few days he would begin an agitation-tour across the nation. He needed the meal, the bath, and the bed.

If he (like other foreigners) expected New York to be absolutely different from, completely superior to, and infinitely richer than the Old World, he (with other foreigners) was disappointed.[2] New York's tallest building was eight stories. Grand Street, the East Side's business street, did not impress those who knew commercial avenues in Minsk, Vienna, Paris, and London; to them, grand it was not. Even Fifth Avenue did not measure up. The greatest visible differences from Europe were the uniformity of the East Side's multistoried houses, the absence of wooden houses, the adjoining fronts of houses with no lawns or gardens in between, and the flat instead of slanted roofs. Come summer, immigrants appreciated flat roofs; people slept there on nights hotter than the immigrants had ever known.

East Side streets were narrow and alleys cramped, pinched between buildings; a beam of sunlight was rare and ephemeral. Into mercantile streets, from storefronts under awnings, pushed barrels and sacks and boxes and racks and stands and piles of food and clothing and tobacco and tools and weapons and liquor and feed. On sidewalks and in streets, in violation of the law, storekeepers packed and unpacked cases, cartons, canisters, and crates. Around them shuffled, over them stumbled, among them scurried, and past them rumbled the maelstrom of immigrant New York—unposed and waiting for Jacob A. Riis: men in rough clothes, long hair, and mustaches (with a ring in an ear now and then); women in full-length dresses, aprons, and shawls (with a tattoo on an arm here and there); men and women with gold in their teeth that glittered when they smiled; urchins and guttersnipes in rags; and horsecarts and handcarts with high, spoked, iron-rimmed wheels that ground and squealed against cobblestone and curb. Right and wrong sides of the street had not been legislated; and polite traffic zigzagged along ways of greatest courtesy or on paths of least resistance, while the powerful clattered down the middle and the rude blustered through everywhere, frightening and scattering people in front and powdering or spattering people behind (like capitalists lording it over the rest of society, Most said). With people thus begrimed and the heat of summer enough to raise sweat on glasses of water, baths were infrequent at the oftenest. Onions and garlic were popular, refuse and garbage rife, and itinerant pigs and free-roaming chickens common; and horses farted, cows shit, and dogs sniffed and pissed while people broke wind and voided with a little more discretion. Riis captured how it looked but not how it smelled. Meanwhile, behind rows of narrow windows, many with panes broken and framed by crippled shutters, throbbed the private life of immigrant New York. In tenements, at once home and sweat-shop, lacking plumbing and heat, and short on light and air, huge families jammed into few and tiny rooms and to subsist cut cloth and rolled cigars. Only landlords and fire liked the tenements. Airshafts and trash fed errant flames, and the era of the tenement was the era of the inferno. In boardinghouses (dovecotes of the poor and warrens of the destitute) little but dirt separated neighbor from neighbor. Riis photographed this New York but left much to imagination. The imagination of reformers like Most produced rage.

The day before Most arrived, ponds froze; and children enjoyed the season's first skating. The day he arrived, under the forest of masts and amid the thicket of jetties in the port, ice stiffened ropes of the ship and numbed fingers of sailors who conveyed him to America's silver gate. There was no snow, but the sun glittered on a New York white with frost. From noses of horses pulling street-cars steam poured in clouds. Steam erupted, too, from dung the horses dropped; and its pungency, carried on chill air, bit passengers' nostrils.

The streetcar on East Broadway in the intellectual center of the East Side (Most's neighborhood) was small, blue, pulled by one horse, and driven by the conductor, who also made change and watched passengers drop nickels into the glass box. Change for dollars, quarters, and dimes he counted into envelopes in advance and handed them to passengers needing change. Like him, clerks at Lord and Taylor's were alert and brisk and ready with change. When it came to money, Americans were efficient and America was on the move. The efficient energetic A. T. Stewart, who invented the department store in New York City, was now a millionaire. Already there were plans for buildings taller than eight stories. Lord and Taylor, outgrowing Grand Street, would soon take their emporium to Fifth Avenue. Seeing money flow from many hands into few, Most called for revolution.

Streetcars shook, rattled, and rolled over cobblestones that delineated the East Side's ethnic sectors. Germans and Irish had departed Hester Street, leaving it artless, unstoried, and unenhanced to Jews who graced it with an exhilarating culture. Theirs was the *Hester Street* of George Luks: a crowded, bustling, always-something-going-on street, more fascinating than a Moroccan bazaar.

On corners around Hester and Grand, Most got on his soapbox, peppered his German with Yiddish, and demanded revolution of Jews who gathered around, peppered their Yiddish with German, and applauded. Late in his career, these Jews were his principal constituency.

With him, many of them urged violence to achieve social justice. Able to see clearly because not blinded by custom or prejudiced by habit or blinkered by patriotism, they chafed at social evils and political corruption and economic wrongs. To organize around a moral leader was in the best of Hebraic tradition; and many Jews organized around Most, whose beliefs resembled, fervor equalled, and knowledge of America exceeded theirs. The Pioneers for Liberty, Jewish anarchists, took after him. Saul Yanofsky, editor of the Yiddish *freye geselshaft*, admired and followed Most when Most was alive and revered and imitated Most when Most was dead. Jews on corners roared with delight when Most said, "What's the difference between the toilet and the stock exchange? In the exchange, papers fall, then comes the crash. In the toilet, the crash comes first."[3]

He lived for a while in the Bowery, neighborhood of outcasts, criminals, and prostitutes, then moved to the German sector, which extended along Second and into side streets above Houston. Here, on summer evenings, Germans sat on stoops, reading German newspapers. Germans frequented beer halls, delicatessens, and book stores where every word spoken and written was German. Germans met in the hall on Second near Houston, and Most gave speeches there. Fritz Schaefer's print shop, also on Second, printed busily in German. Schaefer, friendly, red of face and florid of nose, was short, stocky, blond, and explosive. His typesetters pattered about in slippers and puffed Bismarck pipes. Daily at 10:00 and 3:00 a printer's devil staggered in under tankards of beer and bundles of pretzels strung on a pole, from Justus Schwab's saloon; and typesetters put pipes aside and munched and sipped and were jovial.

The welter of immigrants on the East Side produced a welter of ideas—radical, leftist, and militant often; satisfied people do not emigrate. Samuel Gompers remembered that the East Side harbored French emigrés, Hungarian rebels, Garibaldi's red shirts, German forty-eighters, English chartists, Italian carbonari, Irish home-rulers, and Danish, Austrian, and Russian insurrectionists—men of imagination, courage, and ideals, who sought ends through revolution.[4] The East Side therefore buzzed with circles, leagues, and clubs where ideas were not only food for thought and fare for discussion but also recipes for political, social, and economic reform—and plots for revolution. Book stores stocked Marx, Kropotkin, Bakunin, and Most; and Schaefer's produced pamphlets by Lassalle, Liebknecht, Bebel, Engels, and Most—because a hunger for understanding gnawed at the radicals. They wanted to know the whys and wherefores of their place in the New World and to master the ABCs of revolution. They disliked cheap entertainments and rejected frivolous pastimes. To plebian theatre they preferred lectures on the iron law of wages. Vaudeville was imbecile. But they flocked to Most's plays, which dramatized revolution. Radicalism, not confined to politics or restricted to economics or limited to social change, extended to morals and embraced ethics. Hence the affinity between these radicals and Most; he saw himself as one of them, and they welcomed a radical lecturer.

He was one radical among many; and though he at once became a leader, he was one leader among several.

Another was short slim dark-bearded William Frey, a nobleman born in Russia and there called Vladimir Hines, educated for the military but now a pacifist, onetime professor of mathematics but now a guru. He taught utopian communism, natural religion, and vegetarianism. Once a Comtist, he retained the positivism that agreed with his beliefs. He ate bread kneaded out of his own dough with his own hands into long slim loaves, baked under his own eye, and chewed and swallowed his own way; eating was, like all of life, a religious act. He who ate right lived right and was right.

Another leader, lean bald bearded austere Dr. Felix Adler, founded the Society for Ethical Culture, where he held forth Sunday mornings on the bankruptcy of theology and sterility of religion. He believed that consciousness of morality, not religion, produced right conduct. Since right conduct included social justice and economic rectitude, he spoke for both.

He, Frey, and Most, the East Side's leading polemicists, were so persuasive that some of their hearers confounded their doctrines into an anarchist-positivist-ethical hash, while others bounced from one to another like billiard balls. Shaking his head or his fist, Most said or screamed, "How fickle!"

He liked the East Side nonetheless, and there he stayed. Banned from time to time in many cities, he was never banned in New York City. When Chicago lifted its ban in 1896, he declined to join anarchists there, even though they were more numerous and more cohesive than New York's. Other places were nice to visit, he said, but he wanted to live in New York.

Freiheit's offices he established at 167 William, in the Fourteenth Precinct. He would say, "What's right with the Fourteenth? Everything but McCullagh. What's wrong with the Fourteenth? Nothing but McCullagh. What's rotten in the Fourteenth? McCullagh. He stinks!" McCullagh was captain of the Fourteenth, a hater and baiter of radicals, a martinet niggardly of permits to assemble but liberal with truncheons—Most's enemy. Better to get soaked in cold rain than see McCullagh, better to be pelted by hail than smell McCullagh, Most said, and walked blocks to avoid him.

Most, who loved to walk, walked from home to Battery Park, and from there watched ships passing (How many, he wondered, how many were going to Germany? Would there have been a place for him? Would there be a place?). He walked north to give speeches in Union Square. He walked in his big slouch hat, which covered the upper part of his face and emphasized the lower (his bushy beard then seemed three times its size), and people said he looked like the brigand of a melodrama. On early trips to Brooklyn he took the ferry; the Bridge, though done, was not open. In Brooklyn he rode a double-decker streetcar of the kind Walt Whitman sang.

He oriented himself on the Bridge, the Pulitzer Building, Cooper Union, and Trinity Church. Past, between, and under the towers of the Bridge he went afoot and by horsecar and boat to agitate revolution by speech, rally, and demonstration. In return he felt jabs of journalists' pens dipped in acid, endured harrassment by police, and suffered three terms in prison. Under a golden dome that bespoke the ostentation of plutocracy, the Pulitzer Building stood for a press that ridiculed, abused, and maligned him. He had no sooner landed than the New York *Times* called him an unattractive little man who blustered in the hackneyed style of socialists. Cooper

Figure 2. Most Addressing a Meeting at Cooper Union, 1887

—Culver Pictures

Union meant free speech; and there he gave many a speech, all reported as intolerable, incendiary, and even insane. The spire of Trinity, pointing up from Wall Street (from the den of money changers and plutocrats), spoiled his view of communal ownership, blurred his vision of a classless society, and sullied his clear skies of atheism.

He participated in activities of German clubs: clubs political, athletic, musical, literary, philosophical, educational, and social. Clubs invited him to speak. The Social Revolutionary Club, which called him to New York and met him at the pier, owed to active and influential members its preeminence among political clubs.

Among the Club's members, comrades of his had come by his route: Germany, London, New York: from elementary school to preparatory school to university of leftist education. Justus Schwab, less famous in America only than Most himself, and Moritz Bachmann and Peter Knauer, founders of the Club, met Most on the pier. He shook hands with them like a thirsty man pumping a dry well.

They did not take him at once to a cafe or a saloon, but he got there soon; comrades rallied there. Samuel Gompers remembered saloons as places where pennies bought a glass of beer—and hours of congeniality. Keepers cashed checks and were employment agents. Free lunches sustained many a hungry striker; and a room or hall at the rear, available for nominal fee, might be the only place to hold a meeting.[5] To comrades, saloons and cafes were clean well-lighted places.

For, on the streets, even in their own quarter, in outlandish dress and uttering a foreign tongue, immigrants were strangers, aliens. Americans asked, "Who are those queer fish who flit around corners there evenings?" Some immigrants drank beer with meals, and others believed in militant socialism: examples, to Americans, of barbarous habits and tramontane notions. Forced to menial work, immigrants often drifted from job to job. Compelled to take shabby rooms in rotting tenements, they stayed in them little. Clothes, language, work, habits, ideas, dwellings (all of another world) separated immigrants from natives.

So the comrades were nowhere at home but with their own in cafes and saloons. Hence what coffeehouses and salons had been

to literature in the eighteenth century, cafes and saloons were to
radicalism in the nineteenth century. Recognizing cafes and saloons
as hubs of the revolutionary movement, Henry James and Joseph
Conrad assigned them prominence in novels of anarchism set in
Most's time, inspired by Most's enterprises, and featuring characters modeled on Most and his followers.

Headquarters for socialists and anarchists were Sachs's cafe on
Suffolk, the saloon and hall at 625 East Sixth, and above all, Justus
Schwab's saloon at 50 First Street. Immigrant Germans and Austrians, joined more and more by East European Jews and a few
Irish, Hungarians, Czechs, Italians, Bohemians, and Poles—poor
students, struggling writers, disgruntled intellectuals, impecunious
workers, and professional revolutionaries, a motley crowd—night
after night filled these hangouts with smoke, dirty dishes, empty
bottles, and talk and went home less with heads spinning than with
ideas spinning in heads. To think without speaking was as bad as
to speak without thinking. Whatever the season, leftist doctrine
was on the menu: tables groaned under conjectures of a classless
utopia; and everyone took seconds of schemes for wrecking the
railroads, notions that came as main courses or side dishes, rare,
half-baked, done to a turn and every degree in between, served with
piping hot language and seasoned with a whiff of grapeshot. Marx
was milquetoast.

In no modern lyceum were more ideas exchanged, nor at any
ancient symposium more spirits drunk in the cause of philosophical
discussion, than on a normal night at Schwab's. No lyceum or symposium looked like Schwab's. The bar extended across the front
of the low-ceilinged smoky saloon. Above bottles behind the bar
a bas relief of Marat glowered. Beneath Marat from copper wire
hung a shiny flintlock pistol, said to be ready to fire. Beside the
pistol, notices plastered a bulletin board. In the rest of the room,
tables and chairs crowded a beer-stained player piano that burst
into waltzes, out of tune but jovial. In the next room, chairs surrounded a long green table, which Most once pounded with a full
mug, for order; and stains still marked the spot where the mug
broke, beer spilled, and blood dripped from his hand. *Freiheit* lay
on tables near the piano. Early arrivers would read it, then greet
latecomers with quotations, hurrahs, and "Beer! Wine!" Up an

imaginary aisle a couple might strut arm in arm to the wedding march from *Lohengrin* sung by every voice present.

From behind the bar came the voice of Schwab himself. Schwab stood over six feet, rolled his sleeves above the elbows, folded a Byronic collar around a Michelangelic neck, and belted out songs in a tenor that had promised fame until he rebelled with lyrics of his own, to the tune of the *Marseillaise*. His hair and ideas were red, shoulders and humor broad, and chest and generosity enormous. Leftists needed not go hungry or thirsty, would they but visit his place. Many paid call from Europe and America, so widespread was his reputation. Tourists, too, hunted for First and First (his "anarchist saloon" at First Street and First Avenue) and for him, the president of the Social Revolutionary Club, who sang, looked, and acted like a Wagnerian hero. Even in cartoons that roasted him as an apostle of anarchy and hops, he retained heroic proportions of body, mind, and character and dispensed beer with saintly benevolence and robust charm.

His reputation began in a Tompkins Square demonstration of the 1870s, when he waved a red flag and was dragged to jail singing variations on the *Marseillaise* at the top of his lungs. Because he never bribed, police raided whenever they needed evidence against charges of graft or inefficiency; raids on someone of his reputation made news and exonerated the police. Raids kept him on the verge of ruin, and bribing the police would have been cheaper, but raids enhanced his reputation with comrades. He spoke and they listened. When *Freiheit* struggled in London, he coaxed contributions. *"Freiheit* is dying! Long live *Freiheit!"* He persuaded the Club to bring *Freiheit* and Most to America, which saved *Freiheit* and commenced Most's American career. Then illness wasted Schwab, stole the silver from his voice, and dimmed his eyes. Comrades wept. "Schwab is dying! Long live Schwab!" He died, but his reputation lived.

Comrades mourned the man who fed the hungry. How often they hungered! A certain comrade, who frequently could afford only bread and tea, one evening shouted, "Extra-large steak! Extra cup of coffee!"

The voice thundered from a brawny chest; a high forehead tilted toward the food; intelligent eyes fastened on it; and a strong jaw and thick lips packed it away, as if he had hungered for weeks, which he likely had.

Emma Goldman asked Hillel Solotaroff, "Who is that glutton?" "Alexander Berkman. He can eat for three. But he rarely has enough money for much food. When he has, he eats Sachs out of his supplies. I'll introduce him to you."[6]

So the woman who would become the anarchist orator called Red Emma met the man who was to shoot Henry Clay Frick and become an anarchist second only to Red Emma herself. They met on a typical night, amid a pandemonium of German, Russian, and Yiddish and felt at home, for they spoke all three. All languages addressed one topic: revolution. Later, Most brought in the polyglot staff of *Freiheit*. Babel rose in unison, glasses raised, when he proposed, "The Social Revolution: soon may it come, long may it live, always may it prosper!"

Rising in unison was one way comrades lionized him. They also crowded to meet him the first time he returned from Blackwell's Island. Fifty received him at water's edge at the foot of 52nd, "delirious in their joy over their chieftain's release. They hugged and kissed him. They pressed his hands and embraced his legs. They made dabs for his mouth and struck his ears. They carried him up the steep steps." At the top, another 100 "took him to their hearts and wept with joy."[7] At the offices of *Freiheit*, men and women, typesetters and dispatchers and editors, alike rushed into his arms.

Ida Hoffman, wife of the physician, was more dignified. She appeared at his trial in 1887 and sat inside the rail. Her red hair, blue eyes, pale complexion, expensive dress, and well-known name sent whispers around the courtroom. Everyone stared at her. She told reporters that she and her husband Julius were anarchists and friends of Most's. Julius, Most's surety next year, accompanied Most to court, too, and stood by him like a true comrade.[8]

Others were anonymous. This fact, cheering to Most, bothered the authorities. They feared that anarchists "out there somewhere" would "do something" if they got (half) a chance. Hands, stretched from clusters of people held back by police, reached for him. Admirers wanted to touch him and give him things. One burst out of a throng and tried to pass him cigars, until clubbed aside. Since a cigar was nearly part of Most's anatomy, he regretted missing those cigars.

To the perpetual cigar add a violent manner, an obstreperous voice, burning eyes, twisted face, bristly hair, bushy beard, and boozy attitudes, and you have the Most of the caricaturists. His notoriety caused illustrators and cartoonists to caricature him often. In the golden age of the political cartoon, Most became the cartoonists' prototypal terrorist: wolfish, conspiratorial, and armed to the teeth; even the teeth were weapons. Joseph Keppler of *Puck* helped create that prototype. When Most was in custody in 1886, Keppler studied him "for professional purposes." Of this "first look at a real, live, wild Anarchist" Keppler said, "I hope it will be my last if the rest are like the specimen I saw."[9] Thomas Nast, as angered by Most as by Andrew Johnson or the Tweed Ring, made the donkey the symbol of the Democrats, the elephant of the Republicans, and Most of the Anarchists. Nast's Most boozed and bristled in cartoons that sent chuckles across the nation and furrows across Most's brow.

Perhaps the caricatures encouraged Emma Goldman to go from Rochester to New York City, to ask Most to help her become an anarchist. Their relationship began, as she remembered,[10] when she and Berkman took the Elevated from West 42nd to Brooklyn Bridge, the stop near 167 William. *Freiheit*'s resembled the situations of print shops and newspapers nearby, with windows too dirty for gaslight to penetrate, boxes of dust, wooden stairs, and rat dung. Goldman and Berkman went into a ramshackle building, which Most called a "horribly furnished shelter for wandering comrades and other gypsies," up two dark flights that creaked, through a doorway decked with a blood-red flag and posted with NO REPORTERS PERMITTED, past typesetters, and into a room lined with books, Most's sanctum. Erect behind a stand-up desk was Most, writing. "Standing spares my behind," he said. The blue of his searching eyes was deep. His twisted jaw was obtrusive, voice gruff. Gruffly he bade Goldman and Berkman be seated.

"My damned torturers there," he said of the typesetters, "are squeezing the blood out of me. Copy, copy, copy! That's all they know! Ask them to write a line—not they. They are too stupid and too lazy."

"Angry, this Most," Goldman thought. Was *he* last night's speaker whose oratory had carried her away?

Berkman whispered "not to mind Most, that he was always in such a mood when at work."

Most's appetite for work was still voracious—often he had not slept for days when serving in parliament and editing in Germany —but now he allayed the appetite with outbursts of anger. They varied monotony, relieved tension, and spiced bland work with pungent spleen. They helped him stand all day planted at his desk, writing amid hubbub: type clacking, presses rumbling, envelopes rustling, paper rattling, and voices chattering, singing, shouting, and resounding. Strangers to this hubbub marveled at Most's concentration; in spite of hubbub he wrote the way he arranged a meeting, staged a demonstration, or gave a speech—with fanatical intensity. In the evening, weary, he would stop, cuss out associates—"Toothless old women!" . . . "Cackling geese!"—snatch up his big slouch hat, and repair to dinner and diversion at Sachs's or Schwab's.

Now he thundered, "Here's my pound of flesh, you Shylocks! More than enough to fill the paper. Here, Berkman, take it to the black devils in there!"

Most approached Goldman, who was inspecting books and wondering whether she dare ask him to suggest a course of reading. He was the person to ask; friend and foe alike respected his knowledge. In London, Crown-Attorney Poland had called him "a lecturer and a learned man." Revolutionary history, radical social thought, and leftist political theory he knew backward and forward. Questions about Marx? Engels? Lassalle? Social Democracy? The International? Bakunin? Answers were at his fingertips.

He gave her books, shook her hand, and asked her to return Wednesday to help dispatch *Freiheit*. His voice was warm and friendly.

"Afterwards," he said, "we may be able to talk."

Wednesday, over dinner, they talked. He said that anarchism was the Cause, to which he dedicated his life. Without the Cause, life would be meaningless; and he would kill himself. Aside from the Cause, food and drink mattered. How he had suffered hunger! Stepmother, prison officials, and police inflicted it; and poverty forced eating little or nothing when appetite screamed for plenty. Deprivation engendered cravings, which he indulged whenever he could with rich food and full-bodied wine.

He was indulging now, and the food and wine mellowed him.

While wine was poetic (he continued), woman's love was prosaic. Even in this mellow mood he declared that women neither could nor would climb to anarchism. Louise Michel and Sophia Perovskaya were exceptions. Outstanding women in the American movement? "None at all, only stupids." But he told Goldman he would help her find work and a place in the Cause; coming from Russia, she might be different from the stupids. The Cause needed her.

"And," he said, "I have need of ardent friendship."

"You? You have thousands in New York—all over the world. You are loved, you are idolized."

"Yes, little girl, idolized by many, but loved by none. One can be very lonely among thousands—did you know that?"

She remembered, "Something gripped my heart. I wanted to take his hand, to tell him that I would be his friend. But I dared not speak out. What could I give this man—I, a factory girl, uneducated; and he, the famous Johann Most, the leader of the masses, the man of magic tongue and powerful pen?"

At daybreak he took her home.

She attracted him as had no woman in years.

He touched her hand. "Where did you get your silky blond hair? And your blue eyes?" He looked into them. "This," he said, "was my first happy evening in a long while."

He charmed her. She thought his talents remarkable and found his eagerness for life moving and his yearning for friendship touching.

When he took a lecture tour, his letters to her described people he met or denounced reporters who vilified him. He included newspapers' caricatures of him, with his glosses:

"Behold the wife-killer!"

"Here's the man who eats little children."

His interests and learning extended beyond economics, history, and politics (she discovered) to music, theatre, literature, and art. They saw *Carmen* together at the Metropolitan. Aficionados, they stood through it willingly, after he helped her burning feet out of new shoes.

In succeeding weeks he trimmed his beard, wore a natty suit with a red carnation, and looked younger. He gave her violets and lilacs. When she returned from her first lecture tour, he scolded himself; he would never let her go again, at least not without him. When she was ill, he visited and sent flowers. One day in a cab, trembling, he embraced her, and his kisses covered her mouth. He kissed as if "famished with thirst," she said. "I let him drink; I could have denied him nothing."

He said he loved her, had never longed so for any other woman.

She remembered that her youth made him young, her ardor raised his, and her heart awakened him to new meaning. "I was his Blondkopf, his 'blue eyes'; he wanted me to be his own, his helpmate, his voice." She felt "infinite tenderness" for this "great man-child" who "was hungry for affection, for understanding. I would give him both."

He impressed her as "a man apart, the most remarkable in all the world. She was proud of his confidence and honored by his love. She wanted to show him to her friends. Though long and fiercely against children for herself, she dreamed "how wonderful . . . to have a child by this unique personality!" Of many who knew him, she alone saw through bitterness to his kind, gentle, sensitive self within. She worshipped him, idolized him, and followed him into the public and polemical life of the anarchist.

NOTES

1. *New York Times* 1882: 14 December, p. 8; 19 December, p. 8. *Freiheit*, 16 December 1882.

2. The following discussion of New York City and its Lower East Side: Morris Raphael Cohen, *A Dreamer's Journey. New York Times*, 14-20 December 1882. Abraham Cahan, *The Education of Abraham Cahan*. Gregory Weinstein, *The Ardent Eighties*. Samuel Gompers, *Seventy Years of Life and Labor*. Irving Howe, *World of Our Fathers*. Emma Goldman, *Living My Life. Freiheit*, 16, 23, 30 December 1882. Photographs by Jacob A. Riis.

3. Samuel Blitz to Frederic Trautmann, 5 June 1976. On Most and the Pioneers for Liberty see Norma Fain Pratt, *Morris Hillquit*, p. 10.

4. Gompers, *Seventy Years* 1:50-51, 61.

5. Ibid. 2:176.

6. Goldman, *Living My Life*, p. 5.

7. *New York Times*, 2 April 1887, p. 8.

8. Ibid., 19 November 1887, p. 8. *Freiheit*, 26 November 1887, 15 December 1888.

9. *New York Times*, 15 May 1886, p. 8.

10. Goldman, *Living My Life*, pp. 3-77 *passim*.

7
POSITIONS AND PERSUASIONS

1821: Bartoldi records terrorist practices in *Memoirs of the Secret Societies of the South of Italy.*

1840: Proudhon asks *What Is Property*? and answers, "theft." "Property is theft" becomes a battle cry of the century.

1842: Bakunin publishes "Reaction in Germany," asserting, "The passion for destruction is also a creative passion."

1845: Blanqui coins the term "dictatorship of the proletariat" and affirms Babeuf's components of revolution: secret societies, propaganda, coup d'etat, terrorism, and violence.

1851: Proudhon states the necessity and nature of *The General Idea of the Revolution in the 19th Century.*

1854: Thoreau is convinced that thieving and robbery "take place only in communities where some have got more than is sufficient while others have not enough."

1860: France and especially French-speaking Switzerland (the Jura) are the leftist hub. Germans who know French learn the latest in anarchism. Other Germans become anarchists later.

1868: Bakunin argues *The People's Cause*: anarchism, collectivism, and atheism are the way to freedom.

1880: Kropotkin shows in "The Spirit of Revolt" what a few of the courageous can do when words fail.

Most thought in jerks. Vain it is to search him for fine distinctions.

Max Nettlau, *Anarchisten und Sozialrevolutionäre*

Every change in the wind turns Most this way and that, like a weathercock.

Karl Marx to Friedrich Sorge, September 19, 1879

With Most, social revolution was only skin-deep. Scaling would reveal the anarchist underneath, which, given his propensity to scrapes, could happen overnight.

Karl Schneidt, *Die Kritik*, April 11, 1896

SOCIAL REVOLUTIONARY

I follow four commandments [Most said]. Thou shalt deny God and love truth; therefore I am an atheist. Thou shalt oppose tyranny and seek liberty; therefore I am a republican. Thou shalt repudiate property and champion equality; therefore I am a communist. Thou shalt hate oppression and foment revolution; therefore I am a revolutionary. Long live the social revolution![1]

The atheist recognized in religion the source of authority. Command and obedience in groups from family to nation, and creation and acceptance of social class, began with worship of a god: the first despot, king, lawgiver, father, and in Christianity, chief of the Trinity: a gray eminence to be feared, honored, and above all, obeyed. He ordered people to love Him. Commanding that His name not be taken in vain, He pioneered in suppressing free speech, the Original Tyranny. It followed that monarchs who arrogated divine right, fathers who bullied families, teachers who frightened classrooms, princes who lorded over nations, officials who bossed institutions, and employers who dictated to employees replicated the Creature that laid down the Decalogue. Autocrats ruled because religion satisfied only the impalpable in mankind's intellectual needs and emotional wants. To satisfy the palpable, mankind extended authority from abstractions of God and religion to concretions of authority and submission.[2]

In times gone by, authority empowered religion to pillory apos-
tates, rack unbelievers, and burn skeptics. Today, religion must
content itself to elaborate the lie of God.

And what a lie! God—the all-wise bungler Who created mankind but did not keep them from sin; Who created the Devil yet
failed to control him; Who, though omnipresent, descended from
heaven to see what mankind were doing; Who created planets,
stars, moon, and sun like a magician shaking eggs from a coatsleeve;
and Who, though all-merciful, permitted slaughter of innocent millions and condemned to eternal and infernal fire sinners created in
His image—this was *God*?[3]

The atheist therefore took Blanqui's motto: "No God, no master!"[4] God is bunk, authority a fiction. Away with clerics, in league
with rulers for centuries, who preach, "Obey or be damned." Cure
religious syphilis: strangle rulers with clerics' intestines. Then authority will disperse, superstition dissolve, and in the truth of
materialism, freedom come to a mankind downtrodden since God
gave Adam the first order and subservient since God handed Moses
the first commandment.[5]

The republican wanted people organized into natural units, communes. Associations of like-minded individuals, they will vary in
nature, size, and purpose according to members' needs, wants, and
goals. Only one rule applies to all communes: each member must
be honored as an individual. Communes will govern themselves,
each member participating directly, without law or leaders. No
member will be forced into an unwanted position or constrained
from a desired action.[6]

To the republican, as important as "being for" is "being against."
The republican must bid the tyrant defiance and heed the maxim,
"Tyrannicide the greatest virtue!" The republican must oppose
the ballot, because dictators justify coercion with plebiscites, voting sanctifies oppression, and the individual's vote means nothing.
Parliaments, the republican's enemies, are fraud.[7] When an MP,
Most witnessed how MPs vote in ignorance; he realized how little
business they conduct on the floor and how much in taverns; and
he observed how MPs appropriate unto themselves stationery, ink,
seals, pens, and pencils enough to last not only the session but also
the rest of the year, in amounts sufficient to serve not only official

but also personal needs and in quantities prodigal not only for self and family but also lavish for relatives and friends—proof positive of fraud.[8]

The communist would effect common ownership and acknowledge, "From each according to ability, to each according to need." To stipulate more would encroach on the liberty and infringe on the right of the ideal republic to chart its own destiny.[9]

The revolutionary would obliterate religion, destroy its roots, and poison the ground that nourished it; demolish government, let no authority remain, and pulverize every evidence that mankind once comprised servants and masters; and smash the system of private property, introduce new economic and social relations, and foster liberty, equality, and fraternity. Wreck from top down and rebuild from bottom up—that is social revolution.[10]

Critics cross-examined.[11]

Can this scheme work without authority?

"Experience shows that a spirit of enterprise and sense of purpose will bring and hold people together and direct them to a goal. Authority is either superfluous or tyrannical."

Aren't you asking too much participation per person?

"More than traditionally, true. But more can be expected in consideration of problems of common interest, especially since participants will influence the outcome and see results."

Aren't you forgetting benefits of competition?

"Rivalry among communes, together with communes' freedom of thought and lack of constraint, will produce more progress than ever before."

Won't your commune be as tyrannical as democracy, since people differ and a majority must rule?

"In democracy, millions may be in the minority—millions therefore subjected to tyranny without recourse! And there abound instances when a plurality tyrannizes over the majority. In refreshing contrast, that communes are smaller means that minorities are smaller. A discontented minority can leave one commune and, of the hundreds, perhaps thousands of others, join another in which their ideas meet accord."

Critics persisted. Obliterate, destroy, smash—have you no ethics, Most?

Ethics? Anyone with a scintilla of ethics can see that the exercise of authority and prerogatives of property are not natural rights but privileges of plunder. Anyone's sense of justice should cry out that everything belongs to labor because labor creates everything. But labor will get nothing unless it seizes as today's powers seized. Seizure is the final legality and the ultimate morality. One thrust of the nihilist's dagger is more moral than all tones of every priest's prayer, and more just than all raps of every judge's gavel.[12]

Ethics? The end of revolution is freedom; the end justifies the means. The struggle for freedom is a war; wars are to be won and therefore to be waged with all energy, ruthlessly. If ruthlessness is wrong, then the least ruthless war will be the short war, ended as soon as possible by using all there is to use, including the latest in technology and the finest of chemistry, to kill oppressors forthwith. If killing is wrong, the short decisive war will be best; a few oppressors will perish and their torture of millions and slaughter of thousands cease. To hell with faintheartedness, a tooth for a tooth![13]

Ethics? Necheyev and Bakunin, the noble Russian revolutionists, spelled them out in 1869. The terrorist is obliged first to himself, then to comrades, and then to the community. He must sacrifice everything people call their own. He must renounce beliefs, spurn pleasures, despise traditional morality, suffer pain, and stifle feeling until nothing remains but passion for revolution. Then he must do everything to foment and nothing to deter the Revolution. Having stifled feelings, he will aid and befriend comrades only when aid and friendship advance the Revolution. Having renounced beliefs, he will entertain only such loyalties to the community as will advance the Revolution. What remains intractable he will destroy with his own hands, and those who resist he will murder in cold blood. So help him Justice![14]

Ethics? Since the end justifies the means, propaganda-by-the-deed is right. Furthermore, without propaganda-by-the-deed, propaganda-of-the-word is useless; the execrable social order has not been built on paper and ink, and paper and ink will not destroy it. Propaganda-by-the-deed will unsettle the complacent, agitate the unsettled, and enrage the agitated—terrorize opponents, win comrades, and rouse the masses—by quick, decisive, well-timed violent acts that confound oppressors and inspire the oppressed. But unless directed and aimed at things the masses dislike, propaganda-by-the-deed will redound to damage the Cause. Accordingly, not every act of terrorism is an instance of propaganda-by-the-deed. Blowing up buildings, setting fire to factories, cutting telegraph lines, shooting officials, lynching informers, stabbing policemen, poisoning clerics, and castrating spies are admirable in themselves (any act against tyranny today is an act for a better tomorrow); but if misguided, such terrorism will not secure the future for the Revolution. To attack detestable principles by attacking scoundrels who hold them and to win the applause of the masses, is propaganda-by-the-deed.[15]

To instruct in propaganda-by-the-deed, Most wrote a series for *Freiheit*, then compiled it as *The Science of Revolutionary Warfare*. He explained, to the last detail, with diagrams, how to brew disappearing ink; use codes; prepare gunpowder; spin guncotton; concoct, store, and administer poisons; handle guns, knives, detonating gas, dynamite, Greek fire, and Congreve rockets; and wrap and dispatch his invention, the letter bomb. Daggers, because they glance off bones, should be poisoned. Because curare is hard to get, dip the weapon in juice of oleander or a mixture of phosphorus and gum arabic. Crush twenty-five mayapple seeds, mix with flour, bake in cookies, and feed to flatfoots; they will croak in a few days. For best results, throw the four-inch hand grenade under the table of a banquet.

Enemies laughed. This amateur wanted to foist on ignorant radicals a cookbook to give the Establishment indigestion? The likeliest result was that radicals would blow their own heads off. Bismarck was said to have held *Science* up in parliament, glowered at it through his monocle, and made fun of it. But when the curious stopped laughing and tried *Science*'s recipes, the recipes worked. Most had done research, and not only in libraries, reading manuals and studying experiments with explosives by ministries of war. He also took a job in a munitions factory, where he knew a foreman, to learn firsthand. The foreman was blown to bits, but not before Most had what he needed to write *Science*.[16]

Ethics? The end justifies the means; and when propaganda-by-the-deed echoes in hearts and propaganda-of-the-word strikes chords in minds, the end will be at hand.[17] The masses will pour into the streets. Social revolutionaries will destroy bridges, arsenals, telegraph and railway lines, and buildings, and kill officials. Soldiers will refuse to fight, for they are brothers to the masses; they will turn on their officers. Within hours, revolutionaries will organize the masses and take the cities; and within days they will secure the countryside, where the hypocritical enemy will have failed to rally the populace behind the slogan that all men are brothers. But if revolutionaries fail to consolidate victories, forces of reaction fighting like tigers for dear life will counterattack. Therefore revolutionaries must stockpile food and supplies, turn cities into fortresses, arm the masses, terrorize attempts to mobilize reaction, and pursue reactionaries to the corners of the nation and the ends of the earth. Then the dream will come true: "Long live the Revolution!"

ANARCHIST

"Perhaps never did so few people favor an idea less than the presently infamous *anarchy*, nor yet so many lips utter an idea more than the now savagely detested *anarchy*." So wrote Most in "Anarchy."[18]

Anarchy is said to be general confusion, wild turmoil, which every civilization scorns. Since this condition renders both government and law unthinkable, anarchy means the atomization of society into isolated individuals, who with impunity attack others, until the strong subject the weak in a slavery more terrible than the world has ever seen. Abominable and absurd, the goal of the anarchist! Foul the means by which it is to be attained, namely theft, murder, arson, and all kinds of destruction! Anarchy is therefore a mixture of idiocy and crime. Against it society must defend with all power—legally so far as possible, violently when necessary. At all events, every lover of order is obliged to nip anarchy in the bud as well as eradicate anarchists root and branch from the face of the earth. . . .

Now if people would only think . . . they would see: anarchy (autonomy or freedom) really means, not the criminal chaos just referred to, but the absence of the criminal chaos that archy (subjugation or government) has brought to mankind. Archy springs from the desire of the strong to oppress the weak; and up to the present day, whatever its form, oppression has been its goal.

Archy, always the tool of the propertied, has forever put the screws to the unpropertied. The more barbaric the society, the harsher and more flagrant the archy. The higher the civilization, the more refined the cleverness of the archists in hiding the usurpation of power—without weakening the exercise of power. . . .

If archy in all forms has brought mankind grief, it follows that the remedy is repudiation. The repudiation of archy is *anarchy*. Anarchy is therefore the goal of freedom-seeking mankind. Whoever seeks freedom, advances anarchy. If, among freedom-seekers, a multitude want no part of anarchy (having a false notion of it), that fact does not demean anarchy. The multitude simply do not know that, regardless of the route taken in the search for the rights of man, every route leads to anarchy. It cannot be otherwise; for either one accepts archy or one fights it and advances its opposite, anarchy. Something in between is unthinkable. . . .

The truth that government (archy) is instituted to exploit the poor is a truth the opponents of anarchy blink at; and, counting on the ignorance they have created in the masses, they adduce a hundred bagatelles in archy's favor. They emphasize crime. Were government and law abolished, they say, unpunished crime would peril life and property until chaos rendered existence disagreeable at best.

These sorcerers! In broad daylight they ascribe to anarchy aberrations of their society, when the basis of anarchy is the absence of such aberrations. All crimes—except misbehavior of madmen, which, by definition, is the symptom of illness—all crimes are notoriously the offspring of the system of private property, archy's reason for being. This system mandates a struggle for existence, by all, against all. Greed and the lust for power flourish in the propertied and goad the propertied to crimes that as a rule go unpunished because archy enforces its laws against another kind of "crime": those deeds done out of necessity and in response to brutality. Turn the pages of the so-called civil law: the topic is "yours and mine"; the civil law is the natural result of a society of individuals who want to cheat as much as possible because cheating is the only way to power and wealth. Today's society considers such behavior normal.

Freedom and equality, the conditions of anarchy, would end this ruinous struggle for existence. . . . Law, purposeless, would no longer be needed, nor government . . . and they would disappear.

More important than the arguments of the archists are the arguments from a side that should have the least reason to oppose anarchy. Unconscious anarchists, particularly those called socialists, expend untold time and effort attacking anarchy, even though their goals are freedom and equality (anarchy). . . . These people maintain: anarchy is opposite to socialism. In truth, anarchy is socialism perfected. Because anarchists seek freedom for the individual—the greatest human happiness—other socialists say the anarchists contradict the brotherhood of man. As if the brotherhood of man did not presuppose the freedom of the individual! . . .

This wrongheadedness goes so far as to claim that the anarchists ignore technology and favor cottage industry. . . . But . . . no anarchist wants to reverse technological advances; every anarchist wants more such advances. Accordingly, anarchists recognize, labor and production must be organized, their powers united. And since the lack of freedom today results from private property's control of the factors of production . . . those who want freedom (anarchy) want these things owned in common; that is, they want communism. . . .

Contrary to the old-style communists, however, the anarchists declare for the organization with the greatest validity, *federalism.* . . . From it, "over-and-under" structure—that is, authority concentrated in economic and political hierarchies, and power centralized in the state—would be excluded. Instead, voluntary association would give rise to thousands of special organizations, interconnected horizontally according to purpose or necessity. . . .

Organization is paramount. Indeed, the enemies of the proletariat are so well organized, so unified, that the proletariat commit crime by not gathering all forces and directing them at once at the destruction of the status quo by all possible means. For whether the propertied and ruling classes call themselves conservative or liberal, clerical or free-thinking, protectionist or free-trade, aristocrat or democrat, imperialist or republican—their differences hinder them not from seeing themselves as the propertied against the unpropertied. . . . Nor should be overlooked the monstrous police, military, and legal apparatus that stands at the disposal of the bourgeoisie. Nor should be forgotten the machinations of the black constabulary of priests and the reactionary press; the bourgeoisie can turn them to its purpose, too. . . .

If the rich stick together, why can't the poor stick together? Unfortunately, the cause of discord among those who should be of one heart and a single mind, and who need the profoundest of unity to achieve victory, is nothing but fear of the word *anarchy*. Yet all that a socialist has to get rid of, to be an anarchist, is the idea of the political state, to which socialists who are terrified hold fast, even though Marx and Engels taught that in a truly free society, the state would wither away.

What is the supreme joy of mankind? It is the greatest freedom possible, i.e., the opportunity to realize intellectual and physical potential. Of course, such freedom must not go beyond the point at which it hurts someone, for then a domination of some by others occurs. At the same time, in a civilized society, many goals are not attainable by individuals; they can be reached only by associations with a common purpose. But is that to say: a system must exist in which an individual has by dictate to exist tucked away in the bureau of a centralized state, put there by a higher power and told what to do from birth to death? . . .

What is needed to produce a system in which the freedom of one and all is guaranteed is simply an agreement for a free society! No need for a Providence directing from above; it is only necessary that things are handled correctly from below. . . .

What is the issue? Is it not whether *besides* society a state is needed? The answer, you see, is simpler than many think. We need only imagine what the state has been hitherto. Is it natural, an eternal verity? It is a creature of circumstance, used by a clique to dominate the masses. Let us therefore smash the state to bits. . . . Nothing less must be the climax of the Revolution. . . .

We do not stand alone. The really great minds have long been sure that, without freedom, no perfect society is possible, and that no government, not even a representative government, insures freedom.

John Stuart Mill [the British philosopher and economist, 1806-1873] has said that the only part of behavior for which anyone is accountable to society is that which concerns others; over himself, his own mind and spirit, the individual is supreme. . . .

[Ludwig] Börne [the German journalist and outspoken liberal, 1786-1837] writes that as soon as a child is born, its mother, wet nurse, father, and governess surround it, and later its teachers, and then the policeman and the state. The mother brings sugar, the wet nurse a fairy tale, the governess a rod, the father a reproach, the teacher a cane, and the state chains and the axe. And if the child shows any resistance, it will be coaxed, harangued, or forced. Thus

o

in childhood we become like . . . a goose fattened for its liver. Everything is sacrificed to the liver. We are locked in a stall, not able to move, so we grow fat; we are force-fed moral corn, and we wheeze and nearly choke on morality, erudition, and obedience; and then an old cook of a government paws us, praises us, slaughters us, and uses our liver. . . . What does death find to take in us! But death is a poor dog, nothing but bones its life through—seldom does a whole person fall to him.

Asked what kind of government he preferred, [Pierre Joseph] Proudhon [the French political reformer, 1809-1865] denied monarchy, republicanism, democracy, constitutionalism, aristocracy, and a mixed form. Asked, in desperation, "What are you then?" he said: "I am an anarchist."

Victor Drury [American anarchist, Most's contemporary] rightly argues that freedom is the self-government (sovereignty) of the individual; freedom is order and security, without which no freedom. Freedom means the denial of all government, since it stands to reason that where authority exists, oppression must also exist—and with it all kinds of danger and disorder. It is not the word *anarchy* but the word *government* that means the absence of order and security. The admirer of authority would call that a paradox, but it is simply logical.

Otto Hotzen [German poet, 1830-1899] gets to the heart of things:

> A temple piled high with corpses
> Slain to build the state—
> Who asks if brick and mortar have feelings?
> The welfare of people is not a goal
> Of founding fathers or of slave drivers.
> The state, that Moloch, devours the people that
> "God" has made for this purpose.

Even Friedrich Engels [Karl Marx's associate, 1820-1895] could not avoid breaking a lance for anarchism: "The state is not an eternal verity. There have been societies, finished in every way, but having no suspicion of state and state-power. With us, at a certain level of economic development, which was of necessity connected with the splitting of society into classes, the state became a necessity because of this splitting. We are rapidly nearing a stage of development of production at which these classes are

no longer not merely unnecessary but are a hindrance to production. They will fall as inevitably as they rose. With them falls the
state. The society that organizes production on the basis of free
and equal associations of producers, displaces thereby the machin-
ery of the state to where it belongs: the museum of antiquity, beside the spinning wheel and the bronze axe." . . .

Pythagoras [the Greek philosopher and mathematician, fl. 540-
510 B.C.] said: a people that needs laws does not deserve freedom.

Thomas Paine [the British crusader for democratic rights and
American patriot, 1737-1809] established the truth that a large
part of what we call government is nothing more than arrogance
and effrontery. The higher the civilization, the less reason for government, because civilized people govern themselves. The laws
society should follow are the laws of nature, which require no
human government. Whatever may seem the cause of insurrec-
tions, the true cause is dissatisfaction. The business of government, since the beginning, has been monopolized by the ignoramus
and the rogue.

In the papers of Richard Wagner [the German composer, conductor, and author, 1813-1883] the following sentences occur:
"Freedom means not to suffer authority that is against our purpose and desire. . . . Only were we to consider ourselves ignorant
and without will could we believe useful an authority that showed
us the right thought and true purpose. To tolerate an authority
that we realize does not know and do right is slavery."

Wagner also says: only blockheads and people without will—
those in despair of character—can suffer domination (archy),
while people of sound mind and of strong will resist it.

[Percy Bysshe] Shelley [the British poet, 1792-1822] says: the
true man does not command or obey. Authority is a pestilence that
devours everything it touches. Obedience is the death of genius,
virtue, truth, freedom—obedience enslaves people—obedience is
the true enemy of noble deeds and makes automatons of body and
soul.

Karl Heinzen [the German publicist, 1809-1880] maintains:
"Yes, man alone commits the crime called law, which in its per-
fection appears as penal law. What is this law? Simply a stipula-
tion of conditions under which a person is to be imprisoned, exiled,
or executed. Were an assembly of the best people to consider these
punishments as ways of securing society against its worst enemies,
these punishments would be exposed as tyrannical arbitrariness or

bloodthirsty barbarity; but they are necessary and legal, under any conditions, when done in the name of the "law," which the worst people have made. Within the law, no crime; outside the law, no virtue. Be a monster and you can become a saint, if the law does not affect you. The law alone labels behavior. Again, who makes law? He who has the power to imprison and murder without danger of reprisal, who orders and forbids, and rewards and punishes as he pleases, which behavior he calls legal . . . *he* makes law. Law did not create power, which law uses: power created law, and abuses it. At the side of power stands religion, which crowns power, blesses law, and curses crime. Unless basic changes are made, what if the doors of prisons be opened, the blood of officials flow, the flames crackle? The law will be carried out, crime atoned for, and divine order maintained until a new prison be built, a new scaffold raised, and a new pyre erected."

We could fill a book with such citations, and prove that from time immemorial every great mind has proclaimed anarchy. Is anyone, therefore, narrowminded enough to be afraid of the ideal we call *anarchy*?"

COMMUNIST-ANARCHIST

Most arrived at communist-anarchism, the final version of his ideology, after twenty years of accumulating the ideas of Blanc, Lassalle, Dühring, Blanqui, Marx, Bakunin, Necheyev, and especially Kropotkin.[19] Most's communist-anarchism was therefore a composite of much that he believed earlier. Thus Most the communist-anarchist wanted liberty for the individual, freedom for the group, and equality for all (anarchy) in a society of common ownership and communal economics (communism) achieved by destruction of the old and building anew (social revolution).

He learned from Édouard Vaillant (Communard), Victor Dave and August Reinsdorf (anarchists), Wilhelm Hasselmann (social revolutionary), and several nihilists. At Madame Audinet's restaurant in London, Vaillant and the others talked of anarchism, social revolution, and the latest from the Jura; and Most listened and remembered. He studied wherever and whenever he could; books and pamphlets stuck out of his pockets like quills on a porcupine, comrades said; and he read in the bath. He was hampered and came to communist-anarchism late because he could not read French, the language of avant-garde leftists. Worse, America was far from Madame Audinet's and farther from the Jura. But he made up for tardiness with passion that Kropotkin himself admired.

Most the communist-anarchist retained the anarchist's social-revolutionary credo and still subscribed to what he had written in the Pittsburgh Proclamation. But unlike Most the anarchist, who stressed evil and urged its destruction, the communist-anarchist stressed communist-anarchism's nature, goals, and strategy.

"Anarchism is a world view," he said in "Communist-Anarchism,"[20]

a philosophy of society; indeed *the* philosophy of society, for whoever considers the world and human life in their profoundest senses and their complete development, and then decides on the societal form of greatest desirability, cannot but decide for anarchism. Every other form is a half-measure and patchwork. . . .

Is anarchism desirable? . . . Well, who does not seek freedom? What man, unless willing to declare himself in bondage, would care to call any control agreeable? Think about it! . . .

Is anarchism possible? . . . The failure of attempts to attain freedom does not mean the cause is lost. The facts that the struggle for freedom is clearer and stronger than ever before, that today there are different preconditions to achieving the goal, and that we therefore stand nearer anarchy than had been hoped—prove a development of the desire to wash from the face of the earth what is authoritarian. . . .

Anarchists are socialists because they want the improvement of society, and they are communists because they are convinced that such a transformation of society can result only from the establishment of a commonwealth of property. . . . The aims of anarchists and true communists are identical. Why, then, are anarchists not satisfied to call themselves socialists or communists? Because they do not want to be confused with people who misappropriate these words, as many people do nowadays, and because they believe communism would be an incomplete, less-than-desirable system if not infused with the spirit of anarchism. . . .

Communists and anarchists also agree on tactics. He who negates present society, and seeks social conditions based on the sharing of property, is a revolutionary whether he calls himself an anarchist or a communist. . . . But anarchists are not bloodhounds who speak with levity of revolution by murder and arson. They make revolutionary propaganda because they know the privileged class can never be overturned peacefully. . . .

The anarchists, on behalf of the proletariat, therefore consider it necessary to show the proletariat that it will have to win a gigantic battle before it realizes its goals. The anarchists prepare for the social revolution and use every means—speech, writing, or deed, whichever is more to the point—to accelerate revolutionary development. . . . Can anyone, who honestly supports the proletariat, blame them for that?

The fact that, as a consequence, capitalists, police, press, clergy, and other hypocrites and philistines hate us with all their hearts, all their minds, all their souls, and all their strength all the time— we can readily understand. . . . But it seems unnatural that at every step we meet fanatical hostility inside the labor movement, accompanied by bullheaded stupidity. . . .

The greatest stumbling-block to anarchism among the non-anarchist socialists, which causes much of the discord, is the "free contract." . . . Yet one need not put oneself into a different world —neither on Mars nor in Utopia—to see how the free contract would work. Take, for example, the International Postal Union. The national postal organizations join of their own free will and can withdraw in the same way. These contracting parties agree to what they will provide one another, in order to achieve service of the highest practicality and greatest efficiency. International law lacks precedent for compelling a violator to fulfill obligations, nor can the violator be taken to court. Nevertheless, "free contract" works—because, since every breach of promise carries with it damage to the breacher, it behooves every contracting party not to violate the contract. If irregularities arise, conferences agree on adjustments.

This institution, a model for free associations, is not an isolated example. People who have little else in common form groups, trusts, and pools—organizations musical, gymnastic, commercial, protective, educational, and political; and associations for the advancement of art and science—in all countries, despite contradictory natures of the parties, and despite the fact that the parties cannot be forced to fulfill the agreements. Everything done in these agreements is done because of advantage to each member. . . .

Absurd the claim that these organizations could not work without control by a higher power! Indeed, whenever and wherever government has interfered, it has disturbed and obstructed the organizations. Moreover, where this kind of intervention is happening, the organizations agitate with supreme energy for its abolition. . . . In a society of the free and equal there can be nothing but the free contract; cooperation by force violates freedom and equality.

The gist of the matter is whether, in the society of the future, the various organizations (created and operating according to free contracts) are to be centralized or of a federal nature. We are for federalism as necessary and right, because experience has taught us that centralization must end in monstrous total-power accumulation in a few hands; centralization causes abuse of power, domination by a few, and loss of freedom by many. In addition, we see nothing useful or necessary in centralization.

If we hope and even assume that the social question will be answered through communism, and not in this or that country but in the world, any thought of centralization must be a monstrosity. Think of a bakers' central commission, meeting in Washington, prescribing to the bakers of Peking or Melbourne the size and amount of the rolls they are to bake. . . . Since the people of the future will not be old-fashioned fools, they will not fall into such nonsense. They will regulate their affairs as practice and experience teach.

The shortsighted object. Freedom is now enjoyed in economic affairs, they say, and since government does not interfere, freedom has caused abuses. We accept this argument of our enemies and with it teach them something better. That is, economic freedom *abused by private property* has created the social question. Private property, guarded by the state, increasingly exploits the poor; and the poor less and less use what they produce. If the government did not wholeheartedly maintain this swindle, the masses would not suffer it. . . . Yes, the state is the organized power of property. Therefore the unpropertied must destroy the state, eliminate private property, and establish ownership in common. . . . Communism, contrary to the liberal-bourgeois tradition, needs no state to achieve its freedom and equality. Communism finds the force of the state disturbing and restrictive. . . .

Now we come to the main objection to communism, that in it the individual gives himself up to the whole and leads no existence of his own—a thought fit to frighten away original characters and throw a scare even into common philistines with no individuality to lose. We need do no more than repeat: only under communism does the individual become himself and lead his own life.

Conversely, does anarchism isolate people and dissolve society? No. Our discussions show: the individual develops fullest in the system of ownership-in-common. Anarchism also does not prohibit the cooperation of some, many, or all—whichever is desirable—for the achievement of common goals. . . .

Above all, what socialist, without flushing with shame, maintains he is not a revolutionary? We say: *none*! . . . And the revolutionary . . . favors constant propagation of principles. . . . While we have entertained the contention that a *deed* may make more propaganda than hundreds of speeches, thousands of articles, and tens of thousands of pamphlets, we have held that an *arbitrary* act of violence will not necessarily have such an effect. . . . In short, propaganda-by-the-deed has not become our hobbyhorse, which we ride to the neglect of other propaganda. If on the one side we do not harbor the illusion that the entire proletariat must be enlightened before it can be called into battle, so on the other we do not doubt that as much enlightenment as possible must be produced with oral and printed agitation. . . .

Fortunately, no country was ever more suited for anarchist agitation than present-day America. . . . Here nobody wants to experiment further with the people's state. It has been here more than a century; it has experienced the profoundest fiasco [the Civil War]; and future state-makers had better learn the lesson. Whoever looks at America will see: the ship is powered by stupidity, corruption, or prejudice. Long has the government disgusted noble and intelligent natures; they avoid voting; and they are, even if they don't know it, anarchists. . . . The sharp-minded observer, the upright character, and the independent thinker . . . see in the people's state a crude superstition . . . and are ready to listen to the anarchists.

Finally, whatever else may be said, this much is for sure: the welfare of humanity, which the future can and will bring, lies in communism. It excludes in logical ways all authority and servitude, and therefore equals anarchy. The way to the goal is the social revolution. By energetic, relentless, international action, it will destroy class rule and establish a free society based on cooperative organization of production. . . .

Long live the Social Revolution!

NOTES

1. *Freiheit*, 15 July 1882.
2. Ibid., 5 March and 3 December 1881, 18 March 1883.
3. Most, "Die Gottespest und die Religionsseuche." *Freiheit*, 7 May 1881.
4. *Freiheit*, 11 December 1880.
5. Ibid., 5 November 1881, 9 December 1882.
6. Ibid., 19 November and 3 December 1881, 6 May 1882.
7. Ibid., 23 October 1880, 14 October 1882, 16 June 1883.
8. Most, *Memoiren* 3:57-58.
9. *Freiheit*, 5 May 1883.
10. Ibid., 30 July 1881, 4 March and 14 October 1882.
11. Ibid., 19 and 26 November 1881, 5 May 1883.
12. Ibid., 30 July 1881.
13. Ibid., 4 March 1882.
14. Ibid., 18 September 1880, 18 March 1883. Most's was one of many translations and adaptations of Necheyev and Bakunin's "Catechism of a Revolutionist."
15. Ibid., 30 July 1881, 4 March, 15 April and 11 November 1882.
16. Rudolf Rocker, *Johann Most*, p. 160. Andrew R. Carlson, *Anarchism in Germany*, p. 255.
17. *Freiheit*, 11 December 1880, 4 March and 16 September 1882.
18. Most, "Die Anarchie," *Internationale Bibliothek*, 1888.
19. Kropotkin was his teacher, he often assured Max Baginski; to Kropotkin "he owed much of his mental development." Baginski, "John Most," *Mother Earth*, p. 20.
20. Most, "Der kommunistische Anarchismus," *Internationale Bibliothek*, 1889.

8
PUBLIC AND POLEMICAL

1806: Caulkers and shipbuilders in New York agitate for the 10-hour day but fail.

1828: Women operatives in Dover, New Hampshire, refuse a wage cut, pelt the boss with wads of cotton, and go home.

1845: Thoreau retreats to the woods for two years, two months, and two days, emerging once to spend a night in jail. He says: "That government is best which governs not at all" and becomes an anarchist, American style.

1850: Allan Pinkerton establishes his National Detective Agency. Populists later call for abolition of this "standing army of mercenaries."

1876: The International dissolves in Philadelphia.

1877: William H. Vanderbilt inherits $90,000,000. In 1885 he is the richest man in the world, worth $200,-000,000 despite depression and strikes.

1880: Equal distribution of America's wealth would hand America's 50,000,000 each $1,000. But 2,000 millionaires have half the wealth, while 11,000,000 of America's 12,000,000 families live on an average of $380 a year. One millionaire, Andrew Carnegie, will give away $350,000,000.

1880: In America, 80 dailies, 466 weeklies, and 95 other periodicals are published in German. Daily newspaper circulation in Cincinnati is 28 percent German, in St. Louis 21 percent, and in New York 10 percent.

1881: Burnette G. Haskell founds an International Workingmen's Association in San Francisco.

1881: Benjamin R. Tucker, taken with Proudhon's ideas, begins *Liberty* in Boston.

1883, October 12: The Pittsburgh Congress convenes.

1886: Breaking the streetcar strike, New York police attack a crowd of 10,000.

1886, August 20: The Haymarket anarchists are convicted.

1887, November 11: They are executed. Leftists make the date an anniversary.

1892, early July: Henry Clay Frick, of the Carnegie Steel Company, breaks the Homestead strike with militia and Pinkertons.

Not for 300 years has society been so restless as at present.
The Right Reverend Joseph Gilmour, Bishop of Cleveland,
quoted in the Washington, D.C., *Evening Star*,
April 25, 1883

A pound of this good stuff [dynamite] beats a bushel of ballots.   Albert Parsons, *Alarm*, February 21, 1885

When the Americans start, it will be with energy and violence. In comparison we [European revolutionaries] will be children.
Friedrich Engels to Hermann Schlüter, March 30, 1892

HAYMARKET: PRELIMINARY

When the Social-Revolutionary Club brought Most to America, it asked him to do what it could not, to accomplish what seemed unlikely, and to achieve what looked impossible. "Save the movement," the Club ordered, "and make the Revolution."

The movement was mired in a complication of discords.[1] So many of the International disagreed so much about so many principles, and fought so viciously over more policies, that two groups of dissenters formed the Social-Democratic Working-Men's Party and the Labor Party of Illinois. Two years later, what remained of the International hobbled to Philadelphia and pronounced itself dead on arrival.

The two dissenting parties united into the Socialist Labor Party (SLP). Briefly harmonious, the SLP encouraged the railway strike of 1877 but failed to make the strike general. The failure caused intraparty quarrels that lasted until three years later when the question of arming split the party. The faction that favored arming called themselves social revolutionaries.

Among them the Social-Revolutionary Club of New York took the lead. But other clubs soon differed with the New Yorkers' rejection of everything parliamentary. The Chicago club, for instance, wanted to run candidates for public office. When the New Yorkers declared sympathy with the nihilists, others refused to go that far.

Another part of the Left, the communists, not only quarreled with socialists and social revolutionaries, but also disagreed among themselves. Authoritarian and collectivist communists from Europe clashed with utopian and nonauthoritarian Americans. Each kind of communist wondered how the other dared call itself communist.

Similarly, philosophical anarchists were American and nonviolent, while militant anarchists were European and insurrectionist. The principal of the militant anarchists, Most, loathed idealistic and genteel Benjamin Tucker; and the principal of the philosophical anarchists, Tucker, detested volatile and impulsive Most.

Besides opposing philosophical anarchists, militant anarchists wrangled among themselves—over doctrine, goals, and methods. Even what they called themselves caused disorder and produced friction. Some (including Most) professed anarchism, used *anarchist* to denote what they were, and put *anarchism* on what they believed. Yet some (including Most) also called themselves social revolutionaries; anarchism was their end, social revolution their means. Soon, part of these social-revolutionary anarchists (including Most) began calling themselves anarchists exclusively, though they still advocated social revolution. Then they increased confusion by changing their name to communist-anarchist, after adding a version of communism to their doctrine, while still believing in anarchism and social revolution. They emphasized that their communism, unlike others', was neither authoritarian nor utopian.

Meanwhile, Burnette G. Haskell founded an International Workingmen's Association that held anarchist and social-revolutionary tenets. Affiliating with the London International (which had nothing to do with Marx's), it borrowed much of the London's organizational scheme but repudiated many of its principles, especially propaganda-by-the-deed. Radicals of the Trans-Mississippi West gravitated to Haskell.[2]

He did not attend the Chicago congress of the radical Left, of groups and clubs from fourteen states, which in October 1881 resolved to unify the Left. He doubted the congress could unify. Clamoring and arguing, it passed resolutions of violence to the extremes of dynamite and assassination and passed resolutions of humanitarian ideals to the extremes of love and peace to all, everywhere, always. One resolution designated *Liberty* and *Vorbote* party organs. Yet *Liberty*, individualist and philosophical, was as polite as the high society of its Boston, while *Vorbote*, collectivist and militant, was as rough as the stockyards of its Chicago. Haskell was correct: contradictory resolutions meant more division.

Then, to this complication of discords, Most set out to bring union, purpose, and mission.

Failure seemed likely. His principles were terroristic, and terroristic Wilhelm Hasselmann won little applause and much disdain for speeches the Berlin Political Police (BPP) called "dripping with blood." The BPP also reported American newspapers' telling agitators from Germany to work, not talk. "America needs your labor but Americans hate your teachings."[3] Moreover, the Revolutionary Socialist International Workingmen's party, supposedly formed at the paradoxical 1881 Chicago congress, never met; and the party's information bureau, provided for by the congress, was never organized. With pessimism fading to apathy, the party that should have been the nucleus of the social-revolutionary movement appeared headed from fact to fiction to fantasy. *Freiheit*'s Chicago correspondent said, "Of dire necessity must a man like Most come to America and shake up these sleepyheads."[4]

For all that, Most was optimistic. Had he not helped begin the labor movement in reluctant Austria? Had he not led the drive to revitalize Social Democracy in antagonistic Germany? Had he not invigorated the Communist Workers' Educational Association in unfavorable London? And had he not succeeded in Germany with a party damaged by war, splintered by dissension, embittered by strife, and terrorized by the police? Told, "You'll fall in America, Jack," he said, "Look at my record. Besides, labor is turning left; and the Left is getting radical."[5]

Indeed, unions swelled with immigrants experienced in militancy, practiced in violence, and looking for trouble. In New York City, behind American and German flags, marchers for the 8-hour day sang the *Marseillaise* and *Die Wacht am Rhein*. In New York's Great Strike, 100,000 stayed out for months. In Chicago on December 21, 1873, 5,000 cheered orators calling in five languages for action against unemployment and low wages. In 1874 the Molly Maguires helped provoke and sustain the Long Strike in the coal fields. The 1877 railroad strike took 100 lives and cost $10,000,000 damage. Social revolutionaries joined educational and defensive societies (*Lehr und Wehr Vereine*) and learned to shoot straight.[6]

Meanwhile, police, military, and private forces broke strikes and scattered demonstrations. In the Tompkins Square riot in New York, mounted police, swinging clubs, rode and struck down men, women, and children; and Samuel Gompers dove into a cellarway to avoid a split head.[7] After Tompkins Square, New York police invaded indoor meetings. Platoons would march to the platform, handcuff and gag the speaker, and march out, driving everyone before them and cracking the skulls of resisters. In 1877, riots brought out militia, army, and marines; and the navy carried troops from Norfolk to Washington, D.C., to protect the capital. The Pinkertons became paramilitary.

Although this repression made Most's side angry and his job therefore easier, his job was formidable nonetheless. He button-holed comrades, wrote letters, called meetings, twisted arms, re-established *Freiheit*, and with a speech the day he arrived, began a tour to Boston, Baltimore, St. Louis, Chicago, Denver, and cities between them and New York.

His first speech was in Cooper Union's Great Hall. Newspapers had discussed him for days, and aroused interest and created enthusiasm city-wide. Thousands—*Freiheit* said 5,000—crowded into the Hall, while hundreds struggled but did not get in. Flaunting affiliations, leftists with pink lapel-pins, red carnations, and black armbands—socialists, communists, anarchists—packed themselves cheek by jowl. Pairs of policemen stood back to back, eyes nervous, hands on truncheons, like precarious islands in a treacherous sea.

A roar filled the Hall, to greet Victor Drury, Justus Schwab, and Most. Under the high ceiling, on the platform that made the audience's heads tilt back and eyes turn up, between hissing gaslights, Drury and Schwab gave speeches of introduction, while Most sat in an armchair and nodded at sentences that pleased him. They finished, and he took their place. A man waved a red flag. The audience stamped and clapped.

Most was thirty-six, short, emaciated, stern, hairy, and grim. He extended good wishes from comrades in Europe, then said:

The question is not Will there be a revolution? but When will it break out? [italics added]

Among the thousands, packed row on row, not a sneeze or a cough. Thousands of eyes fixed like one eye, thousands of ears bent like one ear.

And when the Revolution breaks out, history will be rewritten with blood and iron.

Like stones thrown into a pond, the words sent ripples of anger, indignation, horror, and resolution across the sea of faces.

People need only be shown that the enemy is rotten with corruption, tottering, and ready to be smashed.

Bodies stiffened when Most's body stiffened, eyes turned when his turned, and arms shot up when his lifted with his closing words:

I shall stamp on ruling heads!

Applause shook the Hall.

To the roar of "Three cheers for the Revolution!" the house passed motions to support him.[8] Revolutionary socialism, European-style, had come to America.

Within hours he was on tour. The nomadic life of the agitator, learned in Switzerland, practiced in Austria, and perfected in Germany, was second nature in America. He told a Philadelphia reporter, in a loud voice and with a wave of the arm: "I have sounded the war cry; it rang in their ears and roused them from slumber. Now I go among them and form them into societies. We must unite."[9]

Hard times and labor unrest turned out audiences.[10] In Chicago, 6,000 jammed the hall, overflowed the galleries, and blocked the aisles—belying the Chicago *Times*'s prediction that Most would find the beer strong but radicalism weak. In Milwaukee not another could squeeze in, and all breathed fire. In Louisville it took three meetings to quench thirst for words and presence of Most. In Cincinnati a Workers' Hall crowded with attentive, expectant, responsive hundreds gave Most's speech applause throughout that burst into a storm at the end. In Cleveland none were more gripped or clapped louder than the women who comprised a quarter of the audience. In Philadelphia the large first assembly grew for the second and swelled for the third, and the doors of Germania Theatre had to be locked against many who could not enter but demanded entry. The worst of Baltimore weather seemed neither to keep comrades away nor dampen their spirits; they shouted, "We mant Most!" When the tour ended he joined Genêt, Lafayette, and Kossuth—foreigners who made history with tours on these shores.

In April he took another, leaving a trail of hoarse voices, tingling hands, and littered halls. The Washington *Star* said that workers liked him. B. G. McDonald of the tailors' union said, "Do you suppose I would endorse the man if there was not something in him?"[11] In Lawrence, Massachusetts, thousands braved rain a second time because, detained by Boston police, he missed the first meeting; and he gave the Laurentians two hours that whetted appetites that three the next day did not satisfy.

In six months the stranger to America had made two tours, delivered 200 speeches, and became one of America's best-known faces. "He promises to kill people of property and position," said the Berlin Political Police, "and that's why he's popular."[12]

When not on tour he lectured to clubs in New York City, Paterson, and Newark in support of leftist union. Debates followed lectures, pitting moderate against revolutionary socialists, with Most respected as the best debater. The anniversary of the Commune and the memorial to Marx attracted his biggest New York audiences. "If revolutionaries don't cut off heads of reactionaries," he told a Commune gathering, "reactionaries will cut off heads of revolutionaries."[13]

Language equally remarkable, likewise intended to unify, bristled in *Freiheit*. Theory, in language elevated and dignified, was aimed at the reader of intelligence and learning. Exhortation—coarse, sarcastic, violent, slangy, vulgar, and scurrilous—was aimed at the common reader. "Most had perfected such language [of exhortation] in a way reminiscent of the older German polemics, of the kind Luther exchanged with opponents"—unheard in Germany between Luther's time and Most's.[14]

Such language not only cheered and incited radicals; it also angered and roused the establishment. The press caricatured him as the mad anarchist and made fun of his speeches. Counterdemonstrations threatened his meetings. Detroit citizens demanded that city hall do something about this troublemaker, this rabble-rouser. Philadelphians blocked his use of an auditorium. The pulpit in Chicago and Cleveland denounced the lunatic who riled the masses. Pillars of Pittsburgh society said that if the police did nothing about this beast, law-abiding people should hang him from the nearest lamppost.[15]

Neither those guardians of decorum nor various police forces listened to his speeches more intently or gathered data on his agitation more diligently than the Berlin Political Police, who maintained an international network of agents and informers. The BPP feared him because, of many driven into exile by the Anti-Socialist Law, he was likeliest to try anti-German subversion. The BPP reasoned that as Germany dealt him its worst (drove him out of Germany), so he would deal Germany his worst; and he was capable of anything. For years he was the chief villain of BPP reports.

The BPP reported that between December 1882 and October 1883 he multiplied one social-revolutionary club to twenty-four, with 1,500 members in all, in New York City and environs. He multiplied a few clubs in a few other cities into a social-revolutionary party that in thirty cities—notably Chicago, Cleveland, and

Pittsburgh—was more important than the older Socialist Labor party. Indeed, owing to his causing members to defect, the SLP was near collapse. He won allegiance from Chicago's leading leftists, Albert Parsons and August Spies, and turned further left their *Arbeiterzeitung*. The BPP saw his hand in the strikes of 1883. And, to the BPP's greatest concern, he brought a strengthened Left into congress.[16]

Forty delegates wearing red badges mingled with 400 observers at the opening reception in a Turner Hall decked with red flags, while the Masonic Sextette sang revolutionary songs, including some of Most's.[17] Delegates had come to Pittsburgh from every industrial city, and from Paterson, New Jersey; Salineville, Ohio; and St. Joseph, Missouri. Delegates and observers shook hands, exchanged ideas, shared information, swapped tracts, talked politics, and clinked glasses. Comrade Frick, of Pittsburgh, gave the address of welcome, which Comrade Drury, of New York, accepted in a speech of thanks. But the orator of the evening, and of the congress, was Most. When Frick and Drury spoke, the assembly smoked, drank beer, and chatted, with half an ear for the speeches. When Most spoke, smoke dispersed, glasses stayed on the table, beer grew flat, nobody talked but Most, and attention riveted on him. He gripped the assembly, declaring that the congress would unite the workers of America, and they would break capitalism's chains and scatter capitalism's swarm of evils.

Next morning, Sunday, at 9:00, the delegates returned. While they blinked sleepily and coughed phlegm from their throats, Most organized with bright eyes and a clear voice. Four hours' sleep readied him for work; and, atheist to the core, he liked to work on religious holidays.

The congress chose officers, but he was not among them; he could do more if unencumbered. He approved the declaration of purpose—to unify comrades in philosophy, aims, policies, and procedures and to "unite all workingmen, join them in a community of equality, and bind them together for their common welfare." New words in leftist parlance—"unite," "join," "bind"—and "the highest time" to turn them into deeds, he said. Committees on organization, resolutions, communications, and propaganda met, while he circulated, twisted arms, buttonholed, debated, promised, rolled logs, argued, cajoled, and threatened. Committees did what he wanted.

In the afternoon 150 Pittsburghers, women among them, joined the delegates to hear speeches. Parsons (to be executed for participation in the Haymarket riot, a result of this congress) pointed to the red flag as a symbol of liberty, equality, and fraternity. Spies (to be executed with Parsons) predicted revolution—*soon*! Most said that capitalists in America hurt workers more in the last 25 years than crowned heads in Europe hurt them in the last 200; crowned heads and capitalists should be shot.

In the evening, wishes for success were heard from Mexico, Germany, Russia, and France. "The eyes of the world are upon YOU, comrades!"

Monday, in long and hot debate over how to organize the party, Most defeated a proposal for centralization, whose backers, though popular and eloquent, could not prevail against his éclat. He got his federation of small groups. Each was to be independent, free to interpret the federation's principles for itself, unrestrained in adapting them to its needs, and at liberty to disband itself or leave the federation. This was his answer to the paradoxes of the libertarian: how to organize freedom, arrange spontaneity, prescribe autonomy, and legislate independence.

He named the federation the American Federation of the International Working People's Association (IWPA), also called The Black International after anarchism's color. It subscribed to similar principles and exchanged affection of comrades-in-arms but did not affiliate with the International Working People's Association founded in London in 1881.

At the end of the congress, to contradict a rumor that delegates were a feckless lot who did nothing but talk about labor while workers labored, a list of delegates' names and occupations was published: shoemakers, carpenters, bakers, saddlers, printers, farmers, cabinetmakers, miners, weavers, butchers, paperhangers, tanners, and "Most, New York, bookbinder," who had not bound a book for fifteen years.

Rather he had given fifteen years to thinking over, speaking about, and writing on the social question. His answers appeared in the Proclamation, the congress's crowning work, a landmark in

the history of radicalism. For years radicals swore to it, and it was
Most's credo until he died. He was responsible for content, com-
position, and acceptance. The congress approved unanimously. In
English, 100,000 copies were published, German 50,000, and
French 10,000.

After three cheers for the Revolution, delegates departed in the
best of spirits. Everyone, according to *Freiheit*, felt he had done
his duty. Each promised all, and all vowed to each, to carry out
what the congress propounded. *Freiheit* closed its report with: "A
new era in America's labor movement has begun. The word is
ALL ABOARD!"

For three years Most and his Proclamation dominated, guided,
and inspired the radical Left. Then the Left's vitality and cohesive-
ness exploded in the bomb at Haymarket Square.

HAYMARKET

"Johann Most is speaking tonight," said Alexander Berkman to
Emma Goldman. "Do you want to hear him?"

Extraordinary, she thought. The chance to see the firebrand
himself. The man the press called bloodthirsty, criminal, the devil
incarnate. *Him*! She felt on the verge of something wonderful,
something that would change her life.

Berkman took her to a hall behind a saloon, filled with Germans
smoking, drinking, and talking. Most entered. She was revolted.
That huge head, that greyish bushy beard, that twisted face!

He spoke. She heard a denunciation, a satire, and a tirade. His
disfigurement disappeared, and she forgot his repugnant appear-
ance. He became a primal power, radiating love and hate, inspiration and strength. The storm of his eloquence tossed her about: her
soul contracted and expanded to the rise and fall of his voice. Stirred
to her depths, she went to bed teeming with emotions.[18]

She had seen a great orator. Infectious energy, a melodious and
flexible voice, a flair for the dramatic, and an incisive sense of
timing; continual observance and constant rehearsal of theatrical
techniques, modified and corrected in hundreds of speeches; a way
with words; conviction that he knew the truth; devotion to speaking it; a ready mind—these qualities and practices, brought to a

lecture a week in and around New York City and taken on tour across the country, gave him strength that made audiences tremble. They trembled when he said: arm and be ready; violence is the way to right wrongs, to end misery. Shoot or be shot. Better yet, dynamite.

At forty cents a pound it was cheap, the poor man's weapon. It was glorified. Songs were sung in its praise.

> Dynamite today, dynamite tonight.
> Most tells how, he shows where:
> He says all in *Freiheit*
> And his good little book on warfare.

"Johann Most speaks tonight" brought out comrades. "Johann Most speaks tonight" drew them like errant travelers to a lodestar. "Johann Most speaks tonight"; and he looked at them, packed to the aisles and jamming the gallery. Fire glowed in all eyes, and *Freiheit* lay in every lap. He said, "Herrmann Stellmacher's killing of a policeman was not murder. Murder is the killing of a human being, and a policeman is not a human being." (Applause.) He asked nonmembers of the International Working People's Association to join. Many joined. The Berlin Political Police reported 7,000 members in eighty groups.[19] He posed the question of arming. They answered, *Yes!* "Success, success everywhere," he said. "We advance in seven-league boots. All signs point to the Revolution."[20]

Changing times benefitted success. His unification of leftists coincided with new radicalism. Never had so many of the Left agreed on so much, so many of the Left been such partisans of labor, and so much of labor been so militant. Cigarmakers and miners founded national unions on socialistic platforms. The biggest union, the 500,000-member Knights of Labor (which had expelled Cincinnati tailors for striking), did nothing about St. Louis railway strikers in 1886 and considered a statute to permit strikes. The second-biggest union, the Federation of Organized Trades and Labor Unions, directed strikes in industrial centers.

He therefore addressed a growing constituency among labor and the Left. Tireless, he was the IWPA's busiest spokesman; and he got more, larger, and more enthusiastic audiences. *Freiheit* led the seven newspapers published by the IWPA; its readers increased weekly. By popular demand he doubled the pages. His pamphlets, "The God-Pestilence," "The Beast of Property," and "The Free Society," circulated in several languages in America and Europe.

The leadership of the Socialist Labor party was first to learn that Most and the IWPA were strong and getting stronger. The SLP's rank and file defected to the IWPA wholesale.[21] In Chicago, Cleveland, and Pittsburgh (once SLP bastions) the SLP looked ruined. Allegheny, Pennsylvania, had been a stronghold; now its SLP numbered three. The SLP's secretary Philipp Van Patten disappeared, leaving a suicide note: he was in despair over the party. By the end of 1883, influence declining and membership dwindling, the SLP was a creature of principles without power and a tissue of bombast: a paper tiger.

But the Right was no paper tiger. The press advised employers to serve hungry workers hot lead. Employers, dissatisfied with bland menus of the police and the military, hired the Pinkertons. The Pinkerton brothers, detectives' detectives, commanded a private army—trained, experienced, well-equipped, and bloodthirsty. They served hot lead forthwith.

Workers were killed and wounded. But nowhere would courts hear cases against employers. Yet everywhere were police happy to arrest and courts ready to convict strikers for inciting to riot, intimidation, obstructing justice, blocking streets and trespassing.

In retaliation, *Freiheit* trumpeted, "To arms!"[22] Revolutionaries armed. Educational and defensive societies, the *Lehr und Wehr Vereine*, bought rifles and handguns. At picnics, target practice rivaled eating. The Chicago society claimed 1,500 members. Arming reached full speed when Most published *The Science of Revolutionary Warfare*, a standard reference among terrorists. As far away as Denmark, Copenhagen police pried a copy from the hand of Theodor Machner, a terrorist. August Spies packed a revolver. For the first time, Most owned guns and may have carried them. When truncheons broke up a meeting at Cooper Union, Serge Schevitsch roared, "Next time come armed, comrades!"[23]

After years of lobbying, agitation, and strikes, the 1880s arrived with the 8-hour day still a dream. Luckier workers enjoyed a 10-

hour day—10 hours had been the practice on Federal projects for fifty years—but others struggled in the nightmare of 90 hours a week in urban transportation and 100 in the bakeries of New York City.

The ailing Federation of Organized Trades and Labor Unions, to regain members and recover strength, took the lead in the 8-hour movement, resolving that 8 hours shall be a day's work after May First, 1886. Should the law not comply, unions were to strike on May First. Much of labor endorsed the resolution. The Knights of Labor mounted a campaign of oratory and pamphleteering that continued until May First. The date was set for the bloodiest battle ever in the war between capital and labor.

Yet Most, the loudest voice for blood, opposed the movement. He scorned it as misguided, debilitating of energy better spent on the true mission: revolution. The 8-hour day would repair; he wanted to wreck. Why try to fix a rotten system? Why affirm capitalism? Why fresh butter on stale bread? Why beg or coerce a concession from plutocrats when plutocrats' throats should be cut? "To the knife, comrades!"

Despite him the May First idea caught on with the public and found favor in unions. When unions prepared to strike for it, the public was ready to support them. Anarchists and social revolutionaries, former followers of Most's, joined the movement, in defiance of Most.

Meanwhile, employers stood firm; the press backed them; and police loaded guns.

The press opened fire with words. The favorite was *anarchist*. A headline-writer's dream, it echoed in the mouth, crackled in the air, vibrated in print, and hummed in the mind. It brimmed with images: * * * BEARDED BOMB-THROWERS * * * LONG-HAIRED ARSONISTS * * * WILD-EYED ASSASSINS * * *. It burst with associations: * * * TERROR * * * DESTRUCTION * * * MURDER * * *. It made readers tremble. So the press called radicals and radical acts *anarchist*.

Events of 1885-1886 gave opportunity to shout *anarchist*. Two million unemployed, cold and hungry, spread idle hands before fires of radicalism and sat down to banquets spread by revolutionary orators. Most was on the platform day in and day out, and *Freiheit* screamed for action: *To arms!* Terence Powderly declared, "That a deep-rooted feeling of discontent pervades the masses, none can deny; that there is just cause for it, must be admitted."[24] In 1886, over 1,500 strikes hit various industries. In one of the worst, 610,000 struck street-transit systems; and New York police clubbed, stabbed, and punched open the way for scab-operated streetcars. *Freiheit* heralded a new labor era, the era of open warfare. The Chicago *Tribune* told farmers to poison the food they gave the unemployed streaming out of cities; poison was an antidote to anarchy. Agitation, unrest, and strikes continued until May First itself.

The May First idea was strongest in Chicago. The Chicago IWPA, 3,000 members in twenty sections led by the influential Parsons and the forcible Spies, backed the idea there. The IWPA's *Arbeiterzeitung* and its English-language edition *Alarm* publicized the idea. Parsons and Spies, together with Samuel Fielden and Michael Schwab, were fiery orators at eight-hour meetings; and they urged arming for May First. The IWPA and Chicago's Central Labor Union supported the National Eight-Hour Association, founded in Chicago in November 1885. IWPA, CLU, and NEHR agitators played up the fact that soup kitchens could not serve all Chicago's hungry in the winter of 1885. Agitated and hungry, on Christmas day, Chicago labor paraded down posh Prairie Avenue. The ragged horde waved black and red flags and hooted and jeered before millionaires' mansions; the more sumptuous the mansion, the louder the hoots and more brazen the jeers.

Thus, May First, 1886, would be the date and Chicago the place for the showdown.

As the day neared, tension increased. In April, patrol wagons full of doubly armed reinforcements sped to clashes between police and workers. Police broke up brawls between strikers and scabs. Pinkertons broke strikers' heads. Late in the month, demonstrations shook the city. In the largest, 3,000 paraded with flags and music to the lakefront and cheered speeches by Parsons, Spies, and Schwab. May First, and Haymarket, were a few days off.

Still opposed to the 8-hour movement, Most resisted the May First idea. As nothing would come of it, even if there were a few demonstrations and some strikes, better to forget it and aim for the true goal, revolution. By logic and according to the signs, he should have been right; but time and chance disregarded the signs and overpowered logic. Unforeseeable, spontaneous, unlikely, and incoherent events made up a train of circumstances that ran to Haymarket.[25]

Heading the train was the ironic fact that his Chicago followers were preparing to join the May First demonstrations and make them violent. Disobeying him but following his teachings, they issued proclamations, drilled in educational and defensive societies, and assembled firearms and explosives: the man who opposed the 8-hour movement was helping arm for its red-letter day.

Tension increased. Police reviewed old plans and laid new ones.

Cyrus H. McCormick declared the right to hire and fire and locked employees who did not agree out of his Harvester factory.

They struck. Scabs protected by 300 Pinkertons replaced them. Strikers massed and protested.

Police broke them up. Anxiety, fear, anger, and hostility mounted.

Railroad and gas workers, iron-mill hands, meat packers, and plumbers struck for shorter hours before May First. If workers were so eager that they anticipated the day, what would happen on the day itself? Police mobilized every available officer.

On May First, 30,000 struck and more demonstrated, but without violence. On May Second, less happened, still no violence. It seemed that Most was right; nothing would come of the eight-hour movement and the May First idea.

On the 3rd, Spies, though known as an anarchist and therefore anathema to some labor leaders, gave a speech to strikers of the lumber-shovers' union, assembled by chance near the McCormick plant.[26] McCormick strikers happened to join the shovers.

As if wanting to belie the connotations of *anarchist*, usually fiery Spies spoke calmly and reasonably. He asked his audience not to bother scabs leaving the McCormick plant at the end of a shift.

The audience attacked the scabs. Shots were exchanged. Police scattered nearly all attackers and trampled the rest under the hooves of their horses. One person was killed and several hurt.

Spies, driven by rage to mistake bloodshed for carnage, thought strikers were butchered wholesale. He wrote a circular exhorting: "To arms, we call you, to ARMS!"

At the head of the circular, without Spies's knowledge, a typesetter inserted "revenge," and the circular was distributed. An ugly mood worsened.

Labor leaders scheduled a demonstration for May 4th at Haymarket Square. The orators were to be Spies, Parsons, and Fielden —"arch anarchists all," said the press.

Demonstrators crossed railroad tracks, passed tenements, spotted saloons to visit later, and gathered near the Square. Half a block away, in the Desplaines Street station, police prepared for action.

Mayor Carter Harrison inspected the area, told the district captain everything seemed calm, and went home.

From a wagon near an alley off the Square, under a sky overcharged with rain-laden clouds, Fielden told 1,200 what to do with the law: "Throttle it, kill it, stab it, do everything you can to wound it." A fierce cold blast of wind, carrying dust and bits of paper, roared down the street. Signs creaked. Rain fell, and three-fourths of the audience ran for cover, many to saloons spotted earlier. Fielden began his last sentence: "In conclusion. . . ."

Police appeared, 180 strong. They formed for attack. Captains Ward and Bonfield, skull-crackers, ordered the remaining demonstrators, wet and torpid, to disperse. Fielden said, "We are peaceable," and climbed down from the wagon.

A light flashed, a fuse sputtered, a detonator glowed, and the bomb exploded near the front rank of police. The police re-formed around their wounded, opened fire, and charged. The blue ranks and the gray huddle collided: a seething, struggling mass, fighting. Truncheons slammed flesh, clubs split skulls, shots rang out, a stench of gunpowder filled the air, and blood spattered the street. When the uproar stilled and stench dissipated, some victims lay twitching and screaming amid others who would never move or talk again. One policeman was dead on the spot; and of sixty-seven policemen wounded, six died soon. At least ten demonstrators were killed and forty wounded.

The unforeseeable, spontaneous, and unlikely had happened. Even the bomb seemed the deed of an invisible hand; the bomber was never identified. The press called *anarchists* to blame and demanded vengeance.

Most was neither at the Square nor behind the bombing nor even in favor of the movement and the idea that caused the demonstration. But he had much to do with Haymarket indirectly. He gave speeches, wrote articles, and distributed pamphlets urging violence; he published a manual on how to arm and fight; and his exhortations and instructions could have inspired the idea, informed the making, and prompted the throwing of the bomb. Chicago orators, urging arming, had said, "Read Most." Corresponding with Spies, when Spies was secretary of the IWPA's information bureau, Most discussed violence and praised explosives. A week and a half before Haymarket he held up a rifle in public and shouted, "This is the way, comrades!" The "Haymarket anarchists," imprisoned and executed for the bombing, told how the Pittsburgh Congress and its Proclamation hit home to them.[27] Congress and Proclamation were Most's work, work Most took pride in and boasted of.

With reason, then, he was seen at the bottom of Haymarket. The prosecution introduced his *Science of Revolutionary Warfare* as evidence in the trial.[28] Liebknecht toured America saying: Most prepared the Haymarket anarchists' fate and sealed their doom. The press isolated Most as the bacillus that spread terrorism to Haymarket. The *Knights of Labor* spoke of "cowardly murderers, cutthroats and robbers, known as anarchists . . . Parsons, Spies, Fielden, Most and all their followers," outlaws who should be blotted from the earth.[29]

New York authorities could not connect Most with Haymarket officially; but the grand jury, like the rest of the nation alarmed at violence, indicted him for holding the meeting at which he brandished a rifle. Near midnight on May 11th, four detectives drew revolvers, broke down his door, and carried him to detention and trial.

HAYMARKET: AFTERMATH

The press, calling Haymarket *carnage*, blamed anarchists. Carnage the anarchists promised, carnage they were capable of, carnage they have done, and carnage should have been expected of them, said the press. Stop carnage, punish carnage: convict anarchists.[30]

Albert Parsons, August Spies, Michael Schwab, Adolph Fischer, Samuel Fielden, George Engel, Oscar Neebe, and Louis Lingg—

anarchists—were convicted. But not of throwing the bomb or of being behind the bombing; the inside of that story was never learned. Nor by a jury assembled in the customary way; the court's bailiff selected a group from which the jury was drawn—a jury on which served not one workingman, a jury who said they disliked anarchists and knew they should punish these anarchists. Convicted— yet the prosecution could not establish that any of the accused threw the bomb, caused it to be thrown, or knew it would be thrown. Convicted—but not before an impartial judge. On all contested points Joseph E. Gary, openly anti-anarchist, ruled in the prosecution's favor and made insinuating remarks against the accused. Subsequent governor of Illinois John P. Altgeld led many, including William Dean Howells, who called Gary unfair. Convicted— for incendiary writings and inflammatory speeches that could have provoked the bomb. Convicted, in short, by a biased jury and a partial judge, in an atmosphere of anti-anarchist hysteria, and not for deeds but for ideas, for being anarchists. Even an enemy of anarchism, Samuel Gompers, could not stomach the "shocking story of official prejudice."[31]

Not men but anarchy, said the state's attorney Julius S. Grinnell, *anarchy* was on trial. Make examples of the accused, he asked the jury—hang them, preserve American institutions, and save our society. Parsons, Spies, Engel, and Fischer were hanged. Neebe, Schwab, and Fielden went to prison. Lingg, exploding a cartridge in his mouth, killed himself. Anarchy, said the Chicago *Inter Ocean*, "got its verdict."[32]

Parsons, Spies, Engel, and Fischer said good-bye to friends and relatives, wrote letters, chatted with the death watch, and went to bed at 2:00 A.M. Parsons sang "Annie Laurie." The clear tenor voice filled the corridors:

> . . . and for bonnie Annie Laurie
> I'd lay me doon and dee.

Other prisoners raised themselves on their elbows and listened.[33]

Next morning the condemned breakfasted early and with gusto, read the papers, and refused spiritual consolation. Hammering by

carpenters erecting the gallows disturbed them not at all. Parsons
cited Marc Cook's "Waiting":

> My ship has gone down in the waters unknown,
> And vain has been all my waiting.

At 11:30 A.M., in an unsteady voice, the sheriff read them their
death warrants. Two hundred spectators, seated as if in a theater,
watched the condemned, bound and hooded, take places on the
trap. The hangman fixed the nooses, too tightly for Spies. "Adjust
it, please." Then he shrieked:
"There will be a time when our silence will be more powerful
than the voices you strangle today."
Fischer: "Hurrah for anarchy----"
Engel: "Hurrah for anarchy!"
Fischer: "This is the happiest moment of my life!"
Parsons: "Will I be allowed to speak, O men of America? Let me
speak, Sheriff Matson! Let the voice of the people be heard! O----"
12:02. A woman screams. Four hooded men kick air they can-
not breathe, until they can kick no more.
Newsboys shouted, "Extra! Extra! Chicago anarchists hanged!"[34]
Parsons had recited:

> Come not to my grave with your mournings,
> With your lamentations and tears.

Lucy Parsons, his widow, looked with tear-reddened eyes at his
corpse, touched the mark of the rope around the neck, and cried,
"Albert! Albert!"
Parsons:

> Bring no long train of carriages,
> . . . .
> Insult not my dust with your pity.

Perhaps half a million watched the procession to the cemetery.
At graveside 150,000 heard eulogies until nightfall and mourned
men the eulogists called martyrs, victims of legitimized killing.

Parsons:

> For me no more are the hardships,
> The bitterness, heartaches, and strife
> The sadness and sorrow of life—
> . . . .
>   'Tis a pity I should, as I do,
>   Pity you

The star eulogist would have been Most; but promised arrest in Illinois, he stayed home and wrote about the executions instead.

"They are murderers!" he wrote of Grinnell, Gary, the witnesses for the prosecution, the jury, and Governor Oglesby. "They are murderers!" A black-bordered *Freiheit* proclaimed, "Let the gallows of Chicago be a symbol and the 11th of November a beacon in our struggle"; and so they were for decades. "Every year," Art Young wrote, "meetings are held in many parts of the world in commemoration of these martyrs who fell victim to that worst mob of all—respectable legalized vengeance."[35]

Most spoke annually at Haymarket memorials in New York and around the country. "They were martyrs!" he said of Parsons, Spies, Engel, Fischer, and Lingg. "They were martyrs!" Like many leftists he admired Lingg particularly, Lingg who blew off his own head and beat the hangman.

The Haymarket anarchists' lives and deaths became an inspiration to unity and a fillip to action. "If anything could ever have made me an Anarchist," said Joseph R. Buchanan, "my conversion would have taken place in Chicago, in November, 1887."[36] Leftists of every stripe, including Most, mourned at Haymarket memorials, differences notwithstanding. Disputes over the 8-hour day subsided, and speeches smelled alike of gunpowder and in unison hailed solidarity. Emma Goldman and Voltairine de Cleyre, hitherto lukewarm, took up anarchism with fervor. Numbers and anger of European leftists increased, and governments stiffened repression. Haymarket was an international incident.[37] Russian Jews, driven to America together with exiles no longer welcome in London and Paris, rallied around Most. Leftists talked as if they stood on the threshold of the Revolution.[38]

Seeking to lead this aroused and unified Left, Most implored comrades to stop the Haymarket executions by force. He sounded "a fierce call to battle," a "call to individual acts, to vengeance."[39] Only the threat of arrest kept him from agitating at the scene of Haymarket itself. Then a rash speech landed him again on Blackwell's Island. An official there called him one of the "damned Germans" causing trouble in America.

The official was right; the American radical Left was chiefly German. Of the eight convicted for Haymarket, six were German. Non-German leftist immigrants often learned German before they learned English, because leftist newspapers, pamphlets, and oratory were principally in German. In the Socialist Labor party it seemed as if German immigrants were natives and Americans foreigners.[40]

But wage in German the Revolution in America?

Yes, if there were enough Germans. Before the Civil War, more immigrants came from Germany than anywhere outside Britain. Between 1850 and 1890, some four million joined the million already here. In addition, by 1900, native Americans of German parents numbered over five million. These ten million Germans and German-Americans comprised neighborhoods and towns, spoke German (and if possible, nothing else); published in it newspapers, magazines, and books; caused it to be taught in public schools; watched and wrote plays, worshipped, and sang in it. In short, they lived, loved, worked, played, and died in a community conceived and expressed in German by Germans.

But wage in German the Revolution in America?

Yes, if enough Germans were radical, and if radical Germans were radical enough. When Most arrived, many radicals were German. Neither craftsmen nor farmers seeking in a new country more beer, richer butter, and brisker polkas, they were revolutionaries who fled for their freedom or flew for their lives after failing to foment revolution. Those driven out by the Anti-Socialist Law were numerous and militant. Resisters of oppression in the old country, they practiced radicalism with a vengeance in the new. They called themselves socialists, communists, and anarchists—in German.

But wage in German the Revolution in America?

Yes, if enough converts could be won. Many immigrants decided, after arrival, to turn left or further left. For, though they enjoyed freedoms of speech and press, they suffered economic serfdom— especially the intellectuals, the best-equipped voices and likeliest organizers of revolution. Unlike craftsmen able to wield tools in any language, intellectuals worked with language itself and were menials until they mastered English. Stripping tobacco in a cigar factory, an editor might watch the hand skilled with a pen grow clumsy, might feel atrophy of the mind deft at a phrase, and be angered. He had come to America not only for freedom of expression but also for economic betterment—and where was it? Where the prosperity about which he had heard so much? Was he, were those like him, shut up in a capitalist prison for life? Perhaps Most was right; capitalism should be destroyed.

But wage in German the Revolution in America?

Most shouted, "Yes!"

To a Left aroused, unified, and predominantly German he would make *Freiheit* an organ of cohesion, a star to steer by, and a source of strength, if he could find enough money. He was broke, and Schwab and the Club had none to spare.

Fearful for *Freiheit*'s life, he took lecture tours to save "my beloved child of sorrow, which grows more and more dear to my heart, and of which I am proud—the sole joy of my days."[41] Comrades gave him lodging when he was on tour, to help him economize. At home or on tour he was abstemious in diet, frugal with tobacco, and parsimonious in dress. These were sacrifices; he loved to eat, relished cigars, and coveted clothing. Carfare was unthinkable, and he walked. That was no sacrifice; he liked to walk.

Tours netted money, speeches won subscribers, and *Freiheit*'s circumstances improved. *The God-Pestilence*, translated by 1896 into English, French, Spanish, Portuguese, Italian, Polish, Russian, and Swedish, sold 100,000 copies in Germany alone. Though priced at a nickel, of which dealers got a good cut, it produced revenue over the years. How often he despaired of his next meal—would Schwab give another handout, or Sachs put another tab on the cuff?—but found in the mail a check, revenue from *The God-Pestilence*, to carry him and *Freiheit* another week! The pestilence of God was his salvation.

Improved finances did not preclude crises. Again and again and again he begged delinquent subscribers please to settle up, and importuned "any help you can give, comrades."

He wailed, "Hundreds who know about *Freiheit* would buy if it were offered them."[42] He wanted colporteurs like the hunchback called the Jesuit (he had been expelled from a seminary) who sold 700 to 800 a week, twice what anyone else sold. Unfortunately, what damaged him in the seminary (drink) ruined him now; and he vanished owing Most $36.00. Elderly comrades, unsteady of voice and shaky on their legs, squatted on street corners and hunkered in saloons and, in quavering tones, hawked *Freiheit*. But not enough for Most. He coaxed every comrade to carry a few and be ready to push one under somebody's nose. He gave unemployed comrades 25 or 30 each, to sell in the park in summer or in the saloon in winter. But he found their efforts sickly. These lackadaisical colporteurs seemed to expect customers to come to them, while he urged the manner of the streetcorner evangelist: "Catch attention, stick it in front of them, be sincere, wave it before their eyes, shove it into their hands, talk fast, don't take *no* for an answer!"

Still the American *Freiheit* never flagged and missed few issues. In the 1880s, when it was a gadfly to the movement, its eight big pages bristled with revolutionary doctrine. One of the first anarchist journals, it outlasted by far its predecessors and many of its rivals, despite the worst of trouble. It survived even the editor's writing from prison on toilet paper. Its epitaph might have been:

FREIHEIT

1879 — 1909

In its time
the strongest, the lustiest, the loudest,
and the longest-lived
radical journal ever published.

It consisted of:

* Discussions of anarchism, communism, and social revolution: defining and describing *who we are.*

• Statements of goals: *what we want.* "Liberty, Equality, Fraternity" were for the French in 1789, and revolutionaries of 1889 would like to get them. But they want more: "Bread, Rights, Happiness" and "Truth, Freedom, Love."

• Exonerations of goals: *why what we want is right.* When wages are shameful, rents exorbitant, poverty and disease rife, police cruel, newspapers the tools of oppression, capitalists exploitative, schools ignorant, churches sinful, courts crooked, and governments corrupt; when the privileged lie, steal, cheat, and murder, while the oppressed honor and obey; when the elite, tricked out in silk, satin, ermine, and lace, and flaunting gold and jewels, disport themselves while the poor scream, "Bread! Bread! Bread!"; when the destitute, vouchsafed bread, are expected to live by it alone—then "An eye for an eye" and "The end justifies the means"! What else but the knife for Henry Ward Beecher, after he said anyone not able to live on bread does not deserve to live? "Strike for the jugular, stab through the heart, comrades!"

• Justifications of goals: *why what we want is expedient.* As things cannot get worse, so any change will benefit the downtrodden. For a better tomorrow, destroy today.

• Proposals for action: *how to get what we want.* "Deeds must follow words." So: "For traitors, the dagger; priests, the rope; drones, bullets; and despots, bombs." Use *The Science of Revolutionary Warfare,* the rebel's cookbook, to give the plutocrat indigestion today, bloat his belly tomorrow, and spill his tub of guts next week.

• Exhortations to act: *let us carry out our ideal!* With meetings, resolutions, and protests inadequate, petitions silly, the vote a fraud, and democracy a hoax, what else but the sword, the gun, and dynamite? "Storm the bastille of capitalism!"

• Vilifications of the enemy: *identifying the fiends who oppose us.* Judge Gardener sentenced forty-two beggars to six months in jail. "Gardener, you are a monster!" The press is not an engine of liberty but a tool of exploitation; it generates a morphine of misinformation. Kick the habit! Priests and preachers are not spiritual leaders but cultivators of ignorance; they spread the manure of the Dark Ages. Hold your nose!

- Predictions of success: *we shall get what we deserve.* Everywhere, like breezes stirring regions of calm, anarchism is discussed and finds favor. Meanwhile, conservatives thresh empty straw and their words blow away like chaff. To anarchism belongs the future, and the future is now.

- Biographies of great radicals: *examples of how we are to think and act.* Imitate Emil Varlin, bookbinder, who died in defense of the Commune. Imitate the Commune's heroine, Louise Michel.

- Sources of inspiration: *how we are to feel about ourselves and our work.* History was discussed to show that the Cause is glorious and bound to succeed. Novels were reprinted to dramatize points every comrade should remember. Poems such as "The Day Nears" were published to show how the oppressed will free themselves under the slogan: "Victory or Death!" Columns of correspondence and news of locals, promoting comradeship and solidarity, kept group in touch with group and comrade with comrade. Aphorisms and mottoes, at tops of pages and as filler, proclaimed: "Against tyrants all methods legal"; "Agitate, organize, rebel"; and "Proletarians of all nations, unite!" Contemporary affairs were interpreted to give joy: "This society sits on a powder keg and strikes the match."

Accordingly, among radical papers—such as *Arbeiterzeitung* and *Alarm* of Chicago, *Freie Wacht* of Philadelphia, and *Arme Teufel* of Detroit—*Freiheit* led. It excelled in size of readership and power of language. Irony, sarcasm, vulgarity where effective; impudence, derision, logic where necessary; humor, pathos, satire where appropriate; therefore verve everywhere—these qualities distinguished it from competitors and made them banal by comparison. Coarse and vile, an enemy called it, "the most blasphemous of all socialistic papers."[43] It spurted "flames of ridicule, scorn, and defiance," a friend said; it breathed hatred.[44]

For Goldman and Berkman, reading it was *de rigueur.* They delighted in its language, agreed with it on armed uprising, and rejoiced in its promotion of propaganda-by-the-deed. They read: Henry Clay Frick, ignorant of his namesake's genius for compromise, broke the Homestead strike with Pinkertons and militia; workers and a child were dead, and more wounded; and Berkman said:

"I will kill Frick."

Goldman agreed that Frick must be killed and with a bomb. It was the moment for assassination. The country was aroused; everybody believed Frick a murderer. A blow at him "would re-echo in the poorest hovel" and advertise "the real cause behind the Homestead struggle. It would also strike terror in the enemy's ranks and make them realize that the proletariat had its avengers."[45] Hers was a classic definition of propaganda-by-the-deed, learned from Most and *Freiheit.*

Berkman made bombs, following Most's *Science of Revolutionary Warfare.* Goldman tried to be a streetwalker to raise money. He would go to Pittsburgh to kill Frick. She would stay behind to explain the assassination's meaning. Thus they planned the perfect act of propaganda-by-the-deed: one that Most himself could not surpass.

At the Baltimore and Ohio station in New York City, Goldman and Berkman paced the platform, their hearts too full for speech.[46]

"All aboard!"

She clung to him.

They used pet names: "sailor girl" and "Sasha." In moments of emotion, "Sasha" became "Sashenka."

He said, "My sailor girl . . . comrade . . . you will proclaim that I gave what was dearest to me for an ideal, for the great suffering people."

He was aboard, and the plan to put Most's theory into practice was in motion.

Waving, she ran beside the train, calling, "Sasha! Sashenka!"

NOTES

1. Howard H. Quint, *The Forging of American Socialism*, pp. 10-20. Henry David, *The History of the Haymarket Affair*, pp. 54-76.

2. Ira B. Cross, *A History of the Labor Movement in California*, pp. 156-57, 164-65. Haskell's journal *Truth* (San Francisco) records his IWA's early history, January 1882-December 1884.

3. Reinhard Höhn, *Die vaterlandslosen Gesellen*, pp. 74-75.

4. *Freiheit*, 16 December 1882.

5. Ibid., 17 February 1883.

6. "Harmonia Association of Joiners vs. Michael C. Hickey et al.,"

Circuit Court of Chicago, 5 May 1879; reproduced in *Labor Enquirer* (Chicago), 10 December 1887.

7. Samuel Gompers, *Seventy Years of Life and Labor* 1:96-97.

8. *Freiheit*, 23 December 1882. See also *New York Times*, 19 December 1882.

9. *Freiheit*, 14 April 1883.

10. Ibid., 30 December 1882, 6, 13, 20, 27, January, 3, 10, 17 February 1883.

11. *Washington* (D.C.) *Evening Star*, 21 April 1883.

12. Höhn, *Gesellen*, p. 166.

13. *Freiheit*, 2 June 1883.

14. Albert Weidner, *Aus den Tiefen der Berliner Arbeiterbewegung*, p. 75.

15. A. Sartorius, *Der moderne Socialismus in den Vereinigten Staaten von Amerika*, pp. 200-203.

16. Höhn, *Gesellen*, pp. 166, 188-89, 215-16.

17. Detailed reports of the congress: *Freiheit*, 20 and 27 October 1883. *Pittsburgh Commercial Gazette*, 13, 15, 16, and 17 October 1883. A concise account: Carl Nold, "Fifty Years Ago," p. 5.

18. Emma Goldman, *Living My Life*, p. 6.

19. Höhn, *Gesellen*, p. 262.

20. *Freiheit*, 16 February and 14 June 1884.

21. Ibid., 21 July 1883.

22. Ibid., 1 August 1896.

23. Abraham Cahan, *The Education of Abraham Cahan*, p. 327.

24. Terence V. Powderly, "The Army of the Discontented," p. 371.

25. David, *Haymarket*, pp. 157-205. Chicago newspapers of May 1886 covered the event in detail: *Herald*, 5. *Inter Ocean*, 5, 6, 8. *Times*, 6, 7, 8. *Daily News*, 15

26. August Spies, *Autobiography, pp.* 40-45.

27. *See* especially Adolph Fischer's speech at the trial, in A. R. Parsons, *Anarchism*, p. 78.

28. Dyer D. Lum, *A Concise History of the Great Trial of the Chicago Anarchists*, p. 171. Transcripts show the role Most's words and ideas played. *See*, for example, "The Celebrated Chicago Anarchists' Case," pp. 701-86.

29. Quoted by Norman J. Ware, *The Labor Movement in the United States*, p. 317. Seventy-five years later, George Woodcock agreed, in *Anarchism* (p. 464): the bomb "would never have been thrown," nor the anarchists hanged, but for exhortations that poured from Chicago anarchist papers and from Most's *Freiheit*.

30. The *Chicago Times*, for instance, spoke of "arch counselors of riot, pillage, incendiarism, and murder . . . blood-preaching anarchists . . . and fiends"; 6 May 1886.

31. Gompers, *Seventy Years* 2:178 and 181. *See also* Morris Hillquit, *History of Socialism in the United States*, pp. 227-29.

32. *Chicago Inter Ocean*, 21 August 1886.

33. Parsons, *Anarchism*, p. 198

34. Cahan, *Education*, pp. 328-29.

35. Art Young, *On My Way*, p. 123.

36. Joseph R. Buchanan, *The Story of a Labor Agitator*, p. 422.

37. Spies, *Autobiography*, p. 95.

38. Cahan, *Education*, p. 326.

39. Goldman, *Living My Life*, p. 43.

40. Cahan, *Education*, p. 410.

41. *Freiheit*, 7 January 1899.

42. Ibid., 1 August 1896.

43. Richard T. Ely, *The Labor Movement in America*, p. 242.

44. Goldman, *Living My Life*, p. 9.

45. Ibid., p. 87.

46. Ibid., p. 91.

9
PENALTY AND PUNISHMENT

1635: Massachusetts banishes Roger Williams for preaching separation of church and state.

1637: Massachusetts convicts John Wheelwright of opposing fasts and asserting the Elect above law and government.

1638: Massachusetts banishes Anne Hutchinson for heresy.

1656: Anne Hibbins hangs as a witch, in Salem.

1798: The Alien and Sedition Acts promise expulsion of undesirables and aim fines and imprisonment at critics of the government.

1877: June 21 is Pennsylvania's "Day with the Rope." In Pottsville and Mauch Chunk, ten Molly Maguires swing. Seven follow before the year is out.

1878: Ezra Heywood, in *Cupid's Yokes*, includes sexual emancipation among women's rights. He gets two years for mailing obscenity, in Boston.

1883: Sixty-five alleged anarchists, including Kropotkin, stand trial for associating with the International, in Lyons, France.

1890: Heywood again gets two years for transmitting obscenity.

When someone said to Most that here in America he was safe from imprisonment, he answered: such an assumption was false; it was at best only a question of time before the bourgeoisie's beadles overtook him. Time proved him right only too soon.

Most, *Acht Jahre hinter Schloss und Riegel*

If Most is sent up again, it will be interesting to observe whether his "principles" can stand another year of silence, soap and water, and hard work. As a rule these wholesome things are highly unfavorable to Anarchist doctrines.

The New York *Times*, November 18, 1887

OFFICIALS AND POLICE

Twelve days before Haymarket, workers crowded New York's Germania Garden. Like bits of glass in an Arizona sun, their eyes glittered with issues that burned in their hearts, issues they had come to hear Most address: the 8-hour day, the general strike, and the question of arming. He held up a rifle and shrieked, "To arm is not hard. Buy these, steal revolvers, make bombs, and when you have enough, rise and seize what is yours. Take the city by force and capitalists by the throat. Shoot or be shot." Pandemonium shook the Garden.[1]

The grand jury indicted him for that speech, but he was not to be found.

Then the Haymarket bomb rocked the nation. Word was, anarchists threw it—anarchists inspired by Most. Police redoubled efforts to catch him. They raided his home. They cast a dragnet and trawled from West New York to Brooklyn. One squad of detectives searched the anarchist colony in Jersey City Heights while another ransacked Newark. *Freiheit*'s offices went under surveillance.

According to stories later in the press, detectives learned of his fondness for Lena Fischer, an eighteen-year-old "of fine figure and

Figure 3. Thomas Nast's Cartoon of Most, 1886, with caption: "Anarchists' Drill, New Tactics. Generalissimo: 'Double quick, under the bed, march!'"

—*Culver Pictures*

attractive countenance," followed her to 198 Allen Street, and knocked.

"I don't care to tell who is in the room," she answered, through the door.

They broke it open, looked at her, and sniffed.

"You don't smoke cigars, do you, Lena?"

They found Most under the bed. "Here he is, stinking like a skunk in his hole." They dragged him out, ordered him to dress (he had "not very much on," except his cigar), and hauled him to headquarters. He was surly all the way.

At headquarters he admitted being in European prisons "for the cause of liberty." He described himself as twice a member of the German parliament, forty, single, and an editor.

The police emptied his pockets and took a knife, which they secured, along with three rifles and three bayonets and books (including his own) on the manufacture and use of explosives, found at 198 Allen.[2]

His version was different.[3] He hid to avoid unjust arrest. The only person who knew his whereabouts was the emissary between him and *Freiheit*—the clue that brought police to 198 Allen. Seeing their suspicious movements, he sought shelter among comrades. He went out one door while police came in the other. No comrade would shelter him, and every policeman on the street seemed to look at him askance. Exasperated, he said: "I've had enough of this game, and I'm going to end it."

Back at 198 Allen he was taking off his coat when police forced the door, drew revolvers, and surrounded him. One said he would "like to put a bullet through your head, you god-damned son of a bitch," and another, "If you show your teeth or open your yap, we'll shoot you down like a dog," and another, "One bark out of you and you'll feel how we bite." They grabbed from his belongings a rifle, a club, books and newspapers, and a briefcase containing $180 in cash and postage and carried them and him to headquarters.

There his pockets were turned out; and the contents were kept, even his handkerchief. Fists were shaken in his face.

"Let him stew in his own juice," said a voice, while the key grated in the lock.

Another voice, as grating as the key, "And then he can fry in his own fat."

Next morning he asked for a towel; he wanted to wash his hands and face.

Refused. Everyone knew that anarchists do not bathe.

His handkerchief?

No.

Breakfast?

Refused. Everyone knew that anarchists eat little children.

He was photographed for the rogues' gallery, and then "shown up"—displayed while fifty detectives memorized his features, hurling insults and flinging threats meanwhile.

Returning to his cell he met Inspector McCullagh, who laughed, "Ah, there's my friend Most, worst of the worst. This time we've got him so he won't get away. After every country he's been in has arrested and imprisoned and expelled him, he thinks he can work mischief among us. Well, we'll take care of him, too. I wouldn't want to be in his shoes."

Most was furious when he heard the press's story and livid when he saw Nast's two-part cartoon of him: "before," when "his skin is not in danger," a giant with a bugle to his lips, tabard proclaiming, "I am not only there but I am very much there!"; and "after," when his skin *is* in danger, under a bed, only feet and bugle protruding to give "Herr Most" away to the pointed finger of the law. *Lies! Lies!* He said his landlord, his landlord's wife, and their friend Miss Georges saw everything and were witnesses against the lies, *the egregious mendacity*. He charged a reporter named Cohen, of the *Staats-Zeitung*, and another named Cuno, of the *Volkszeitung*, with inventing the story; those rascals and their papers would go to any length to calumniate him, do any outrage to slander him. Indeed, a few months before, Cuno trumped up the story that Most hid behind the curtain in the Concordia Assembly Rooms while police battered comrades black and blue. Cuno admitted deceit when an angry Most pointed out that in the Concordia, no curtain was big enough to hide behind.

Cuno's confession did not change popular and official attitudes. Most remained a public enemy. Police, reacting against anarchist strength and responding to anti-anarchist opinion, grew more hostile.

Newark police closed the hall where he was to speak.[4] Another was gotten. No sooner was he done speaking than police appeared, furious that *the cur* had fooled them. Next day the Office of Licenses and Inspections ordered that the owner of any place of business in which Most spoke be subject to arrest, fine, and loss of license. Making himself a test case, Comrade Edward Wilms, Newark restaurateur and saloon-keeper, invited Most to speak. Wilms was arrested, lost his license for a month, and paid $50. Thereafter, police shook him down whenever they thought he might be aiding and comforting Most, or (according to Most) whenever they needed to shake someone down to raise themselves in public opinion, or (again according to Most) whenever they wanted to train rookies in shakedowns, or (still according to Most) whenever they obeyed their bestiality. When police wanted Most for his speech on the execution of the Haymarket anarchists, they arrested Wilms for keeping a house of ill fame. Officials and police erected a wall around Newark, Most said, "a wall, not in Turkey or Russia, but in New Jersey."

The wall encircled the state after Most went to a picnic with comrades in Weehawken. Deputy sheriffs, deciding the flags, slogans, speeches, wine, and beer were distilling into an explosive, brandished revolvers and fired into the air. Liable to arrest on the flimsiest of pretexts, Most fled. Comrades roughed up the deputies and threw them off the grounds. Next day, newspapers described a riot instigated and led by Most. New Jersey ordered his arrest, should he be found in the state henceforth, and interdicted distribution and sale of *Freiheit*.

Banned in New Jersey, as well as Brooklyn, Chicago, and Philadelphia, and fearful of arrest where he was not banned, he kept to New York City for years. And there Pinkertons and police, in disguise, tried to get something on him. One day a wild-looking man in an army uniform, pretending to be out of breath, burst into 167 William and told Most:

"I am a deserter. Give me different clothes. I will do anything for the Cause."

"Tell me more," Most said.

"Let me into your organization, the inner circle. Assign me a mission, an act of propaganda-by-the-deed."

Most showed him the door. Leaving, the man accompanied "God damn!" with an unmentionable gesture.

Another hooked his cane over his arm, tipped his homburg, and laid on the table in front of Most a dollar "for the Cause." Most took it and said thank you. A few days later the homburg was back, with questions. Where did the comrades meet? Most told him. No, the homburg wanted the place of the secret meetings.

"We keep no secrets. Secrecy is a form of authority. We oppose authority."

The homburg grimaced like an orangutan, took a deep breath, looked around, lowered his voice, and offered to enter the lists for the Haymarket anarchists—would Most see to it? Most threw him out.

His worst enemy in New York, the *Times*, wanted anarchists' requests for citizenship denied and citizenship of naturalized anarchists revoked; believers in riot and murder should not be countenanced with the dignity, let alone aided by the power, of the vote. Most made himself a test case, to see whether officials had changed with the *Times* or were continuing as befitted the land of the free and the home of the brave.[5]

According to the *Times*, four of Most's followers, "as pale as the dirt upon their faces would permit at their leader's reckless daring," craned their necks around the doorposts of the courthouse and watched, awestruck. He, out to "beard the monopolistic lion who acts as Clerk of the Superior Court," strode in with "the strut of a hero in a Bowery theatre" and said, "I am Herr Most, and I want to declare my intentions."

Thomas Boese, the lion, showed his claws and let Most take no steps toward naturalization, an action nearly unprecedented. Most, happy, had proved his point; newspapers published it; and the world knew that the United States had sunk to the depths of capitalist infamy. There ended the case of "Citizen Most," after the *Times* fired its parting shot: of bad character, hostile to the Constitution, ill-disposed to happiness, and inimical to order, Most was a blackguard who deserved rejection.

The *Times* hailed the arrest of the blackguard for a speech on the Haymarket executions. Days before, Superintendent Murray ordered precinct commanders to watch anyone (and especially Most) who might cause trouble over the executions. Murray enjoined McCullagh to diligence in the "hotbed of anarchism, the Fourteenth Precinct," where Most lived. McCullagh had Most shadowed.[6]

Louis Roth and John J. Sachs, German-speaking detectives, in gray shirts, slouch hats, and piebald neckties, shadowed him to Kraemer's Hall, 134 East 7th. He disappeared. They went into the saloon in front of the hall and sat among the crowd drinking beer. Roth and Sachs ordered beer, talked to people, and listened for word of Most. Word was, he would speak in a few minutes. Roth and Sachs followed the crowd into the hall. It was forty feet long, packed with people, hung with banners in socialist red and anarchist black, and thick with tobacco smoke. Roth and Sachs stood to the left of the door, twenty feet from the platform. Most entered pulling off his coat and began speaking at once.

Next day, McCullagh had a transcript of the speech, addressed to "Fellow Slaves" and asserting, "I would give ten years of my life to know the executioner. I would never rest until I strangled him as he strangled our brothers. . . . Death to the butcher. Anarchy will live forever." Solomon Dreyfuss had supposedly taken it down, in the presence of Roth and Sachs. (Most snorted, "Took it down? He cooked it up.") The *World* published it, with scornful annotations and sarcastic glosses. Roth and Sachs submitted their own statements, then accompanied Inspector Byrnes, loaded with evidence, to the grand jury.

The jury indicted Most as "an evil-disposed and pernicious person, of wicked and turbulent disposition . . . wickedly and maliciously intending to disturb the public peace, and to excite the good citizens of this State and the United States to hatred and contempt of the Government, and to provoke riot and insurrection and obstruct with force the execution of the laws." He had assembled with "other pernicious persons" and threatened to procure arms and "kill and murder." Empowered by the indictment, Roth and Sachs joined Detective-Sergeants Crowley and Maguire, who were shadowing Most. The four climbed to the top of 167 William and burst in on Most and comrades sitting down to a steaming Irish stew and a foaming growler of beer. A typesetter shouted, "Police bloodhounds!"

"Put on your hat, Most," one of the detectives said.

He rose to protest. A hand restrained him. A voice told him he could protest in court. He was pushed downstairs, marched around the block, hustled into a carriage, and taken to City Hall.

The arrest sobered his comrades. Captain McCullagh toured leftist rendezvous and reported the Fourteenth quiet. Radicals were not much in saloons, for a change. Justus Schwab joined all his customers in a game of pinochle. He said he had heard of the arrest but would say no more. "I'll draw the line just here," and he made a sign as though knotting a rope around his neck.[7]

The *Times* spoke without being asked. The arrest was "a good thing" even if Most were set free. "All the obstruction and discouragement that can lawfully be put in the way of his business is in the public interest. It is to be hoped, however, that his detention will not be brief."[8]

His fate was up to the courts.

HEARINGS AND TRIALS

On a chilly morning in May, comrades jammed the Court of General Sessions and filled the street outside. Those outside shivered, buttoned tighter their coats, stamped their feet, and kept their eyes on the door. Behind it, Most was on trial. He pled not guilty to inciting to riot, holding an illegal meeting, and disturbing the peace.

Yes, he said, he urged workers to arm. It was their right, their duty. Look at East St. Louis. Police there killed a dozen men, women, and children. Armed, they would be alive now. No, he was not the poltroon and the footler depicted by the press. "My conviction means the downfall of free speech! Then will be the downfall of freedom of the press and the end of the Republic!"

Assistant District Attorney Fellows, the prosecutor, a former colonel in the Confederate army still addressed as Colonel, cautioned the jury against Most's "mouth bombs" and retold the story of the arrest under the bed. Fellows scolded like a fishwife with a Southern accent, Most said.

Recorder Smyth, presiding, told the jury: Most's speech was

riotous. The jury returned. "Guilty," they said. "The law, I regret, does not permit me to impose what I should deem adequate punishment," Smyth said. For, to ignorant foreigners, Most advocated dynamite, murder, and arson; and he told servants to poison employers. "A more wicked and atrocious scoundrel" did "not disgrace the face of this earth!" Smyth imposed "the extreme penalty of the law," $500 and imprisonment at hard labor for one year, imprisonment to be extended one day for each dollar until the fine was paid.[9]

Most vetoed comrades' plans to appeal; a favorable decision was not likely. Later he learned that had New York not locked him up, he might have stood trial for causing Haymarket and had his life shortened by a stretched neck.

Released two months early for good behavior, he went back to agitating the Revolution with all his strength, and to envisioning anarchist society with all his fancy, every waking hour. The model prisoner was not the model citizen; his speeches were more pugnacious than ever.

Among the police, the New York *Times*, and the grand jury, his speech the next year, on the Haymarket executions, November 12, 1887, caused more concern than any speech of his before. The jury issued, under Section 451 of the Penal Code, an indictment for illegal assembly and inciting to riot. The *Times* believed he could be charged with murder if anyone followed his advice, but was language capable of inciting riot punishable if no riot followed?[10] He knew the answer: yes. He had gone to Blackwell's Island the year before for riotous language that caused no riot.

He was therefore too nervous to read the newspapers when brought from the Tombs and arraigned in the Court of General Sessions. Newspapers fell from his trembling hands into a heap at his feet, and his shuffling feet twisted and trampled them into a crumpled dirty pile.

Judge Cowing entered and sat down. His chair creaked. As if the creak were a signal, Most and counsel Willard F. Howe bent over the defendant's table and put their heads together, whispering. Howe, "The Lion of Centre Street," was portly and pompous. Rings spangled his hands, and jewelled studs glittered on his shirt. People said he was the city's best public defender.

"Your Honor, we plead not guilty."

Behind the prosecutor's table District Attorney Delancey Nicoll rose, natty in gray pinstripe and resplendent in starched and snowy shirt front. The intent of the law was not to prohibit free speech, he argued, but to stop abuse of that right. He took up the evidence against Most, beginning with a definition of anarchy.

Howe objected that the definition was irrelevant.

Sustained.

Nicoll called Detective Roth, who said, Most entered Kraemer's to "Here comes our leader!" and on the table put a handkerchief, ready when needed to dry the sweat that drenched his brow before the speech was done. Roth heard him mark for assassination the authorities responsible for the Haymarket executions. " 'Fellow slaves,' Most said, 'arm yourselves. They killed five of our brothers in Chicago; we will have 500 for every one they murdered.' " The words had brought the audience near delirium, and one man had shouted: " 'Why not tonight? We're ready.' " Roth claimed perfect German; he could not be mistaken.

According to Most, Roth and Sachs were chosen for the credibility their smattering of German would lend to their testimony; and they memorized Dreyfuss's distortion of Most's speech and parrotted it as what they heard Most say. Howe cross-examined Roth in that light.

"What is German for *fate*?"

"I don't know."

"How did the defendant end his speech?"

"I don't remember."

"That will do, sir; you can go."

Nicoll called Sachs. He testified to the truth of Roth's account. What were Most's first words?

"Fellow anarchists."

Howe observed: Roth said the speech began with "Fellow slaves."

Howe asked Sachs to say "fellow anarchists" in German.

"Bruder Anarchist."

Howe pointed out that Sachs had given the singular; the plural was wanted.

Dreyfuss corroborated Roth's and Sachs's accounts, but to Howe he admitted that he had not transcribed on the spot. He had gone to the police station and transcribed.

Howe's first witness, Adolph Schenck, named by Sachs the chairman at Kraemer's, denied having been near Kraemer's; but to Nicoll admitted that as an anarchist he believed in neither God nor law.

Moritz Schultz, typesetter for *Freiheit*, said he, not Schenck, chaired the meeting. Most's speech was harmless, a quiet wordy dirge. Most did not demand revenge and did not request 500 killed for every anarchist hanged at Chicago; he said: "For each of freedom's soldiers strangled, 500 will rise in his place." The speech produced, not rage, but tears.

Howe recalled Dreyfuss, who admitted being fired from two newspapers; but under Nicoll's cross-examination he maintained that being fired had nothing to do with competence or integrity. He had talked to nobody but his brother about Most's speech before submitting the transcript. Contradicting Dreyfuss, James Creelman said that Dreyfuss told him about the speech; but to Nicoll, Creelman admitted that Dreyfuss told him only that the speech contained nothing worthwhile. Charles Gudis said that Dreyfuss left the meeting before Most finished; but to Nicoll he admitted that as an anarchist he, Gudis, believed in law not at all but in dynamite galore. Emil Koss, a peddler who came to Most's speech to sell corn plasters, said the speech was not illegal; but to Nicoll, Koss admitted that he did not know whether the United States was a republic or a kingdom. Had he heard of Grover Cleveland? Yes, somewhere.

The fifth day, comrades jammed courtroom, corridors, entranceway, and street—coming to see Most testify. They were comrades who gave too much to the Cause to have enough for clothes, ragamuffins who looked like a beggars' army mustering for a last stand. Those outside, in the cold of November, huddled before the door, turning backs to the raw wind and feeling it bite through threadbare coats. A mounted policeman kept watch, sitting motionless except to roll a frequent cigarette, grateful for the warmth of his horse. A vendor positioned himself where the fragrance of his roasting chestnuts would carry to the crowd; for hot chestnuts on a cold day they must have enough money.

Howe said to Most, "Tell the court and jury what you said."

Most straightened and brightened. His tones were dramatic, his gestures theatrical. Yes, he called murderers the people responsible for the executions; but he also called murderers the press, Terence Powderly, Henry George, and workingmen who repudiated their partisans. If five anarchists were dead, Anarchy was alive—invigorated by their deaths. What the cross was to Christians, the gallows would become to anarchists. But he did not say he would give ten years for a chance at the executioner, nor that he would strangle him; nor did he threaten to kill 500 capitalists for every hero hanged. Such blather by an anarchist during an anti-anarchist outcry, in the presence of reporters and police, would have been "very silly."

His eyes flashed for the ten minutes of that recitation. Sweat stood on his brow.

Cross-examining, Nicoll educed that Most had been imprisoned in Suben in 1869, in Chemnitz in 1872, in Plötzensee in 1874, again in Plötzensee in 1877, and in Clerkenwell in 1881. (A spectator shouted, "A regular jailbird!") Most had expounded terrorism, vilified leaders, denounced emperors, and hailed regicide. In short, for breaking laws in three countries, he had spent seven years under lock and key. Then he had fled to America, advocated revolution, and been clapped into prison. (A juror said, "It's time this jailbird's wings were clipped.")

Arms waving, Howe objected, shouting, "Irrelevant! Prejudicial!" Overruled.

Admitting membership in the International Working People's Association, Most stated its purpose: to further anarchism and advance social revolution. Yes, savages who murdered comrades "will suffer for it." Did he demand a terrible accounting for every drop of anarchist blood spilled? Perhaps. Was he an author? No, an editor, though he wrote books and pamphlets.

"Such as?"

"*The Hell of Blackwell's Island.*"

(Laughter in the gallery.)

"Are you the author of *The Science of Revolutionary Warfare?*"

Howe: "Don't answer!"

Nicoll held up a copy and pointed to "Most" on the title page, then called a translator and asked for passages to be read aloud.

"Out of order," ruled Judge Cowing. "Strike it from the record."

Nicoll resumed with Most.

"You favor overthrow of the government?"
"Sure. But not any particular government."
"You believe in force?"
"No progress without it."
"Dynamite?"
"Dynamite."

Most, the last witness, was done. Prosecution and defense addressed the jury. Howe stressed the inconsistent testimony of the prosecution's witnesses; expressed doubt about the capacity of the prosecution's witnesses to understand, remember, and record; and argued that Most was on trial for a speech, not for his books or his past life. Nicoll played up Most's books and life and cast aspersions on testimony from men who believed in dynamite but neither God nor law.

Cowing charged the jury to be honest, diligent, impartial, and cautious about conflicting evidence. The jury retired, and everyone else went to dinner.[11]

The New York *Times* said Most was as innocent this time as he was guilty last. That time he held a gun and urged violence. This time he did neither. Besides, threatened or attempted riot was not criminal unless "accompanied by the power of immediate execution of such threat or attempt." At worst, the blackguard may have called people murderers by name and have threatened an executioner he could not name. But such fulminations, however loud, however repulsive, did not break riot laws.[12]

On the other hand, the prosecution declared him, and he boasted of being, a champion of a doctrine so obnoxious it earned him prison term after prison term. A defendant's beliefs could influence a jury more than guilt or innocence of the crime charged; the anarchists he glorified in the speech for which he was on trial were hanged, not for the bomb, but for being anarchists. In similar circumstances how would he fare?

He returned from dinner smoking a cigar and glowing with a good digestion. He sat with his back to the defendant's table, facing the railing, and across it regaled onlookers with tales of European prisons. At 10:00 P.M. the door opened, Cowing took his seat, and the jury returned. The verdict could be read in every juror's face.

On the first ballot, they had stood 7-5 for acquittal. On the

second, 6-6. Expectations had been that deliberations would last beyond midnight. Dinner had been brought in. An hour later, Cowing had ruled that, failing a verdict in thirty minutes, the jury would stay until 11:00 A.M. next day. In twenty minutes, unanimity.
Howe requested that the jury be polled.
By unanimous vote: Guilty.
Most hissed, "It is unjust!"
Howe asked to move for a new trial.
Granted.
Howe argued one question of fact and three of law. Fact: the jury misinterpreted conflicting evidence and therefore lacked sufficient reason to convict. Law: the charges did not constitute crime. Law: when the prosecution paraded Most's *Science*, it prejudiced the jury, even though ruled inadmissible. Law: the court erred in letting the prosecution ask witnesses whether they believed in a supreme being.
Cowing denied the motion. True, he conceded, the evidence conflicted; but juries were entitled to evaluate evidence and empowered to draw conclusions; orderly and impartial procedure, and the integrity of the jury system itself, demanded that juries be respected. Granted all rights and enjoying every safeguard, Most got as fair a trial as possible. But Cowing agreed that the questions of law raised points worthy of review; and he granted a stay, pending appeal. He looked at Most.
"What have you to say why judgment should not be pronounced?"
Holding a manuscript in hands violently trembling, Most read in a thick accent a statement asking Cowing to recognize that, in addition to misinterpretation of facts, free speech was infringed—a right more important than the privilege of a jury to err. Please use "such discretion as lies within your power." He bowed his head.
Cowing sentenced him to a year in the penitentiary, to be postponed during the stay pending appeal, and ordered his release on bail meanwhile.
Cowing drew a deep breath. His chair creaked. "In your case, Most, the great trouble—I want to say it to you—is this: your tongue and pen have constantly brought you into difficulty," so much difficulty that the mass of the people, who loved their country, considered him its enemy, a threat to its institutions; so much diffi-

culty that it might be impossible to find twelve who would not be prejudiced. But "I have always been averse to interfering with findings of fact by a jury where the evidence is conflicting, even though I might have come to a different conclusion upon the same evidence." Furthermore, law and order were necessary; and government must exist to enforce law and maintain order, even in America. Indeed, "All happiness comes from obedience to law and all misery from disobedience." Therefore "Most, study our institutions, understand the rights of American citizens," and "try to do as much good as you can" instead of "undertaking to create discord." So "print your paper, but do right."[13]

Captain Lindsay and three detectives, with Most the center of a quincunx, went up the street to the Tombs. Nearly all faces in the crowd were doleful, a few lachrymose. But the mounted policeman flung away his cigarette and smiled. The chestnut vendor had gone at dusk, his pocket full of coins, smiling too.

Next day, Ida Hoffmann posted $5,000; and Most left the Tombs carrying his belongings in a bag over his shoulder. Comrades greeted and lifted him, bag and all, onto their shoulders.

His case was appealed. Meanwhile, Nicoll went elsewhere. The man who replaced him, an enemy to the New York *World*, determined that the *World* (which had done its best to get Most convicted) should not have the satisfaction of seeing Most sent to the Island. Two and a half years later, Nicoll (a friend to the *World*) became district attorney again. The appeal was denied. Most was arrested and sent to the Tombs, to be transferred to the Island at once. The carriage was at the door. Deputies came with handcuffs. He flailed and kicked.

Comrades routed Howe out of bed. Bleary-eyed and lacking rings, shirt studs, and shirt itself, he panted into the Tombs and flourished a writ of habeas corpus. Most was released.[14] His case went from the New York State Court of Appeals to the appellate division of the New York Supreme Court.

Comrades established and *Freiheit* advertised a defense fund that grew with dimes and dollars from across the country. The money retained Howe to argue the appeal. After a year the appeal failed.

Freiheit explained that the court (like all American courts) expressed the will of plutocrats and that Nicoll, who became attorney general in time to influence the courts against the appeal, was the tool of the "Upper Four Hundred" who ran New York. They wanted to suppress leftists, subdue labor, squelch agitators, and above all, jail anarchists.[15] Therefore Most was on Blackwell's Island for the second time.

JAILS AND PRISONS

Most was enjoying a glass of wine at Schwab's when Moritz Schultz burst in and waved a letter from Howe. Appeal was denied. Most had better see Howe at once. Newsboys: "Extra! Extra!" Schultz handed Most an extra. The police wanted Most, it said; every available officer had been ordered into the search. Brass buttons flashed at the door. Most dove under the table, too late.[16]

They locked him in the museum at headquarters, until they could take him to the Tombs. He studied burglar tools: drills, crowbars, jimmies, and fret saws. And axes, hatchets, hammers, knives, razors, rifles, pistols, and shotguns—weapons of murderers and suicides. Each pair of hundreds of hoods and nooses bore name and photograph of the person who died in them. He shuddered. How typically American, to make a show of savagery.

In swarmed reporters. As if he were a museum piece they looked him up and down and over, noting shape of head, color of shoes, and defiance of attitude. His head was like an obelisk, one said. Whether his shoes were gray or black remained moot. But they agreed that he was belligerent. The reporter for the New York *Tribune* recorded a malformed head, heavy unsymmetrical jaws that a thick bushy beard could not hide, and a snarling red mouth studded with yellow fangs. The reporters asked questions point-blank and rapid-fire and wrote in notebooks while paying little mind to what he said. Tomorrow "interviews" would appear in the papers, paid for at a penny a line. No wonder these literary highwaymen stared so hard, wrote so fast, and left in such a hurry!

Cell 125 of the Tombs—no ventilation, close darkness, full chamber pot—resembled the toilet on a ferry. In the dark, with his fingers, he ate dinner: bread that tasted like sawdust and meat that smelled as if it were cooked in the chamber pot.

The cells of the Tombs were full, creating a population density appalling to rats. To the peephole in the door of each cell some prisoners rushed when a visitor passed, as if for deliverance; while from it others shrank as if in shame. Except the rare prisoner who purposely exercised, this rushing or shrinking was a prisoner's exercise; walking in open air was unheard-of. Clothing hooks had been removed after prisoners hanged themselves, but suicides continued. Hence the name "Tombs."

Sunday, self-styled brothers of charity and self-appointed sisters of mercy came singing, shouting, and whistling to save souls. Then one began to preach. From cells:

"Shut that guy up!"

"Throw him out!"

"Kick him in the ass!"

Squelched, the preacher looked at his companions, who burst into "A Mighty Fortress Is Our God." Then they went individually from cell to cell. A curly-haired blond youth spoke through the grating.

"You're Herr Most."

Most ignored him.

"Don't you know, all you must do is believe in Jesus, to be saved?"

"Saved from you, I hope."

"Really, Most—shame on you."

"Don't waste your time and mine."

"Oh, I know, you're an anarchist—*the* anarchist. You don't want to hear of God. You think anarchy will take away the sins of the world. Only, you won't see it. You'll be in Hell—you and the Devil."

Most roared. The would-be apostle ran, shouting over his shoulder: "Anarchy won't take away the sins of the world. Anarchy *is* the sin of the world."

Most realized why rats and mice had disappeared since his last lockup here. Six days a week they could tolerate bedlam, but pandemonium every seventh was beyond tolerance.

Besides confinement at the Tombs, he knew arrest at headquarters, detention in the courthouse, and imprisonment on Blackwell's Island.

Arrest at headquarters meant being thrown into a closet eight feet by four by six, with a bare bench as chair and bed combined. If lucky enough to have an overcoat, he either rolled it into a pillow and forgot blankets or used his arm as a pillow and the coat as a blanket. Whichever the choice, sleep was improbable not only because filth turned his stomach and the bench hurt his body but also because ants, lice, and bedbugs bit him. In the corner, where a faucet dripped above a drain and waterbugs scuttled one after another, he was to bathe and drink, and urinate and defecate. He doubted a civilized person could do more than two *there*.[17]

Detention at the courthouse meant being herded into a room with at least twenty other unfortunates. Whereas the hole at headquarters was dark, lights glared continuously here. Detainees used one another for pillows, obviating that problem but losing privacy —a considerable loss when it came to urinating and defecating. Rats, mice, and fleas joined ants, lice, and bedbugs in assault on cleanliness, decency, and self-respect. Blessed with a strong stomach, Most did not mingle his vomit with the vomit of the queasy, which stank in the corners.[18]

Headquarters and the courthouse disgusted but the Island terrified him. Once from a boat he and Emma Goldman saw stately trees and stone buildings on a green island. To her, after tenements, a pleasing sight. She turned to him, to share the pleasure.

His face was ashen, fist clenched.

"What is it?" she cried.

He looked at the island: "Blackwell's Island Penitentiary, the Spanish Inquisition transferred to the United States. Soon it will again hold me."[19]

Soon the ferry brought him and others, handcuffed together, to the Island.[20] When the gates clanged shut in the receiving station, cuffs were removed, beards shaved, and hair cropped. Keepers, barbers, and inmates stared and jeered at his face. On command he stripped and took a bath. Joining stares and jeers then: lewd jibes and obscene gestures. Shamed by stares, pelted by jeers, and needled by jibes, he winced at gestures, shivered in a puddle dripping from his body, and hid as best he could behind his hands, until given black-and-white striped trousers and a blue-and-white striped shirt. These zebra stripes, which he would wear for a year, reminded him of what heretics in the Middle Ages wore to their executions. "I see many stripes but few stars here in America's asshole."

On command he donned the trousers but held the shirt. He was measured, weighed, and asked name and religion. "Atheist" caused indignation.

"A strong back," said Deputy-Warden Osborne. "Put him in the smithy, starting tomorrow. Take him to his cell now."

Cells lined one side of a corridor; loopholes admitted half-light on the other. Always the half-light, because at night, lamps burned but dimly. In winter, six stoves roared but could not heat 300 cells. From fall to spring, prisoners suffered cold feet and colds in the head.

His was cell 16 on the first tier of the old section, a grave of stone and iron, seven feet by three by six, in which he felt buried alive. That space admitted neither table nor chair nor bench nor shelf nor chest. The bed was of sailcloth on a hinged iron frame that, when let down, spanned the cell. Bedding: two blankets and a pillow. A filthy wooden bucket with a crippled cover fouled the air. Above the bucket, signs: no smoking, no writing, no talking, no singing, no whistling; in other words, behave like a dog or be punished like one.

The hundreds of other prisoners were out at work, leaving silence fit for a grave. Through a loophole sunlight sparkled on waves. He heard a boat's whistle, then saw an excursion boat, crowded with people, laughing. He turned to the mirror, looked at his newly shaven face, and shuddered. He went to bed and lay with his face to the wall.

After a long night a bell rang at 5:00 A.M. Jailers burst into the corridor and unlocked locks. Most's neighbor shouted to Most, "Push on your door!" A second bell. Prisoners pushed doors open and in the corridor formed a column. The turnkey commanded, "Face this side!" Then, "Head on!" The march in lockstep began. One man out of step meant chaos. Most was out of step. The turnkey snapped, "Most, I thought you were a rebel general, but you can't march!" This was Assistant-Keeper O'Keefe, turnkey, whose voice outdid a hound's baying the moon. "When he dies," Most said, "from his casket will fly words for the pallbearers: 'Keep step! Close in! Cover down! Dress up! Eyes right!'"

Five hundred missteps and five hundred curses later, the column reached the washroom. On command each prisoner grabbed a pail, filled it from a vat, and washed himself—for a minute. Then: "Back out!" Each prisoner struggled for a piece of towel. Then the return, in lockstep.

At 6:00 A.M. another lockstep, to breakfast. On command, Most sat, like each of his 900 to 1,000 fellows, on a small bench at a narrow table among many benches and tables in a great hall, and in five minutes ate a slice of bread that tasted like sawdust and drank a cup of yellow water called coffee but tasting like the essence of sawdust. Guards on high stools, brandishing truncheons, prevented talking.

Half an hour later, lockstep again. He, like each of his fellows, gripped his excrement bucket in one hand and clutched his cap in the other. Outdoors, on command, in unison, the column put caps on. At the edge of the river, on command, the column faced the water and dumped buckets in unison.

Next, in the assembly area, columns converged into compact formation like a regiment on parade. They stood at attention and listened to the calling of names of dischargees. When dischargees marched away, the rest went to work, in lockstep. "Here I am, the enemy of militarism," Most said, "being taught fundamentals of soldiering."

He worked in the smithy with about fifty men, many of them immigrants: Germans, Chinese, Irish, French, and Italians. He drilled holes in locks, hinges, bedsteads, and carriage fixtures. When drilling did not fill the day, he washed windows, stacked iron, or tended forges. In cold weather their heat warmed him, and pumping the bellows drove rheumatism out of his arms. The boss's voice penetrated everywhere (even to the disruption of Most's deepest thoughts), fuming, ordering, scolding, cursing.

At noon the boss struck an iron with a hammer. Work stopped. Hands washed without soap were dried on handkerchiefs and shirt-tails. Three times a week the column marched, in lockstep, to soup, bread, and meat; twice to pork and beans; and once, Fridays, to potatoes and fish. Only a fool would willingly dawdle: good not to see more than necessary of the slop, better to escape its stench, and best not to remember what food could be like; but the prisoners were kept an hour, sitting at attention, permitted neither to doze nor talk.

Back to work, in lockstep, at 1:00 P.M. During Most's first after-

noon, twenty officials in a group stood around him, to see the anarchist of whom they had heard so much.

At 5:30 P.M., work ended. The column marched, in lockstep, to
the same meal as breakfast, except Sundays, when it was cornmeal
mush and syrup.

The Monday-through-Friday routine changed on weekends.
Prisoners spent Saturday afternoons and Sundays in cells, idle,
unless they went to chapel.

Thus weeks passed—week in, week out. "What can be new
among automatons?" said Most. "Weekdays I am a day laborer,
earning room and board in hell. Weekends I am Diogenes, living in
my barrel and needing no lantern." Weekends he suffered the hours,
slow and heavy hours, without conversation, books, newspapers,
or writing materials.

Empty hours, however slow and heavy, were better than chapel.
The first Sundays the chaplain asked him to come. The chaplain
looked in, between the bars, a moon-face in a clerical collar, holding a Bible in both hands. "I know you are not to be converted,
but can't you come for diversion?" Next week he added: "I'll make
the sermon short." At last: "Two pretty girls are going to sing
today." Giving up he muttered that Most could fry in hell.

Only serious books were prohibited; the library bulged with
trash, which Most refused to read. Newspapers were prohibited.
Food and tobacco could be received, and he got them from wife
and comrades. Each prisoner was allowed to send one letter every
four weeks, and for it was given a few minutes and one sheet of
paper. *Freiheit* published Most's—one letter to answer many from
wife and comrades. Prudent, he watched what he wrote; letters
being censored, the wrong word could land him in solitary. "My
heart is full of poison and gall, mockery and scorn, and love of
freedom and disdain for the world," he said, "but I dare not put
them into a letter" (and that statement was a risk). Other writing
material and writing were forbidden. Once a month a prisoner
could receive visitors in the mess hall for twenty minutes, but a
change of clothes was forbidden; visitors saw prisoners in the shame
of rags. Reporters visited Most (he was often news) whenever they
liked, asking his view on current events; but he said nothing to
irritate the authorities.

For he knew that punishment at least meant no food from outside, no letters, and no visitors for as long as the warden decreed. Worse, sentences were lengthened; one of Most's fellows got eight months extra for talking at lunch. So Most was a model prisoner; he wanted to be out and fit for the Cause. Suffer he did, but the minimum, thanks to circumspection.

He avoided the severest punishment. Leaving a spoon in the mess hall, talking, spitting, faulty work, disobeying—each could bring a day of solitary confinement; and insubordination, cursing, or smuggling, three days. More serious infractions brought longer stays. The confinee saw nothing (darkness was total) and heard naught but his own breathing—or retching, when he gagged on stench from the excrement bucket. He could stand up as long as his legs could bear shackles and sit or lie on the floor as long as his body could take chill and endure hardness. From isolation there was one relief. After hours of standing, lying, and sitting—after an eternity of isolation—the fortunate passed out. Once a day the door opened, a light glared, and a voice growled, "This one's alive," or "This one's loony," or "This one's dead." With the live the voice left a quarter pound of bread and a cup of water. On the sixth day, a warm meal; and every sixth thereafter. For the majority, by the first sixth day, the voice growled, "This one's loony" or "This one's dead."

Though able to escape punishment, Most could not evade torment. Other prisoners stole his food and tobacco, even picked it from his pocket. In front of him, glad he heard, his workmate said, "When I look at him, I see myself as an organ grinder with my monkey." Most also heard:

"He's behind the trouble in this country."

"The bastard's neck should be stretched."

"When they're done with the son of a bitch here, they'll ship him to Chicago. He'll get what he deserves there."

"I'd love to tighten the noose myself."

"And to think the prick only got a year out here."

Strong-willed, he bore this abuse and the other horrors. Even a sterling character could be tarnished here; only the toughest did not become beasts. Food had to be wolfed. There were no towels for personal use, nor sheets or socks. Blankets were shaken every six months but never washed. Bathing was a moistening of hands and face. If he could not see dirt on gray blankets, he could see it on himself. Lice flourished. One word described everyone: savage. As if to confirm that prisoners were animals in a zoo, the prison was open to the public. The main attraction was "the anarchist," "the one named Most; what's he look like?"

Sickness was rampant. Death proved it. "Better to die than be sick," prisoners whispered on winter mornings when they carried corpses like logs, frozen stiff ahead of rigor mortis. "Better dead than sick." For the sick were to report to the dispensary at noon, before eating. If they returned that day, others had eaten their food. At the dispensary, medical students tapped, cut, and probed; prisoners were for experimentation. Chief treatments were colodion and pills of universal application but doubtful potency. "Take them or solitary." Prisoners sick enough for a hospital were given pills, slapped, called goldbricks, and shoved back to work. "You don't go to the hospital," the saying was, "until your death certificate is in your pocket."

Worse off than the physically were the mentally ill. Many went insane. A young slender music teacher with blue-veined hands and long delicate fingers arrived normal. Breaking rules too rigorous for him and refusing medicine that sickened him landed him in solitary once a week. Soon he shrieked like a child and babbled inanities when bundled off to bread, water, silence, and shackles. Enraged by shrieking and vexed by babbling, guards punched and clubbed him comatose and bloody. Again and again, Most saw him with a gory face, unconscious. The "physicians" prescribed laxative, enough for a horse. It worked. And worked and worked. Physicians and guards laughed themselves into stitches.

Freiheit feared that Most would not survive the first term, but he survived both. "From the small I returned to the big prison," he said.[21] "Soon may the world be a prison no more. Long live the Revolution! Hail Anarchy!"

NOTES

1. *New York Times* 1886: 12 May, p. 2; 28 May, p. 3. Most, *Acht Jahre hinter Schloss und Riegel*, pp. 71-72.

2. *New York Times* 1886: 12 May, p. 2; 22 May, p. 2. *Volkszeitung*

(New York), 24 May 1886.

3. *Freiheit*, 15 and 22 May 1886. Most, *Acht Jahre*, pp. 72-74. Most, "Zwischen Galgen und Zuchthaus," *Internationale Bibliothek*, 1887, p. 16.

4. *Freiheit*, 5 September 1896.

5. *New York Times*, 13 September 1887, pp. 4 and 8.

6. Ibid. 1887: 15 November, p. 1; 18 November, p. 1. *Freiheit*, 5 September 1896. Most, *Acht Jahre*, p. 79.

7. *Freiheit*, 19 November 1887.

8. *New York Times*, 18 November 1887, p. 4.

9. Ibid., 3 June 1886, p. 8; see also 29 May 1886, p. 8. *Freiheit*, 5 June 1886. Most, *Acht Jahre*, pp. 74-75.

10. *New York Times* 1887: 15 November, p. 1; 19 November, p. 8.

11. Ibid., 24 November, p. 1; 26 November, p. 8; 29 November, p. 5; 30 November, p. 1; 9 December, p. 1. Most, "Zwischen Galgen und Zuchthaus," pp. 3-9. *Freiheit*, 5 September 1896.

12. *New York Times*, 30 November 1887, p. 4.

13. Ibid., 9 December 1887, p. 1.

14. *Freiheit*, 20 June 1891.

15. Ibid., 11 July 1891.

16. Ibid., 8 February 1890.

17. Ibid., 22 May 1886.

18. Ibid. Most, *Acht Jahre*, 73-75.

19. Emma Goldman, *Living My Life*, p. 63.

20. Most, "Die Hölle von Blackwell's Island," *Internationale Bibliothek*, 1887. *Freiheit* 14 August, 6 November, 4 December 1886; 8 August, 6 September, 28 November 1891; 23 January, 19 March, 3 April 1892. Most, *Acht Jahre*, pp. 75-78.

21. *Freiheit*, 23 April 1891.

10
THE WORLD HE LEFT BEHIND

1881: Leo Walecka begins four years' confinement for smuggling *Freiheit*, in Vienna.

1884: Martial law in Vienna exiles 500. Heads of families never see their families again.

1885: A knife penetrates the overcoat, coat, vest, shirt, and undershirt, and pierces the chest, right lung, and heart of Frankfurt's chief of police. A bloody hand points to a 21-year-old shoemaker. After reiterating, "I am innocent," Julius Lieske leaves the courtroom, shouting, "Up with anarchy!" The evening of November 16th he eats half a goose, drinks schnaps, and says, "It was the feast of my life." Next morning the axe beheads him and splits the block, and blood gushes into the split.

1887: The Imperial Tribunal throws the book at John Neve in Leipzig. Beginning a 15-year sentence at Halle, he writes "1902" on the door of his cell. In 1896, insane, he dies of tuberculosis.

1891: The Social Democratic party, resurging after the fall of Bismarck, strengthens its Marxist philosophy. Anarchist sympathizers, cold-shouldered, leave the party.

1893: The British home secretary, Mr. Asquith, and the leader of the opposition, Mr. Balfour, agree that anarchists threaten order. Anarchist meetings are forbidden.

167

Some sinister anarchic underworld, heaving in its pain, its power, and its hate.

Henry James, *The Princess Casamassima*

What a pleasure to see how lively "Young Germany" [a group of anarchists] is in Berlin! For them (alas!) I was born thirteen years too soon.

Most, *Freiheit*, January 23rd, 1892

A revolution of the greatest magnitude, beginning in the little circle of our district, then the province, then . . . the whole world. Because a just idea cannot but be fruitful.

Levin, in *Anna Karenina*, by Leo Tolstoy

For a decade after Most came to America he inspired terrorists and harried authorities in Europe. Social-revolutionary clubs, burgeoning as a result of his agitation, raised money and gathered materiel in America, to ignite sedition in Europe. Radicals expelled from Europe formed an elite of terrorist moguls and their nabobs, each qualified as a master, if not a doctor, of insurrectionary arts; and they swore allegiance to Most. They studied his *Science of Revolutionary Warfare*, bought dynamite, contrived devices for sabotage, laid plans for assassination, and exported infernal machines—all at his direction.

Worse than infernal machines were the ideas exported. In *Freiheit* he taught terrorism, incited terror, praised terrorists, and applauded terrorist acts. Orators took texts from *Freiheit* and read columns aloud. Agitators quoted it. It passed from hand to hand in fields, factories, and workshops; and angry mutters by the dissatisfied against the authorities and by the authorities against Most followed it. When posters plastered Elberfeld, Germany ("Dynamite, help us!"—"Long live the Revolution!"—"Up anarchy!"), the authorities saw Most behind this outrage. When Franz Glöcker killed his boss with a pickax in Gotha, Germany, the authorities said: Most caused this atrocity. When the Berlin Political Police assembled these and a thousand other pieces of evidence, they reported that Most informed what was wicked on the European left.[1]

"Mostianers" in Switzerland threatened European and especially German security. They ran the station on the underground railway that smuggled *Freiheit* into Germany. Organized into cells in Zurich, St. Gallen, Bern, and Geneva, they set up printing presses and broadcast propaganda the way Most directed in *Freiheit*. They planned murders. Michael Kumics met with them in St. Gallen and Zurich, then robbed a bank and bludgeoned to death a banker in Stuttgart. Fresh from Switzerland, Anton Kammerer and Hermann Stellmacher killed Austrian policemen. Kammerer surrendered after wounding four and gave up a revolver, a file sharpened into a dagger, and two kilos of dynamite. Stellmacher wounded one before handing over two pistols, ammunition, and a knife.[2] Terror thus crept out of the Alps and swept north with more menace than any foehn for a hundred years, and Most was behind it.

European governments, striving to interdict it at the source, succeeded in 1885. Swiss authorities, pressured by the Germans and others, and alarmed at a plot to blow up parliament, jailed smugglers of *Freiheit* and cracked down on leftists, especially foreign anarchists, many of whom fled to Britain and America.[3]

Meanwhile, Austria suffered terrorism of its own.[4] Arrests and cutting lines of terrorist communication proved futile. Police struck down terrorist-inspired demonstrations, with little effect on terrorism. A ban on leftist publications drove leftist publications underground.

Many, used to the hothouse environment of a free press, wilted. Already underground, *Freiheit* flourished because Andreas Scheu, directing distribution in Austria, could put it into more hands when censorship killed competition.

Freiheit warned: Vienna would see such violence as it had never seen before. *Freiheit*'s manifesto to Viennese labor: HAIL MURDER! *Freiheit* declared among its comrades the robbers and killers of the shoemaker Merstallinger and urged more of such constructive atrocities. Banks were held up, public buildings dynamited, and officials assassinated. *Freiheit* promised the knife for priests, the rope for policemen, the gun for capitalists, and the bomb for tyrants. Anarchists took up counterfeiting, the bogus money to buy arsenals for the battle against tyranny. Circulation of *Freiheit* increased, as conclaves of anarchists adopted it as their organ and its methods as their plan. Dynamiting continued. Police morale sank. Terrorism, caused by Most, "struck roots so deeply that only the future knows whether governmental measures can succeed against it."[5]

Freiheit assured Austrian comrades that Most had not forgotten and would not forsake them; their loyalty to the Cause deserved praise, and their terrorism merited imitation. For Stellmacher, hanged in Vienna, Most organized a memorial and gave a speech. For Kammerer, likewise executed, he published a black-bordered *Freiheit*.[6] In praise of Austrian comrades' daring, skill, and success with gun, knife, and bomb, he said, "Study the Austrians, imitate their élan and learn to be terrorists."

Austria, in self-defense, went foursquare against terrorism. Martial law in Vienna forbade associations and suppressed publications. Bigger police forces rounded up more suspects, harsher courts found more guilty, and angrier judges meted out stiffer punishments. Special tribunals dealt with "anarchist criminals." Police morale rose. Raids nabbed counterfeiters; uncovered drugs, disguises, disappearing ink, and phony identification papers; and destroyed bombs, guns, grenades, Greek fire, mitrailleuse, Congreve rockets, and dynamite.[7]

Such repression might itself have subdued Austrian terrorism. In addition, fearing dissipated energy, Most concentrated on Germany, more and more to the neglect of the rest of Europe. Germany was the haunt of his genius. At Germany he aimed *Freiheit*, to Germany he sent emissaries, and in Germany he expected to foment the Revolution. In Austria his influence waned, and terrorism declined.

About Germany he was optimistic. Radicals in Berlin went for *The Science of Revolutionary Warfare* like tourists for the latest Baedeker. His works enjoyed pride of place among those of Stirner, Mackay, and Kropotkin.[8] His propaganda contributed to low voter turnouts.[9]

But in Germany greater difficulties and more enemies than in Switzerland or Austria opposed him. After exiling him, the Anti-Socialist Law drove comrades after him, or underground, or to change their ways. Worse, Social Democrats, to clear themselves of guilt by association and to curry the government's favor, worked against him. While police raided, arrested, and suppressed, Social

Democrats dissuaded, informed, and denounced. When *Freiheit* lauded terrorism, *Sozialdemokrat* lambasted it.[10] Social Democrats bragged that they threw the first bombs against anarchism. Yes, said Most, stink bombs—as foul as the hypocrites who made them.

Social Democratic hostility and police repression reduced his followers to a confusion of disintegrating cells struggling for life. They distributed fewer *Freiheits* in fewer cities. How many cells, what number of *Freiheits*, in which cities? Nobody knew. A cell vigorous one day might disappear the next, as palpable one day and as null the next as the bundles of *Freiheit* it burned and scattered in ashes to the wind.

John Neve set out to save the movement.[11] He formed new cells, taught old new tactics, and improved and extended the underground railway that smuggled *Freiheit*. The Berlin Political Police feared him nearly as much as Most. After conferences in Switzerland and meetings in Germany, Neve was arrested in Vienna under the name Ernest Stevens, an Englishman from Bath. Unable to disprove his alias or fault his English, the Austrians turned Mr. Stevens over to the Germans, who gave him six months for carrying forbidden literature—six months that ruined what he had done to save the movement.

After release, failing to restore organization in Austria and disappointed in rebuilding the underground railway in Switzerland, he smuggled *Freiheit* through Belgium. Success provoked Berlin's chief of police to call him "one of the greatest fanatics." An aroused and angry police, after months of investigation and weeks of planning, arrested him in 1887. This time they would "hear no cock-and-bull" from Mr. Stevens.

While he had been trying to further propaganda-of-the-word, Germany's fiercest terrorist tried to wreak propaganda-by-the-deed. If Neve was the life and soul, August Reinsdorf was the right arm of the movement.[12] His solution to German tyranny was to kill Wilhelm, Bismarck, and other celebrities of Wilhelm's reign. Opportunity knocked when they gathered to dedicate a monument. But Reinsdorf sprained his ankle and turned the plot over to henchmen. They exploded sixteen pounds of dynamite under a hall, thinking Wilhelm and the others inside. The explosion wrecked a nearly empty hall, deafened a bartender, and spattered a caterer

with goulash but touched nobody and hurt nothing else—except
public opinion. The public affirmed renewal of the Anti-Socialist
Law and approved the Anti-Dynamite Law. Used against terrorists, both weakened the movement.

The Laws' strictest enforcer, Dr. Carl Rumpf, chief of Frankfurt
police, sent an *agent provacateur* into Most's organization. Most
wrote: "Revenge! Revenge!"[13]

He seemed to get revenge when an assassin, allegedly Julius
Lieske, stabbed Rumpf. The prosecution adduced from *Freiheit*,
"L. in B.—Success to you," and contended that the message was
to Lieske in Basel. Most said that typesetter Hugo Schlag, needing
to fill a column, composed the message with nobody and nothing
in mind. If not secretly behind the assassination, Most publicly
backed Lieske, writing, "Ten bloodsuckers will die for Lieske"
and, as principal speaker in the New York memorial for Lieske,
saying, "Lieske is another in the pantheon of martyrs, one more to
be avenged."[14]

But vengeance there was none, nor revolution either; for *Bruder-
krieg*, the struggle of comrade against comrade, began. The seat
was London, where a new wave of exiles, driven off the Continent
by new repression, plotted to expel tyranny from the Continent by
new terrorism. Joseph Peukert, former friend and onetime lieutenant of Most's, joined them—and brought trouble.[15]

He wanted to replace Most as head of the movement. He was a
philosopher, Most an agitator; he a thinker, Most an actor; he an
introvert, Most an extrovert. Clash was inevitable. Conversant in
Kropotkin's communist-anarchism, Peukert tried to disabuse comrades of Bakinin's collectivist-anarchism, advocated by Most.
Peukert published *Autonomie*, which he believed should replace
Freiheit. True to the maxim that estranged friends make deadly
enemies, they exchanged epithets like *dictator* and *ass*.

When comrades took sides, *Freiheit* spoke for Most's, *Autonomie*
for Peukert's. Comrades identified themselves by reading one and
scorning the other. A comrade seen with both might explain that
one was for reading, the other for wiping.

John Neve tried to mediate. Surely more than Peukert, probably
more than Most, and perhaps more than Necheyev himself, Neve
lived up to the credo that nothing matter to the anarchist but the

Cause and the Cause and the Cause. To It and for It he renounced time, money, and pleasure first, then comfort and freedom, and finally life itself. With him, as with Fred Hoff in *The 42nd Parallel*, "A man's first duty's to the workin' class." To Neve the Cause was Lent before the Easter of the Revolution. Yet if a fanatic, he was not fanatical; nobody recorded dislike for him. Who could dislike one who wanted harmony and was harmonious? He was respected too, for dedication and intelligence that flung into the face of tyranny a network of terrorist cells and that sustained *Freiheit* when bankruptcy threatened. Unobstructed by vanity and free of need for self-gratification, he saw farther and thought straighter than Most and Peukert; and he wanted unity. Most's best friend and enjoying cordiality with Peukert, he knew the reasons for division and the terms for reconciliation. Capable and congenial, a natural arbitrator and a born diplomat, sincere and knowledgeable, he was the one, the only one, to make peace.[16]

But he went to prison. Not only was the mediator liquidated, but also his demise became the strongest reason for the factions to hate one another. He meant much to many on either side, and all took positions they stuck to like leeches. His name always provoked something: rejoicing, laughter, cheers, or a toast before his imprisonment; regret, tears, rage, or a fist fight after. Victor Dave (leader of the London faction) and Peukert accused each other of betraying him; and Peukert hinted that Most might be guilty too. Peukert could not marshall proof to win anyone who doubted. So Peukert's faction took Peukert's word; but others doubted, and the reputations of Dave and Most suffered not at all.[17] Against Peukert, Dave and Most mustered so much evidence that Peukert worked the rest of his life, twenty years, to clear his name but failed.

Although Most exploited the case against Peukert, arguing it in speeches and *Freiheit*, he could neither preserve his influence nor save the movement in Europe. Dissidents remained dissident, and dissidence damaged the movement. When *Freiheit* fell behind *Autonomie*, he stopped *Freiheit*'s European edition and mailed a few of the American instead. He was out of Europe; and new signs—*Révolté* expelled from Switzerland, Kropotkin convicted in France, *Zukunft* suppressed in Austria—said "stay out."[18]

His circle narrowed. As he could not return to Europe, so he could not run from America. The Revolution had to be made in an industrialized country, and Europe would not have him. Once author of terrorism on two continents, he was bound to America now, in word and deed. When new anarchism rose in Germany in the 1890s, it knew little of Most and less of the old anarchism, it cared nothing for either, and it paid scant heed to Most's officious advice on how to run its affairs. In America, and America alone, he had to make the Revolution—or die trying.

NOTES

1. Reinhard Höhn, *Die vaterlandslosen Gesellen*, pp. 166, 189-90, 200, 201, 216, 236, 262. *See also* Leo Stern, *Der Kampf der deutschen Sozialdemokratie in der Zeit des Sozialistengesetzes*, pp. 237-38.

2. Höhn, *Gesellen*, pp. 210 and 257. *See also* E. V. Zenker, *Anarchism*, p. 291. Andrew R. Carlson, *Anarchism in Germany*, pp. 260-63.

3. Höhn, *Gesellen*, pp. 257-58, 310.

4. Karl Kautsky, *Erinnerungen und Erorterungen*, p. 362. *Arbeiterzeitung* (Vienna), 19 April 1926.

5. Höhn, *Gesellen*, p. 212; *see also* pp. 164, 186-87, 211.

6. 16 August 1884.

7. Höhn, *Gesellen*, pp. 234, 258, 284, 302-303, 331. Rudolf Rocker, *Johann Most*, p. 193. Ludwig Brügel, *Geschichte der österreichischen Sozialdemokratie* 4:13.

8. Albert Weidner, *Aus den Tiefen der Berliner Arbeiterbewegung*, pp. 11-12, 21.

9. Karl-Alexander Hellfaier, *Die deutsche Sozialdemokratie*, pp. 113-14. Ernst Drahn, *Johann Most*, p. 15.

10. Höhn, *Gesellen*, p. 225. Eduard Bernstein, *Sozialdemokratische Lehrjahre*, p. 122.

11. Höhn, *Gesellen*, pp. 225-26.

12. Most, *August Reinsdorf und die Propaganda der Tat*, p. 13 and *passim*.

13. *Freiheit*, 11 July 1885.

14. Ibid., 5 December 1885.

15. Carlson, *Anarchism*, pp. 328-37. Rocker, *Most*, 272-74. Höhn, *Gesellen*, p. 251.

16. *Freiheit*, 26 December 1896. Carlson, *Anarchism*, p. 343. Rocker, *Most*, pp. 88-89.

17. Weidner, *Tiefen*, pp. 50-52.

18. Max Nettlau, "John Most," p. 14.

PART III

In Decline: America, 1893-1906

11
PERSONAL AND PRIVATE

1889: Richard Braunschweig repudiates Most's leadership as heavy-handed and rigid. Sixty comrades join Braunschweig, form the Independent Revolutionists of New York, and vow: no support of Most, no reading of *Freiheit*.

1890: Joseph Peukert arrives in New York from London. He heads the New York section of Group Autonomie.

1890: Emma Goldman begins her career as an anarchist orator. She speaks in Rochester, Buffalo, and Cleveland.

1891: Alexander Berkman finds a life but no livelihood in anarchism, so he packs shirts and rolls cigars, then learns printing and sets type for *Freiheit*.

1892: Berkman and Goldman run an ice-cream parlor in Worcester, Massachusetts. The ice cream is ordinary, but she makes good sandwiches, brews delicious coffee, and bakes tasty pastry; and the anarchists succeed at capitalism.

1893: Most and comrades, forbidden to meet in Chicago's Art Palace, meet in the *Times* building, owned by the mayor. Later the authorities learn that the anarchists planned, under the mayor's nose, to cut fire-alarm, telegraph, and telephone lines and to set fire to the city.

1893: Goldman begins a year on Blackwell's Island for inciting to riot in a speech at Union Square.

1893: Morris Hillquit, socialist leader, 24, becomes an attorney.

There is joy once more in William-street, and hilarity and beer reigned in the office of the *Freiheit* yesterday afternoon. The great mogul of Anarchy was at home again, and held a reception of his delighted followers. . . . A plump, black-haired young woman . . . rushed into the arms of the apostle and kissed and hugged him effusively. Then Associate Editor Schultz and the compositors took their turns at kissing and hugging.

The New York Times, December 10, 1887

Devastation and idleness are the doctrines that he endeavors to teach, and this wins for him the adherence of tramps and others willing to live by the sweat of another's brow.

The Denver Times, of Most, June 4, 1884

Prosperity is ephemeral. . . . If times and circumstances change, a man will be ruined if he does not change. But we do not find any man shrewd enough to know how to adapt; either because he cannot do otherwise than follow character, or because, having always prospered one way, he cannot persuade himself to change.

Machiavelli, The Prince

Emma Goldman, "a mere slip of a girl, without experience,"[1] met Most and Berkman about the same time and became lover to them both. When she told Berkman of an evening with Most, Berkman's face darkened. Not that he was angry at sharing her; anarchists believed in free love. He was angry because Most violated revolutionary ethics by spending on himself money given to the Cause. Most and Goldman went out together often, and Berkman grew angrier.

Opening a world to Goldman, Most introduced her to books, theatre, music. He became her idol, she said. "I worshipped him."[2]

Yet she was uneasy, as if sensing herself the center of a gathering storm. Charmed by Most, she appreciated his talents, liked his thirst for life, delighted in his eagerness for friendship, and was drawn to him, deeply moved. She called him Hannes, he was her friend and lover, yet he awed her. But Berkman, her Sasha, attracted her too. Most or Berkman? She did not have to choose—yet.

Most told her she had talent for the platform; he would make her a public speaker, to take his place when he was gone. She objected that what he did she could never do, his place she could never take. But he inculcated her with his doctrine, coached her in oratory, and sent her against the 8-hour day. He said:

Be brave.

Don't take too seriously the usual audience—they're dullards. Make them laugh.

Be bold.

Don't worry about the structure of the speech; speak the way you tell stories.

Be arrogant.

Expect to be afraid at first.

At first how her heart pounded, stomach turned, knees shook! Yet she became the pioneer woman orator in the American movement and the greatest anarchist orator, greater than Most himself. Though her career took her years, miles, and worlds away from him, she remembered him as her teacher.

But on her initial tour an older man asked whether it was wrong to want the only reform likely in his lifetime. Opposition to the 8-hour day was wrong, she decided.

Back in New York City she met Most. His beard was trimmed, he wore a new suit with a red carnation, and he was happy. But when she broached the 8-hour day, he roared, "Who is not with me is against me!" They quarreled.

She met Berkman. Seeing flowers Most gave her, Berkman exploded, "Violets at the height of winter, with thousands out of work and hungry!" Most was a spendthrift, a traitor. Besides, he cared for women only carnally. She was a terrible revolutionist if she took his gifts. Choose between him and me, Berkman demanded.

She chose Most.

He told her he loved her and hoped she loved him in spite of his face. He was sorry they had quarreled. Fearing he would lose her when she declared independence on the 8-hour issue, for she re-awakened his yearning for a great love, he had quarreled with her, the one he loved and wanted. Now, equanimity restored, he asked for friendship.

She took his hand; his was the confession of a man tormented. They kissed. Her tears covered his face.

"It was beautiful now," she said.

But they still disagreed about the 8-hour day. Critical in her independence, she began to doubt his sincerity. He cooled. When she refused him favors, he said he did not have to beg; he could get Helen anytime. "Helen" was Helen Minkin, who confided in Emma love for him. Emma asked of his feelings for Helen.

He answered, "The girl simply needs a man."

Berkman was right, Emma decided. Most was interested in women as females only. She no longer cared for him, despite his intellect, his personality, and the sympathy he aroused for his suffering. He had too many resentful traits.

Then he called Berkman an arrogant Russian Jew. Choose, he said, between me and the arrogant Russian Jew.

She cried out. She, too, was a Russian Jew. Was Most, the anarchist, anti-Semitic? And how dare he want her for himself? Was that anarchism? Or was Berkman right that Most had ceased to be an anarchist?

These words knocked Most down. He lay at her feet, hands clenched, moaning like a wounded animal and sobbing like a child.

She lifted him, in hands that would be trained to nurse, with compassion deeper than training could impart.

He looked into her face and whispered, "Sasha is a lucky dog to have such love."

He left town. She did not see him off.

Soon, liking *Autonomie*'s position on freedom, she and Berkman joined Group Autonomie, Peukert's group, Most's enemies.

The enemies produced *The Anarchists: A Tragicomedy*, portraying Most as Captain Jack, who cowers in a sewer until dragged to jail, blubbering.[3]

The play was a sign of feuding that wrecked the solidarity Most held dear. Conflict over his personality and policies and his quarrel

with Peukert split American comrades as it split European. Furthermore, after years of advocating violence and encouraging propaganda-by-the-deed, Most shocked comrades by calling Berkman's
attempt on Frick *inane*. Many never spoke to Most again. Justus
Schwab, his best friend, snubbed him. Circulation of *Freiheit*
dropped. Most grieved.

Goldman kept faith in him; she had been his lover and still felt
his charm. She went to him, to console him and to convince him
that, for the Cause, he must stop fighting with Peukert.

He greeted her, "What do you want with me, now that you are
with that dreadful group?"

A surly Most—how different from the affable one!

She asked if they could talk, for old friendship's sake.

"Old friendship's sake!" he said. "You have seen fit to go with
my enemies and you have preferred a mere youngster to me! Whoever is not with me is against me!"

He continued angrily, but he was no longer angry. His was again
the voice that moved her, that she loved, that she understood in its
ringing the changes from severity to tenderness, and that scaled
heights and plumbed depths of emotion. She took his hand.

"Please, Hannes, come, won't you?"

He embraced her. "I love you, I will come."

As usual, wine transformed him. On their first evening he had
emptied the bottle and ordered another before she could sample
half a glass. It smoothed care from his face and erased acrimony
from his manner. Animated, attentive, witty, sympathetic, gracious,
charming, he became as sparkling as the wine itself. Now they
drank again, she consoled him, and they enjoyed amity and decorum. They did not mention Peukert.

Next day she read and reread a letter from Most. He wanted a
woman who would care for nothing but the man she loved and the
children she bore him. Helen would give him what he wanted.
Emma, though he loved her, left him at war with himself, unhappy.
Besides, *Freiheit*'s straits, the feud, his imminent return to prison—
they were enough to destroy composure and render him inept.
Would she understand? Would she, please, help him find peace?

She drifted into reverie. . . . So he wanted children! She had been
against children for herself, but the thought of a child by such an

original stirred her. She would have to have the operation, but. . . .
But she was committed to the Cause! She loved Berkman! But. . . .
She agonized the night through, so strong was Most's grip.

Most answered none of her letters to him in prison, and he did
not see her after release. He and Helen lived together, Helen was
expecting, and they planned to marry. A gulf opened between Goldman and him. She devoted herself to the Cause and to Berkman.

After Berkman tried to kill Frick, she went to a speech by Most,
to hear what Most would say about Berkman. He said nothing about
Berkman until the end: "It is probably the usual newspaper fake."

She castigated him for giving a speech drunk. Or was he afraid
of the detectives at the door?

He left without answering.

Then he came out against Berkman, laughing at the boy who
fired a toy pistol. This derision was the talk of the Left, a topic as
hot as Berkman's attempt itself. The world's leading terrorist was
deriding an act of terrorism! Goldman thought Most was venting
dislike of Berkman. Bitterness welled up in her. She vowed to
strike back.

Continuing to deride Berkman, Most derided her as well. Then
his "Reflections on Assassination" played false to everything she
had heard him teach. Most, revered for advocacy of terror; Most,
imprisoned for glorifying tyrannicide; Most, the voice of terror incarnate; Most was repudiating assassination! Hatred of Berkman,
desire to avoid charges of complicity, change of heart—whatever
his motive, she thought, he was betraying friends and ideals.

"Coward," she said. "Traitor."

"Liar," he retorted.

At his next lecture she was in the front row, a horsewhip under
her coat. He rose to speak, and she rose "to demand proof of your
insinuations against Alexander Berkman." When he muttered about
"hysterical woman," she pulled out the whip, leaped onto the platform, and lashed him across the face, then broke the whip over her
knee and threw the pieces at him. Friends saved her from the anger
of the crowd.[4]

Those friends, and others, strengthened the anti-Most faction and
deepened the split in the movement, which hurt Most more than
the whipping.

To the end of his life, though she mellowed and tried to salvage something of their friendship, he stayed angry. At the reception on his release from Blackwell's Island, she saw him—face ruddy, hair white, eyes shining—and they nearly collided. He snubbed her. At the memorial for Louise Michel they stood side by side, and the audience applauded the reunion. He did not greet her but turned away without a word.[5] When she spoke at Clarendon Hall, he (drunk) kept saying in a husky voice: "Rats! Rats!" Dragged to the door, he protested that people had made a fool of him, "and now they let that woman talk."[6]

Citing such incidents, enemies called him a lush. Friends admitted he drank too much. "Lemonade and coffee!" he fulminated in jail in Long Island City. "Lemonade and coffee they give you here! I want something to *drink*!"[7]

He had that complaint and others, but he was not a complainer. In prison he asked, not for pity, but for eyeglasses, a muffler, books, food, and tobacco. He wrote to his wife and sons in a tone of affection, sent kisses, and glossed over hardships. Looking ahead, he planned to take Kropotkin and Nieuwenhuis as models for how to live and work. He vowed to organize time and marshall energy to advance the Cause. He wanted to expand *Freiheit*. He intended to write memoirs and produce the studies of anarchism teeming in his mind.[8]

Relaxing from this work, he enjoyed picnics where beer flowed. At a picnic on Staten Island, eighteen kegs flowed by 6:00 P.M. More slaked thirsts between then and dusk. He was late, arriving at 2:00, after writing furiously since 4:00 A.M. He filled a mug and drank. He laughed when a pig was labeled "Capital" and driven off with jabs and kicks. He refilled. He ate bratwurst, sauerkraut, pumpernickel, and cheese. He went from keg to keg, and the group around each patted him on the back. The choir sang and he applauded "Our Flag is Red" and "Anarchy is King." Firecrackers exploded, and he made a face at the stench of burned powder. Prevailed on to speak, he said, "It stinks—the powder and the government stink to high heaven." He called elections monkey business. Instead the president should be the winner of a prize fight between candidates. A horse race should decide state offices; a ballgame, county; and pinochle, the rest.[9]

At another picnic, according to newspapers that did not like him,[10] he stayed in the saloon on the edge of the park. He wore a black Prince Albert, greasy and glossy and whitened with cigar ash; a buff vest buttoned to his throat; and a white straw hat pushed back on his bald head. His puffy face, where it could be seen through his grizzled beard, was a deep dull red. His eyes were small and they glittered. He did not speechify, only gossiped like a crone, and recalled good old days when thousands met him with *Hail!* on their lips and fire in their bellies and thunder in their throats and lightning in their eyes. Around him now, German gutterals and wreaths of tobacco smoke. A drunk pounded a doubtful waltz from a sick piano, a hurdy-gurdy artist ground out "My Pearl's a Bowery Girl," and a few couples tried shakily to dance. Fuming, a black-eyed woman with poppies in her hat stood in the center of the room, her back to the bar, and watched a stout woman in red caress Most. From the bar came: "Dot beer she is er getrinken will put her in proper shape fer ter hop der hull outfit." Cords in black-eyes' neck quivered like strings of a harp when she screamed for beer. She kept Most in view until the bartender wheeled her away in a wheelbarrow. Most ignored her, shook himself free of the one in red, and alternated beer with milk punches. Eighty kegs had been provided for an anticipated 1,500 radicals, but the actual 120 drank only twenty. Hence the talk, obtruding above the clack of billiard balls and cutting through the wail of the nickelodeon, was not of bombs or the Rights of Man or the Revolution, but of beer: how to drink and how to pay for it. Dusk fell on Most sitting in a corner, in the glare of the wrath of the saloonkeeper standing over him, fingering papers, turning over invoices, and miscounting coins, trying to settle the bill. Before nine o'clock he stumbled out, crawled into a cab, and went home to the tune of "Put Me Off at Buffalo."

If he fell asleep forgetting he was to stand trial, he awoke remembering the court's order to retain counsel. He went to the rising young Morris Hillquit, a leader of the Social Democratic party, a conservative socialist hostile to anarchism. Most was asking an enemy to represent him because he wanted to defend himself and because he and his comrades had no money for fees. Expecting Hillquit to refuse, he planned to tell the court he could not retain counsel; counsel would not have him.

Hillquit said he would take the case.

Most tried to be difficult. No money for a fee, he said.

"I am not interested in the fee." Hillquit would take the case because freedoms of speech and press were at issue.

Most was stubborn, but Hillquit prevailed. Most acceded with little grace, but Hillquit saw a twinkle in Most's eye when Most said, "Well, then, go ahead and try to defend me."[11]

Hillquit tried, in three courts, but failed. Most liked him nonetheless. If not friends, they were friendly the rest of Most's life.

Hillquit remembered that Most looked older than his fifty-five years. A ruinous life, worsened by imprisonment, had damaged that robust constitution. A year later he returned from the Island broken —indifferent, cynical, and sluggish. He lived four more years, going through the motions of the anarchist-publicist. Though he never lost his reputation as the arch-terrorist, he was not the spirited and impetuous Johann Most anymore.

NOTES

1. Emma Goldman to Max Nettlau, 24 January 1932, in Richard and Anna Maria Drinnon, eds., *Nowhere at Home*, p. 100.

2. Goldman, *Living My Life*, p. 40. The Most-Goldman relationship in the following pages is taken from the same work, pp. 35-106 *passim*.

3. A. Sartorius, *Der moderne Socialismus in den Vereinigten Staaten von Amerika*, p. 197.

4. Goldman, *Living My Life*, pp. 105-106.

5. Ibid., pp. 379-81. *See also* pp. 234 and 313.

6. *New York Tribune*, 13 October 1896.

7. *Freiheit*, 28 September 1901. *See also* 1 August 1896.

8. Ibid., 13 September 1902, 28 February 1903.

9. Ibid., 11 July 1896. *New York Times*, 5 July 1896, p. 8.

10. *New York Times*, 7 September 1897, p. 2. *Volkszeitung* (New York), 8 September 1897.

11. Morris Hillquit, *Loose Leaves from a Busy Life*, pp. 125-28.

12
POSITIONS AND PERSUASIONS

1872: The International expels Bakunin and his anarchists as too militant.

1876: A congress of anarchists propounds propaganda-by-the-deed as a weapon of minorities against authority; in Bern, Switzerland.

1879: Kropotkin begins *Lé Revolté*. In it appears his "Spirit of Revolt."

1881: Kropotkin and Malatesta attend the international anarchist congress that propounds propaganda-by-the-deed as a weapon of individuals against authority, in London.

1890: Sixty-five percent of Chicago's population is foreign-born.

1891: Kropotkin publishes *Anarchist Communism.*

1891: Oscar Wilde, charmed by Kropotkin, publishes *The Soul of Man under Socialism.* Wilde's artist will find freedom where, "of course, authority and compulsion are out of the question."

1897: Kropotkin lectures in the USA and meets Most in Buffalo.

1901: Kropotkin lectures in the USA and visits Most in New York City.

1905: Delegates from forty-three labor organizations form the Industrial Workers of the World, in Chicago. The IWW's methods are propaganda, the strike, the boycott, and direct action.

I explain so often and so simply, yet much is not understood. I don't stop. I explain and explain and explain, from
all possible angles, each time trying to make another aspect
clear.   Most, *Freiheit*, September 21, 1901

Liberty can be got only by taking it in defiance of authority;
that is, by rebellion.
"The Principles of Anarchist-Communism,"
Freiheit, August 23, 1890

Send the priests to heaven and the politicians to hell; we'll
rule ourselves.
'Most, speech to the Manhattan Liberal Club, May 17, 1890

IN DEFENSE OF FREEDOM

Asked, "What is communist-anarchism, in a word?" Most would
answer, "Freedom." Freedom above all; not bread itself over freedom. Freedom is the meaning of life, the reason for effort, the goal
of struggle, and the standard of progress. Freedom is therefore the
purpose of revolution. Freedom will foster the good society. What
is natural, beneficial, and enjoyable will flow from freedom.

"What do you mean by freedom, in a few words?"

"We deny God and fight the God-pestilence, religion. They are
a swindle, a mummery. They befuddle. Befuddled, humanity can
be oppressed.

"We obey neither ruler nor policeman; we thumb our noses at
law; and we seek liberty for the person, secured by liberty of the
people, which is anarchy.

"We consider private property, reform politics, and traditional
morality foes of liberty; therefore we sound the tocsin of atheism,
trumpet the truth of communism, and beat the drum of revolution."[1]

He found defending freedom hard.[2] "Difficulties surround and
obstacles block us." There were blind faith in law, pernicious faith
in authority, narcotic faith in religion, imbecile faith in capitalism,
inane faith in coercion, and bewildering faith in democracy. *Democracy*—humbug of charlatans praising themselves, scandal of

panjandrums disporting themselves, hoax of opiated masses kow-
towing to fraud! Then there were claims for peaceful evolution of
society, for centralization, and for state socialism. And infecting
the masses like an epidemic, there was the lie that called anarchism
opposite to law, antagonist of order, and destroyer of peace: the
enemy of society.

Freedom needed defending especially against democracy, which
sells itself wholesale as freedom's locus. Tyranny does not threaten
freedom; people know what tyranny means and seek to overthrow
it. But people accept democracy; they cannot see the teeth of oppression or feel the claws of exploitation, which glib and crafty
politicians hide. People swallow the sop of the state's provisions
for welfare and thereby stomach the state's poisoned equality and
adulterated rights. Hoodwinked and drugged, people believe democracy purifies equality and sanctifies rights. Yes, it purifies equality, by suppressing all but an elite alike. Yes, it sanctifies one right,
the right to choose masters. People do not realize they are no more
able to change or remove a democracy than to change or remove
a dictatorship. People do not appreciate a democratic state's power;
stronger than despotism, it routinely collects taxes no Czar or Khan
could dream of collecting. In short, democracy does not sin by
imposing obedience; democracy desecrates by creating willingness
to obey.

Therefore, to achieve freedom, eradicate the idea as well as
abolish the fact of majority rule; and establish free association
and free dissociation with or from anybody and anything. In the
resulting unfettered living and open discussion, truth will be embraced and falsehood rejected. Tyranny of the majority will disappear. Minorities, each its own way, will learn right from wrong
through experience. Nor will liberation of individuals and tolera-
tion of minorities be only expedient; they will also be just. For they
will straighten obliquity that calls enlightened dissent treason and
that lauds oppression of minorities as patriotism.

Let history speak. In the Middle Ages, reject the Bible or make
up your own mind, and the rack and screws followed, by law. A few
hundred years ago, when superstition yet held sway, deny balder-
dash any sane person would deny now, and be burned alive or
hanged, by law. Galileo spoke truth and was called criminal. A

surfeit of superstition has subsided, but on the leftovers the moral
gorge rises in disgust, leftovers wrapped in law.

The anarchist therefore opposes law, knowing that lawlessness,
or freedom, will improve everyone and thus benefit society. For
freedom begets responsibility. With freedom, no dictates of an over-
bearing but remote few to an unwilling and therefore negligent
many. Responsible for self and related matters, everyone will attend
to them with care. Free and responsible individuals, free and responsible minorities: happy and prosperous society.

Still, suppression of individuals and tyranny over minorities are
not democracy's worst faults. Its worst is duping people into thinking they rule themselves because every two, four, or six years (or
whatever number is magic) they choose from among scoundrels
one to be their dictator. Some self-rule! Unfortunately, people are
less miserable and more compliant under a government that puts a
shoe on their necks rather than a boot in their faces. Less miserable
and more compliant but hardly happy! People must be taught freedom and trained to revolt.

But socialist and workers' parties block awareness and impede
revolution. These parties cannot find words enough to praise democracy. Words like "Send the right man to Congress" and "Joy
to the people: destroy capitalism by all legal means" are nonsense
of reform, babbled when the word should be *revolution*. These
parties would replace foul practice and rotten procedure with practice and procedure so similar they run to identical corruption.
Needed: drastic change to communism and anarchism.

Let us be clear about communism's meaning, Most said; clarity
is essential here. Communism, contrary to misguided communists,
refers neither to Utopia nor Leviathan. Communism means the
commonwealth of property that permits freedom in abundance and
produces liberty by crop after bumper crop. Therefore communism
is at once the precondition and consequence of anarchy. "Communism is conceivable only in anarchy, and anarchy is possible
only through communism."[3] To avoid misunderstanding I call myself a communist-anarchist, Most said.[4]

Belief in communism distinguished his from individualist or philosophical anarchism that (he said) would favor certain individuals
and destroy freedom. Individualist anarchism will demand com-

petition, which will turn life into a racecourse, where friend runs against neighbor, brother against brother, and man against wife. This mandatory competition will engender overriding of the weak by the strong and incite overreaching of the good-natured by the brutal. Conversely, communist-anarchism's cooperation will provide for everyone's needs and demand competition of no one. Voluntary competition will occur in science, art, crafts, and all other endeavors beyond needs, to the happiness of people and the benefit of society. Voluntary competition will promote discovery, practice, and development of every talent, to the benefit of the individual and the glory of freedom.[5]

While he differed with individualist anarchists, he clashed with state socialists. Although on the wrong track, individualist anarchists (he said) have the right faith and proper goals. But state socialists, demanding obedience above all, want to concentrate production, centralize power, and create a bureaucracy policed down to the individual and enforced in every detail. Each pigeon will have its hole and had better be in it, or suffer terrible consequences.[6]

Communist-anarchism, by contrast, is the manner and means of looking after one's own without direction, oppression, and exploitation: the best way of life ever conceived, the reason to foment revolution.

FOMENTING THE REVOLUTION

"Society is illogical, unjust, intractable, and insufferable—in general, in particular, inevitably," Most said. The problem was fundamental. Righting wrongs, exposing injustices, and reforming malpractices, even passing and with murderous authority enforcing laws would no more cure society than shaving will eradicate whiskers. With society evil at the root, only violent total *social* revolution would solve the problem. Therefore how to prepare revolution, what it would be like, and the nature and delivery of the coup de grace were concerns of the communist-anarchist.[7]

Agitation, necessary to prepare revolution, was hard in America because the audience was heterogeneous. The agitator had first to distinguish between foreign-born and native-born.[8]

The foreign-born were significant enough to form a movement. New York had as many German proletarians as Hamburg, more Jews than Jerusalem, and as many Czechs as any Czech city of second rank, not to mention thousands of Poles, Scandinavians, French, Hungarians, Spanish, Italians, and Russians. In other cities the ratio of foreign-born to native-born was high. The foreign-born were receptive to agitation, could be stronger than any European labor party, and might pull the native-born to revolution, if organized and agitated. Agitation among the foreign-born must proceed as fast and as intensively as possible. "To work, comrades! To work, to work!"

The native-born were full of patriotism, full of superstitions about foreigners, full of pride in a mendacious system of pseudo-freedom, full of the swill of the world's vilest press—in short, stuffed with hokum. Revolutionary doctrine? To the native-born, a raving in tongues by foreigners who competed with Americans for daily bread. Consequently, agitation among the native-born had to start with agitators' learning English and using it to change the native-borns' attitude. "Learn, comrades, learn! Knowledge is power!"

Agitation was so important that each comrade must agitate and every comrade follow instructions.[9]

• Associate widely and mingle creatively. Join groups, especially ones in which the social question might be discussed. Gain respect for yourself. Make friends. Learn what they want in life. Broach atheism, communism, and anarchism as answers to the social question and as ways to get what they want.

• Distribute literature. Make bookselling a cooperative undertaking and give it the attention it deserves. Organize colportage along military lines and enlist in the army of colporteurs. Buy as much literature as your means allow, do not rest until you have distributed it, and distribute it carefully and systematically in places and to hands where it will have greatest effect. Imitate the colporteurs, servants of the Cause, who load themselves with bundles of truth and go in and out of doors regardless of weather, and up and down stairs however steep, day in and day out! Flood meetings—picnics, parties, and all congregations of proletarians—with literature, especially with agitation-numbers of *Freiheit*; forget the "table in the corner"; spread the word from hand to hand. Remember workers on strike as susceptible to literature; but since they lack money, give them back issues of *Freiheit* and anything else you can afford.

• Advertise meetings everywhere and by every medium—flyers, handbills, newspapers, posters, and word of mouth. Play up the liberality, stress the quality, and play down the cost of the refreshments. Appeal to everyone; make the meeting seem educational to the serious and entertaining to the frivolous.

• Practice follow-ups. When giving literature or speaking to a prospect, look him in the eye and remember him. To everyone at a meeting hand a card appealing for membership on one side and asking for name and address on the other. Return to people thus contacted; be friendly, ask how they liked the meeting, or the literature, or what you said. Draw them out, invite them to join, and offer subscriptions at bargain rates (and pay the difference out of your own pocket). Pursue the interested with vigor. Bring them to meetings.

• Give speeches as if the life of the movement depended on them, because the life of the movement does depend on them. Read *Freiheit* and learn what to say and say it with force. Study and imitate great orators. Remember: literature transmits ideas; oratory starts and propels revolutions.

• Stop agitating as if still in Europe. End the scandal of feuds brought from there to rage in agitation aimed at Americans. Why should atheists trying to convert Catholics and Protestants war like Catholics and Protestants trying to convert Hottentots?[10] Kick the habit of quarreling. And don't follow a German or an Austrian plan of agitation; you wouldn't bring a snow shovel to Bali or a sarong to the Arctic, would you? Let your models be comrades in Russia. Their example glows like an ember in the anthracite of anarchist achievement.[11]

• Finally, teach what the Revolution will be like and how it will be fomented.

It will be different from past revolutions. The likes of 1789 will not be seen again. Such uprisings now would be struck down with the ease of a man swatting flies. Witness the Commune, the last revolution in the grand style: heroically waged and brutally suppressed.[12]

Past revolutions wanted to take over public buildings (symbols of power) and install new officials in them. Fighting therefore raged around them, in centers of cities. Tactics included throwing up barricades at key junctures, to interdict troops moving to and from fighting. Narrow short twisted streets encouraged rebels to stack cobblestones into a foundation and on top pile furniture, or tip over a carriage to block the street, or erect cobblestones and furniture behind an overturned carriage. Rebels sortied from behind these barricades and overpowered, often with bare hands, enemy cavalry and artillery, useless in these narrow confines. When infantry might have defeated rebels, people in nearby houses passed to rebels food, drink, munitions, medical aid, and encouragement; and on infantry poured boiling water, ink, shoes, flower pots, stones, slops, vases, table legs, cabbages, and oftener than many an infantryman would live to remember, bullets. Rebels, thus ensconced and so reinforced, won battles.[13]

But that era was over. It disappeared with old cities. With them vanished short crooked narrow streets. Artillery fired down long straight avenues, and cavalry wheeled about spacious boulevards, commanding life-lines and protecting centers of cities now. Bourgeoisie hostile to rebels lived nearby. Rebels, therefore unable to erect barricades and lacking allies, could not stand against grapeshot and saber. Thus, during the revolt in Milan in 1898, bourgeoisie gathered on balconies, watched battles through lorgnettes, and shouted to troops slaughtering rebels, "Bravo, soldiers! Aim straight and shoot fast; we want to go to tea this afternoon!"[14]

Modern revolution, then, must be social revolution, and its way the general strike.[15] A collective disobedience and a unified uprising violent in later stages, the general strike would suspend production, interrupt communication, block services, and thereby disorganize in order to destroy. The general strike was therefore modern, appropriate to industrial society.

Wouldn't the general strike be impossible until the majority struck, and then superfluous because the majority could prevail peacefully and legally? In truth, nothing would happen until a minority leavened the "great inert mass" like yeast turning dough into the staff of life. A minority began every revolution; let one begin the Revolution.

The general strike was thus the theory of coup d'etat adapted to modern circumstances. A small but resolute body of revolutionaries would rise, show the proletariat how to revolt, and then lead the Revolution. When severity and violence were necessary, revolutionaries would disrupt, seize, and assassinate. Propaganda-by-the-deed would scatter the enemy, propaganda-of-the-word unite allies. Kropotkin argued compellingly the likelihood of success, given favorable conditions and passionate rebels. Nor was he the first to put faith in a few to overpower the many. The Gunpowder Plotters, working in a Continental tradition and inspired by the gunpowder-explosion murder of King James's father, plotted to blow up Parliament and take control of the government. A tunnel dug in five laborious months by men unaccustomed and indisposed to labor, barrels of powder, and Guy Fawkes (taken with fuses and tinder in his hands) proved faith in a few to overpower the many.

Revolutionaries will do better now. Given interlocking industries, a strike in one will spread to all. Were coal stopped at the mine or in transit, for example, industries dependent on coal will stop; then industries dependent on the stopped will stop; and at each stop, strikers will board the Snowball Express to victory.

The general strike might be peaceful at first, with individuals and groups refusing to work. Employers will lock factories. Strikers will refuse to pay rent. Police will get tough. Strikers and non-strikers alike, manhandled and hungry, will become militant. If some men still hesitate, women, out to quiet children's screams of hunger, will force doors of butcher shops and smash windows of bakeries. Violence, laying a train of powder, will ignite violence. The strike's leaders will loot, burn, dynamite, and assassinate. Beginning in anticipation of social revolution, the general strike thus becomes social revolution itself.

Yesterday's motto was, "In union there is strength." Today and tomorrow, in the era of local autonomy and individual liberty, the motto will be, "In dispersion there is strength." Dispersion is characteristic of the general strike. Having no choice, the enemy will fight the battle of dispersion and lose.[16]

The reason: their forces cannot concentrate in hundreds of thousands, to brutalize a few workers; those days, like the days of the barricade, are over. Watch will have to be kept' on buildings, trains guarded and run, telephone and telegraph lines patrolled, industries protected, services maintained, scabs defended, and arsenals and warehouses secured, around the country—scattering into impotence the enemy's forces, however large, armed, and disciplined. The enemy will mobilize the reserves, but reservists will be rebels who will colonize the regulars; and the filthy slogan "God and Country" will deliquesce in the air of rebels' "Liberty, Equality, Fraternity." Desertion will be wholesale among enemy forces, mutiny rife.

Meanwhile the enemy will try to reassert themselves by directing scabs, police, and troops to intimidate, bully, and browbeat. The enemy will appeal to order, execrable order, euphemism for tyranny. Strikers will laugh in their faces, spit in their eyes, and meet force with force; but not in the old foolish head-on collision of proletarian flesh with bourgeois steel. Rather, a handful of sand thrown into generators will plunge cities into darkness. Under its cover, strikers will blow up centers and burn symbols of authority: post offices, courts, police stations, offices, and banks. Strikers will seize arsenals and warehouses and take weapons, munitions, clothing, bread, and meat. Again, a snip of shears through telephone and telegraph lines or a blow of a hammer into railway switches will leave the enemy without supplies or intelligence, helpless.

Wails of whistles of trains rushing to carnage in the night will signal the end.

The sun will rise on the wreck of capitalism.

The way will be clear for the erection of the good society.

THE GOOD SOCIETY

To Most a plan was authoritarian; change, the first fact of life; the future, uncertain; and contingency, the watchword. Who but a visionary dare prescribe, who but a tyrant dictate? In unashamedly general terms, therefore, he discussed the good society, under four heads. "Comrades of tomorrow, citizens of the good society: choose, modify, reject—as you see fit!"[17]

Political. Government will have neither place nor purpose. People in the good society will realize that their forebears revered government the way they revered God, and reverence for one is as asinine as reverence for the other; because, no source from which blessings flow, government is organized legalized coercion, an instrument of exploitation. Naturally, where government does not exist, law does not exist. The good, the anarchist society will be of neither law nor government but of liberated individuals and free associations. Politics will be passé.

Free associations, like the communes of Most's social-revolutionary doctrine, will solve economic, scientific, educational, and social problems; secure harmony; answer questions and manage affairs that individuals cannot answer and manage; and encourage individual and collective happiness; and in this way the good society will be mutualist. Labor unions will become associations that run factories, and in this way the good society will be syndicalist. Associations will name officers, firsts among equals, who will not dominate but serve. Associations may join (reserving through free contracts the right and option to secede from) federations created to do what single associations cannot do. In turn, federations may interconnect until society runs in harmony like a clock but without central control.

Economic. Private property in land and capital will be abolished; everyone will share land and capital equally. Commodities will belong to the association that produces them, until distributed to individuals who need them. The means of production will belong to society but be entrusted to associations that use them. This and all trusts will need no policing, because no individual will benefit by violating a trust.

The good society will boast free enjoyment of all commodities by everyone. Supply will be no restriction; the bountiful earth, in the hands of the good society, will produce more than enough of everything for everyone. Accordingly, as money (like real property) will not exist, so nobody will be able to accumulate wealth. Were an incipient capitalist to hoard a vault of bread or a lake of beer, it will amount to nothing but mold and swill, because everyone can always take freely of these and any necessities. The good society having learned that to eliminate property is to destroy evil, everyone will have no reason to act other than fairly and honorably.

Common ownership, common production, common enjoyment of what is produced will all exist in a decentralized commonwealth; the good society will be communist in the fundamental sense.

Social. Education, conducted by free associations, will begin as soon as child can leave mother, in institutes where the latest in educational science will develop the body and enlighten the mind. As educational science will not be the superstition that passes for pedagogy now, so the institutes will not be the barracks that pass for schools. They will afford the best in architecture and the finest in sanitation, to facilitate the supreme in teaching and the maximum of learning. Neither religion nor patriotism will dirty the curriculum. Today's failures—ignorant children, alienated adults, cruel society—mandate more classrooms, more teachers, more years of schooling, and fewer daily hours of instruction. Education, available until death, will be encouraged regardless of age. Enlightenment in youth, together with free time resulting from a communist economy, will provoke interest, create capacity, and promote leisure to study throughout life.

Instead of man's injustice to woman, rife now, women will enjoy rights and privileges men enjoy, in every respect. With children sent in infancy to institutes, women's ties to home and family will loosen. Women will be free to enter any sphere, activity, or undertaking, according to strength, talent, and inclination. No line of work will be closed. If because of actual and potential childbearing, women are oftener unfit for work, women thereby earn dispensation from work; discrimination inflicted by the accident of sex is injustice enough, without the design of society inflicting more. The ancient atrocity of women in bondage will cease. Humanity will replace barbarism.

Marriage, as an institution of tyranny, will end. Women will no longer be subject to husbands, legally, morally, or physically. People will be allowed but never compelled to marry in the society that recognizes no compulsion. Mutual inclination will create and sustain intersexual relations among free people, a behavior ethical and natural. In other words, free love will supplant marriage.

Religion will disappear. The clergy, true to their authoritarian bent, will have sided with reaction and been destroyed; and heavenly as well as earthly authority will have suffered anti-authoritarian an-

nihilation. Church property, like all real estate, will become property of society. Churches and synagogues will become museums of
their own antique mummery and serve as galleries, theatres, meeting halls, and ballrooms. They will make superb granaries; a church
can be filled to the ceiling through the steeple, as if created by God
to hold man's grain. People enlightened by rational education will
never want to restore religion but will wonder how their forebears
could have been religious so long.

Crime will not exist. No laws to break, ergo, no criminals, which
will not be a paradox. Because everybody's needs will be satisfied
and nobody will be able to take advantage of anybody else, laws
will be irrelevant. Robbery, fraud, and corruption, and beggars,
vagabonds, and prostitutes, will disappear with the conditions that
produced them. The Octopus of Law and the Fury of Justice will
vanish in the sink of the old depraved society. Police, courts, execu-
tioners, and bloodsucking attorneys will go the way of necromancers
and witch doctors. Only insanity will provoke antisocial behavior;
and the insane will be understood for what they are, people ill, and
treated accordingly.

Personal. Nobody will have to act contrary to taste, preference,
or inclination. Multiplicity of places and diversity of associations
and freedoms of movement and choice will insure an agreeable
situation for everybody. Nobody will have to answer to a master,
either in the persons of parent, employer, official, landlord, and
political leader or in the abstractions of religion, money, law, and
tradition. Restraint and compulsion will become museum words,
as icons and crucifixes will become museum pieces.

Cooperation, not competition, will be the hallmark as much of
interpersonal as of economic affairs. A capitalist shibboleth, competition will never dignify an ear of corn or signify any stream but
a sewer. "Individual achievement," a euphemism for somebody's
getting the better of somebody, thriving in darkness of greed, will
die in the good society's sunshine.

Exploitation and privilege will be extinct. No aristocracies, no
elites, whether of title, intellect, or talent; equality will prevail.
Superiority will not occur, either by inheritance or purchase or
theft. Thus in theater and stadium, admission and seating will be

free and first-come, first-served. In short, class and its tyranny will disappear.

Everyone will share equally in riches of the earth and partake alike of fruits of enterprise, produced in abundance and distributed in amplitude exceeding everyone's needs: a nutritious and satisfying diet; enough attractive clothing, proper to season, climate, occupation, and occasion; and a pleasing domicile. There will be no concern and little time and energy demanded for things of the body, therefore much time and bounteous energy for things of the mind: education to the limit of ability and inclination; enjoyment of art and appreciation of science; enlightenment arising from open and unbiased education, free thought, and unrestricted discussion; pleasure in knowing that the burden of work is borne by all alike in a two-hour workday, the result of equal sharing of work; and the harmony that is the birthright in the society founded on anarchy.

Enjoying the ultimate in freedom, everyone will be as free as possible from distasteful necessities. For, though healthy, well-fed, well-clothed, well-housed, well-educated, and without constraint or compulsion from outside the home, not free is the woman who has to care for children, cook, clean, and sew when she would rather read, draw, travel, rest, or do whatever else she likes. Though well-paid and without domestic concerns (having a wife to polish his shoes), not free is the man who must travel to work, dress according to society's dictates, and eat socially acceptable food in stipulated ways at prescribed times. Free is the person who dispatches the distasteful quickly and easily. The communist-anarchist (the good) society, because of political, economic, social, and personal rationality, by providing independence and security, eliminating want and care, and fulfilling potential while dispersing responsibility, will minimize the distasteful and maximize freedom. Free, that society will be happy.

NOTES

1. *Freiheit*, 23 August 1890. *See also* 12 January 1895.
2. Ibid., 26 August 1899.
3. Ibid., 10 June 1899.

4. Ibid., 3 May 1890.
5. Ibid., 12 September 1899.
6. Ibid.
7. Ibid., 2 July 1892.
8. Ibid., 9 and 16 January 1892.
9. Ibid., 27 February 1892.
10. Ibid., 3 September 1898.
11. Ibid., 31 January 1903.
12. Ibid., 2 July 1892.
13. Ibid., 13 January 1903.
14. Ibid.
15. Ibid., 24 January 1903.
16. Ibid., 31 January 1903.
17. Ibid., 22 April 1892. The following scheme has been assembled from Most, "Die freie Gesellschaft," *Internationale Bibliothek*, 1887, and *Freiheit*, 24 June and 1 July 1899, 16 March and 21 September 1901.

13
PUBLIC AND POLEMICAL

1886, September 19: Wilhelm Liebknecht, Edward Aveling, and Eleanor (Marx) Aveling speak to 3,000
who wave red flags and cheer in New York City.

1889: Michael J. Schaack, captain of Chicago police,
publishes *Anarchy and Anarchists*, a 700-page
exposé of the menace to America.

1892, July 23: Alexander Berkman stabs and shoots but
fails to kill Henry Clay Frick in Pittsburgh. Thirteen days later, Berkman is in the Allegheny
County jail and Frick is back at his desk.

1893: Pullman Palace Car Company pays $2,520,000 in
dividends, out of a $25,000,000 surplus, and cuts
wages twenty to twenty-five percent. Employees
seek arbitration. Pullman: "Nothing to arbitrate."
In 1894, breaking the strike, troops kill twelve
strikers and jail the leader, Eugene Debs. He becomes a socialist. In response to protests about
troops, President Cleveland says, "If it takes the
entire army and navy of the United States to de-
liver a postal card in Chicago, that card will be
delivered."

1900: Nightly, Leon Franz Czolgosz takes to bed a
newspaper clipping that tells how Bresci killed
King Umberto.

1901, September 6: Czolgosz shoots President McKinley and says: "I done my duty." The dragnet for
coconspirators takes Emma Goldman in Chicago

> **September 10. McKinley dies in bed September 14. Czolgosz dies in the electric chair October 29.**
>
> **1902: New York (April 3) and New Jersey (April 30) pass criminal-anarchy laws.**
>
> **1903: Laws exclude anarchists. Carl Schurz calls the laws a threat to freedom. In the name of the laws, immigration officers throw John Turner, British anarchist, into a cage designed for the insane and fit for a gorilla, on Ellis Island. The Free Speech League engages Clarence Darrow and Edgar Lee Masters, but Turner is excluded.**

Most's splenetic attack on a fellow Anarchist who had been ready to die for the Deed was a stunning betrayal from which the movement in America never fully recovered.

Barbara W. Tuchman, *The Proud Tower*

From what the papers said you might think there was an anarchist or two skulking in every alley . . . with a basket of bombs under the arm. . . . It was all a parcel of lies, of course, but the people were crazy to be lied to, and the police, having nothing better, fed them lies.

Robert Herrick, *The Memoirs of an American Citizen*

I treated anarchists and the bomb-throwing and dynamiting gentry precisely as I treated other criminals. Murder is murder.   Theodore Roosevelt, *Autobiography*

THE END OF UNITY

Comrades changed color and fell away like autumn leaves, and Most led an expiring movement and spoke for a lost cause. How different the days when Social Democrats, fearful of his popularity, called him a burning limb to be cut from the trunk of the party!

Welcoming him to America then, comrades had packed Cooper Union, shook it with cheers, and filled him with hope for concord. But next day this comrade took him aside, and that one pulled him into a corner, and another buttonholed him on the stairs, and then one cornered him in the bathroom. This one was tall, that one short, this one fat, and that one thin; but all were bilious. The first wanted to turn him against the second, the second against the first, the third against the first and second, and the fourth against the other three plus half the movement besides. A minute later they turned on *him*, scowling and cursing: What did he mean, putting *Freiheit* into the hands of Schwab and cronies? Didn't he know, not the Schwab gang, but *they* were the ones to get it?[1]

They were assorted leftists of sundry persuasions. Recently arrived in America, uncertain of purlieu, they joined the social-revolutionary movement for want of something more amenable to their beliefs and more gratifying to their tastes. For a while Most induced them to unity around the Pittsburgh Proclamation. But under the surface of unity, discord boiled; and behind conventions of cooperation, hostility throbbed. Indeed, in his lifetime, radical leftists of neither Europe nor America knew unity long; divisiveness was a property of the radical Left.

He exacerbated divisiveness by opposing the 8-hour struggle. Part of the International Working People's Association left him and backed it with a vengeance that provoked Haymarket. When the struggle failed, advocates blamed him, calling his opposition more damaging than that of capital itself. Unity was hurt.

Then Berkman tried to kill Frick. Comrades looked to Most, expecting a call to rally. They knew that Most was the voice of terror; he not only urged terrorism but also taught how to commit it.

It seemed as if he would issue the call. Ten days after the start of the Homestead strike he wrote in *Freiheit* of "brave strikers who show us how to behave" and called workers "to arms!" A week later, the day of Berkman's attempt on Frick: "Workers, defend yourselves!" The following week, vilifying Frick in an article entitled "Fricktion," he shrieked hatred with every syllable. Next week, strikers surrendered and tempers cooled; but he spoke more hotly than ever. Newspapers and the authorities talked of arresting him as head of a conspiracy responsible for Homestead and behind the attempt on Frick, so clear was his position.

Then he published "Reflections on Assassination." Not only was Berkman's act a failure, it was also a mistake. In a country without

proletarian consciousness, terrorism was futile because workers did
not understand it. Moreover, unlike countries where terrorism was
the way to make a statement, in America propaganda-of-the-word
was possible and should be used. Berkman was therefore misguided
and feckless.[2]

Comrades were shocked. Berkman asked: this from my friend
and teacher? Goldman: this from my teacher and lover? Others:
this from Most—the opposite of what the voice of terror boomed
for years?

Unity was shattered. Robert Reitzel, anarchist publisher of *Arme
Teufel* in Detroit, defended Berkman with "In the Heat of Summer
a Shot Rang Out." Justus Schwab, once Most's best friend, denounced Most and praised Berkman. Goldman snapped that Most
"declared war—so be it!"[3] Michael Schwab, Haymarket anarchist
pardoned by Governor Altgeld, turned the Chicago *Arbeiterzeitung*
against Most.[4] Factions formed. One stayed loyal to Most, another
joined Peukert, and others declared independence. Some erstwhile
"Mostianers," who cared nothing for the factions, enlisted in the
Socialist Labor party, while others scattered. William Merten,
Most's friend from London, opened a rooming house in Brooklyn
and served leftists pancake suppers regardless of affiliation. If pan-
cakes quelled strife at Merten's, elsewhere it stayed vicious. Voltairine de Cleyre proposed to bring to visit Goldman a follower of
Most's and destroyed Goldman's hope for a close friendship with
de Cleyre.[5]

Comrades asked, "Why Most's about-face?" Goldman, and many
who defected, called it personal antagonism; Berkman had chal-
lenged Most, and Most was taking revenge. Most said, "To save
my own skin."[6] Talk of arrest and rumors of deportation frightened
him. He had been in prison twice in America, he had been denied
citizenship, and the New York *Times* advocated his deportation.
He wrote of Blackwell's Island as Hell. Deportation meant return
to Germany, where in every trial for high treason since 1881 he
was alleged a cause of the crime. Policemen there dreamed of winning sergeant's stripes or bagging captain's bars, and district attorneys of becoming attorney general or gaining a seat on the bench,
by getting him. In the 1870s, Tessendorf had harassed him; now

fifty Tessendorfs would swarm at him. "If I set foot on German soil, John Neve's fate will be mine: living death."[7]

Fear of that fate blinded and embittered him. Rigid, sarcastic, and insulting, he ruined chances of reunification. He told comrades: "Whoever is not with me is against me." He blinked at the appeal, to leftists, of Lawrence Gronlund's explication of Marxism, *The Co-operative Commonwealth*, and lambasted Edward Bellamy's fictionalization of it, *Looking Backward*. Bellamy's novel not only looked but was backward; its popularity be damned! Personal feelings meant nothing when they conflicted with public action, Most believed, and social graces were silly if they blocked social revolution; revolutionaries should live by the code of Necheyev and Bakunin. Rather than compromise and conciliate, he stepped on the toes of comrades who stood in his way and rapped the knuckles of comrades who tried to restrain him. After 1892, more and more kicked back in anger and lashed out in reprisal.[8]

He made enemies when he included the editors of the New York *Volkszeitung* among the complacent who lulled workers comatose instead of agitating them rapt. "History is to be made with iron," he told Serge Schevitsch and Alexander Jonas, "and you stick-in-the-muds better learn that fact pronto."[9] Taking umbrage, they restored the Socialist Labor party and led it to victory against his International Working People's Association. The victory spelled doom for the IWPA.

When Most and Schevitsch squared off, Most was not less but Schevitsch more appealing to many. Schevitsch, tall and distinguished, married to the diplomat's daughter for whom Lassalle died in a duel, and fluent in five languages—versus Most, short and stout, married to an immigrant worker, and a fool in every language but German. Most's platform style was becoming eccentric, fine if you liked it but easy to dislike. A red rose flamed in his lapel beside a white beard, while he talked out of the corner of his mouth, looked out of one open and one drooping eye, and gestured with the right eyebrow while waving his notes in the left hand. His was the whirlwind delivery of old, grown wheezy.[10] By contrast, people forgot how Schevitsch looked; moved by what he said, they lost interest in his looks. He spoke at such points of agitation as Union

Square in New York City, and on tour; and leftists marked his words there and in the *Volkszeitung*, the leading Marxist newspaper outside Europe.[11]

He and the Socialist Labor party, as part of the program to restore the party (ravaged by Most a few years before), brought to America Most's enemy Wilhelm Liebknecht, who toured on behalf of the party. His fame preceded him; and leftists turned out to see the leader of Social Democracy—gray, bent, wrinkled, but able yet to stir audiences. Reminded he was past sixty, he said: "When it is necessary, I am not sixty but twice thirty." With him were Marx's daughter Eleanor (Mrs. Edward) Aveling and her husband. Abraham Cahan called Aveling "a handsome graybeard" and Eleanor "dark, beautiful and charming"; she "spoke brilliant words of fire."[12] Most was eloquent, but so were they. Most was ugly, but they were beautiful. Most appealed, but they appealed as he could not. The trio appeared at fifty mass meetings in major cities, with Liebknecht speaking German, Aveling English, and Eleanor both; and they said what they thought of Most and his ilk. Liebknecht's accusation that Most's screaming caused Haymarket fell on receptive ears.[13]

Socialists, angry because press and public lumped them with anarchists and thereby associated them with Haymarket, welcomed these orators who told what was wrong with anarchists and right with socialists. Socialists rejoiced: Liebknecht's oratory enlarged the size and increased the numbers of German-speaking locals of the SLP, while the Avelings' did likewise for the English-speaking.[14] The SLP grew, the IWPA shrank. *Vorbote* left the IWPA and joined the SLP; and to *Vorbote*, *Freiheit* lost 1,000 subscribers.[15] At the SLP's convention of 1896, ninety-four delegates represented seventy-five locals in twelve states. By that year, the IWPA was dead.

Under creative, forward-looking Schevitsch, the SLP took advantage of changing times, while the IWPA, under rigid Most, refused to recognize change. Liebknecht called tactics a question of practicality, to be revised every twenty-four hours if circumstances demanded it. Schevitsch took note, while Most sneered at "that chameleon Liebknecht, that hypocrite." Consequently, in the hard times notable for violent strikes in the early 1880s, the IWPA followed Most and flourished; political action would have been silly.

But the later 1880s were milder; harmony, compromise, and political action were right; and the SLP entered politics and throve, while the IWPA, rooted in Most's now-arid doctrines, withered and died spurning politics.

In 1886, for example, the SLP supported Henry George for mayor of New York, even though the SLP faulted his theory of property and questioned his advocacy of a single tax. Because *Progress and Poverty* made George famous, socialists believed he could win the election; and they wanted to win first and concern themselves with principles later. George, like Most, landed in New York from London in 1882 and was cheered in a packed Cooper Union. George for mayor, not because of his single tax but in spite of it, said the *Volkszeitung*, speaking for socialists willing expediently to accept George as more progressive among a poverty of candidates. With Most, no such compromise; the SLP was a bourgeois party behind a leftist mask, its lies would bring exposure in the press and defeat at the polls, and George was a screwball: chicanery, this election—tomfoolery! George finished behind the Democrats' Abram S. Hewitt, but socialists helped George beat the Republicans' Theodore Roosevelt by 8,000 votes.[16]

Similarly, the SLP recognized the rising power of organized labor and sought association at least, and affiliation if possible, with the unions. The SLP made overtures to the Knights of Labor when the Knights were at their strongest. Meanwhile, Most lambasted the Knights' Grand Master, Terence V. Powderly. "You rat, Powderly —you expel locals with anarchist leanings, and you tell your union not to give money and not to express sympathy for the condemned of Haymarket. You are the Grand Master Rat!"[17] When Daniel De Leon began his career in the SLP and joined efforts to associate the party with organized labor, Most called him a parvenu and a prima donna who stank like a bourgeois while putting on the airs of a proletarian. Later, when the American Federation of Labor drew thousands from the Knights and promised to be the strongest union ever, Most had contempt for it and hard words for its head, Samuel Gompers.

One evening at Schwab's, Gompers, Schwab, and others listened to Most attack leaders of British unions. Gompers bristled. Most lit into leaders of American unions, particularly Adolph Strasser of the United Cigarmakers. Gompers, himself a cigarmaker, grabbed Most by the throat and shook him. They never spoke to each other again.[18]

Thus the SLP greened and the IWPA withered on Most's doorstep. Unless he could command a following among Germans and Jews, he could not command a following at all; and if he could not command one in New York City, he could not command one anywhere. Beginning in 1885, the United German Trades of the City of New York (once friendly to him) supported the SLP; and after 1888, the United Hebrew Trades of New York turned from the IWPA to the SLP.

At last nearly everybody left him. Abraham Cahan, for example, a Jew close to the heart of the leftist and labor movements, had been an anarchist who admired Most. Then Cahan searched his own mind, studied political theory, and discussed the social question with fellow leftists, concluding that Most's terrorism was absurd. Most's speeches, which once rang with truth, now echoed with lies. How could a handful of rebels beat the military and police of a nation of millions? How could a few foreigners make revolution here? How could anarchism be a viable theory of society when people need organization and direction? Marx made sense, Most nonsense. Cahan, like many leftists of the years of Most's decline, exchanged anarchism for socialism. Passage from Most to Marx was like passage from a fog-bound ocean to the shores of light.[19]

Most's following declined until he complained in typical overstatement that he could have invited all, including each of *Freiheit*'s subscribers, to dinner at Schwab's and not filled the place or emptied his wallet.[20] How different the times when comrades packed Cooper Union and bought 8,000 *Freiheits* a week!

THE FUROR AGAINST ANARCHISM

After Haymarket, fear of anarchists spread and hatred of them increased. People in Galesburg, Illinois, welcomed news of the executions with glad howls and: "Well, they hanged 'em!"[21] Carl Sandburg's parents were pleased, because anarchists killed and so ought to be killed. Anybody on a soapbox was apt for arrest. Martin Irons, tobacco-chewing leader in the Knights of Labor, was convicted as much for wearing a dirty shirt and spitting in court as for encouraging riots and leading boycotts; radical behavior was anarchist. People hurt people who favored the Haymarket anarchists. John Peter Altgeld, governor of Illinois, called their trial unjust, denounced the penalty of death carried out on some of them, and pardoned the rest. In turn he was cheated out of his fortune, he ran again for governor and lost, and he ran for mayor of Chicago and lost. The press called him an anarchist: the nastiest invective they could find, in their hatred, in times when being called an anarchist gave grounds for suit. Like vultures they stripped him to the bone, Edgar Lee Masters said. Word was that Altgeld died of a broken heart. Masters' Carl Hamblin was tarred and feathered, his Spoon River *Clarion* wrecked, for ridiculing justice "on the day the Anarchists were hanged in Chicago." Twenty years after Haymarket, portraits of the anarchists were hung in a gallery of criminals, in the same spirit in which the anarchists had been hanged among murderers, robbers, embezzlers, and other bandits.[22]

Supporters of the Haymarket verdict argued that, as an essential freedom is freedom from fear, so a free society can neither brook terror nor shrink from madmen's threats. To James Ford Rhodes, the state's attorney Julius S. Grinnell, "an ideal prosecutor," rightly defined the defendants as accessories to murder. Knowledgeable intelligent heroic Judge Joseph E. Gary, who had risen from the carpenter's bench to the jurist's, ruled correctly. And the supreme courts of Illinois and the United States verified the wisdom of his ruling. Rhodes cited Henry George, who studied the case with the help of a lawyer and agreed that the anarchists were guilty of murder, premeditated, willful, and deliberate. Rhodes cited Michael J. Schaack's *Anarchy and Anarchists*, in which masked men greet ladies in black, while the reader wonders if everything will explode on the next page, so often is dynamite mentioned. Schaack saw more anarchists than hell could hold. Thus Rhodes, a dean of historians, approved the trial as a contest between anarchists who attacked out of malice and the society that defended itself under law.[23]

Among Schaack's anarchists was Most, chief anarchist. An eminence manifest and gray, he could be written about in superlatives: what newspaper could resist attributing the most to Most? He was the most dangerous, most criminal, most bloodthirsty, most evil, most dastardly, and most god-awful man in America. The Portland, Oregon, *Telegram* called him a "rabid red-flag follower."[24] To the Chicago *Times* he was the wild-eyed communist, a red revolutionist, and the rampant socialist.[25] The New York *Times* labeled him blatant hyena, mad anarchist, dynamite-eating editor, museum freak, detestable and despicable scoundrel, arch anarchist, loathsome and bloodthirsty blackguard, and exponent of the art of slaying. Was he late to a meeting, the *Times* wondered, because he detoured to put a banana peel on the mayor's doorstep or because he stopped to rob the blind beggar on the Bowery?[26]

To other newspapers he was the red-mouthed jackal of distorted physiognomy and sinister leer, the drawn-up puffed-out creature with a vicious eye and a lump. When he smiled, the lump gamboled over his features; and when he frowned, it sank into the slough of despond. His face registered base and brutal passions; no dignity, no nobility, no charity, no calm—only envy and malice, craft and cowardice, and vacillation and venom. He swaggered with the bravado and staggered with the braggadocio of beer. In court he looked like a whipped cur. And there, or in any closed place, your nose confirmed what your eye surmised: a filthy anarchist, stinking of liquor, onions, tobacco, garlic, and layers and years of dirt and sweat.

How he talked was equally reprehensible. Actually he did not talk or speak, or even orate or speechify. He breathed, exhaled, roared, screeched, bellowed, shrieked, and spat flames, coals, embers, lava, hellfire, brimstone, or at the coolest, molten words and blistering epithets. He relieved his mind of rodomontades, hurled diatribes, spouted tirades, discharged harangues, fired blitzes, belched vaporings, disgorged bombast, and slunk around the country howling. He ranted and raved, railed and blustered, and frothed and foamed. To emphasize points he squealed and reddened. When he threw back his head and shook his arm he resembled the braggart calling names. He did not practice persiflage. He did not palter or chaffer. He wore to speeches a black frock coat and striped pants, his hair on end like the quills of the fretful porcupine. He rushed to the platform waving his notes. He stamped, shook his fist, raved. He trembled, the bristling bang on his brow quivered, and his teeth clicked like a wolf's. He was all animal. So excited that his mouth could not express his thoughts, he spluttered and hissed. So red that his scalp gleamed through his hair, he was a communist beacon. He was mouth personified and lip incarnate.[27]

The English language was this ripper's victim. He hat knotting to zay to dee *Vorlt*. He hated dat baber. Unt dee *Thaimss* aboossed heem yoost like dee udder babers. Dey vanted to half heem hangt unt expelt. Ach! vass dat fair? Vo vass dee boasted-uff Amerikaan liberty uf speech unt uf dee press? Dee kapitalistik babers vanted all dee zay demzelfss. Vy shoot he not half dee right to express opinionss een meedings unt een heess baber?[28]

According to the press, his broken English and sturdy German spread arson and instigated murder. In Europe he inspired the assassination of the Czar. In America, having influence over the foreign-born, he caused uprisings and strikes. In Chicago, anarchists "took him at his word and murdered policemen under the impression that they were following his teachings."[29]

His cronies were rowdies and hooligans—unkempt and uncouth, wild-looking, wilder-acting, long-haired, and demonstrative of the absence of soap. Nightly they crowded scorbutic saloons, drank beer, guzzled wine, slurped whiskey, smoked foul pipes, puffed vile cigars, cursed capital, and worried the authorities with bluster of dynamite. These madmen massed in meetings like mad dogs in packs, and snarled and drooled and snapped. Massed in meetings the shady revelers stank. The odor of their cigars, strong enough to do manual labor, exceeded the odor of their innocence of bathtubs. And the cigars were likelier to labor than the loafers who smoked them. Having no work freed and fitted this lazy and malefic bunch for carousing, and then they transmuted spirits of the flask into the spirit of hanky-panky. When not brawling, when not ridiculing law and order, they imbibed anarchist ambrosia and lay drunk together among exhausted bottles, empty casks, and drained barrels, singing revolutionary ditties and humming conspiratorial dirges, some written by Most himself.

To get money for their hellish cause, and with Most's encouragement, they insured their apartments and then set them afire. Benjamin Tucker wrote in "the firebug article": an exploding kerosene lamp caused each of the rash of fires in anarchists' apartments, each apartment was insured in excess of value, and in one case claim was made before the agent had time to register the policy. Most denied all. Then the New York *Sun* published a list of fires, together with names, addresses, and indemnities paid. Most was not incriminated, but scandal drove away followers and friends.[30]

As with the man and his company, so with his theories and doctrines. What could be more noxious than threatening with guns and bombs a free and democratic America? What more loathsome than a foreigner, a guest, teaching assassination and preaching a gospel of the bludgeon, stiletto, bullet, and grenade? Despising blood and abhorring destruction, Americans rejected a utopia built on the shards and ashes of the broken family, gutted church, and smashed state. Americans were too upstanding.

They doubted that his theories could work. Even the dedicated must weary of maintaining the indolent, the extravagant, and the incompetent; and anarchism could not abolish indolence, extravagance, and incompetence. Worse, he was quoted: "All measures are legal against tyrants" and "A tyrant is a person who has more money than yourself." Thus "if two laborers earn ten dollars a week each, and one saves three dollars, while the other spends all in rum, the former is a tyrant to the extent of three dollars, and it is the duty of the latter . . . to knock down and rob his more thrifty companion." But "as soon as he succeeds in getting the 'tyrant's' wealth, he is himself a 'tyrant,' and it becomes logically the duty of his followers to turn upon him." Hence the chaos of anarchy.[31]

Personally wicked, socially vicious, prophet of evil, sinister chucklehead, leader of ruffians—Most deserved retribution and earned punishment. The day he arrived in America and every day thereafter the Chicago *Times* was for deporting him. The New York *Times* detested his grumbling about his treatment in the courts.[32] When the courts, in their democratic weakness, were absurdly lenient—how dare he grumble? Hard labor and compulsory washing were mild for so coarse a malefactor, so nefarious a scoundrel. Was the rogue dissatisfied with a trial that should have put him away for life or sent him to the chair? Did he want a new trial, the cur? Ship him back to the old country!

Ship him back and help rid America of its worst enemies, the fiends who sought to destroy everything, by any means, however criminal. So spoke some of the once-cool heads who joined the anti-anarchist furor now. One of them, Carl Schurz, seemed to fear a greater threat to the Republic in 1897 than in 1862.[33]

Leon Czolgosz justified the furor and confirmed the fear. Calling himself an anarchist, he identified his inspiration, Emma Goldman, in a speech at the Liberty Association in Cleveland, May 5, 1901.

Police pricked up their ears. Goldman, eh? Chicago newspapers wrote that during Kropotkin's visit, at a leftist redoubt called Hull House, Kropotkin, Goldman, and Czolgosz plotted the killing of McKinley a la Russe.[34] Kropotkin, Goldman, and Czolgosz, eh? Wheels of investigation whirled, and out poured results: anarchist hyenas, in cahoots, stuck together like leeches and lived to assassinate; and Czolgosz was the tool of an anarchist conspiracy.

Formation of the FBI was over twenty years off, and interagency cooperation was unusual nationally; but a dragnet thrown wide and set deep caught suspects in St. Louis, Buffalo, Pittsburgh, and somewhere in New Mexico; and in Chicago, Red Emma herself.

Officials, trying to torture Czolgosz to admit her complicity, tortured until the last day, the final hour.[35] Czolgosz walked the last mile with face mutilated by torture and head bandaged to stanch wounds of torture. He took his final seat. Again the warden spoke of "that bad woman."

"Emma Goldman betrayed you, Leon. Why do you shield her?"

From under the black mask: "She had nothing to do with my act. I did it alone . . . for the American people."

Goldman went free, after Czolgosz paid for the death of the president.

But not only Czolgosz paid. For while police and marshalls around the country pursued anarchists, police in New York City pursued the chief anarchist. Fifty-five years old, gray in service to the Cause, Most was nonetheless vigorous—publishing *Freiheit*, lecturing in the city when not on tour around the country, and urging revolution: a dangerous character still.

In the *Freiheit* distributed hours before the assassination, an article praised tyrannicide. Written by Karl Heinzen in 1849, it was "true yet today," Most told readers. Hearing of the assassination, he ordered the issue withdrawn.

Too late. The police had a copy and directly they had him. They snorted at his disclaimers. The article and the assassination on the same day—coincidence, you say, Most? Poppycock! You hate McKinley and want him killed. Item: the Chicago *Times-Herald*'s report: Most's speech on the anniversary of Haymarket denounced McKinley as " 'the clown of Mark Hanna, himself the clown of the trusts.' "[36] Item: the New York *Tribune*'s report: Most sat in the saloon at 69 Gold Street, holding three inches from his mouth a piece of meat that dripped grease onto his waistcoat, and said McKinley and Roosevelt must be killed. About McKinley he said, " 'Who is he, anyway? He's only a man. He has no right there.' "[37] To Most's disclaimers the court was as unsympathetic as the police.

Arrest and conviction of the chief anarchist in New York seemed to encourage harrassment and persecution of anarchists elsewhere. Gangs beat up anarchists in the streets. In Tacoma, Washington, and Spring Valley, Illinois, mobs attacked anarchist colonies as if they were hives of wasps. Justice Davy of the New York Supreme Court ordered anarchists of Rochester indicted for conspiracy. The excise board of Newark refused licenses to establishments that served anarchists. Mayors in New Jersey and chiefs of police in Boston, New York, and Philadelphia said they would go to the limits of the law to crush anarchism. Cleveland police closed the Liberty Association, where Czolgosz heard Goldman; and a US marshall and a Post Office inspector ransacked the Association's records. The Cleveland *Leader* demanded that Czolgosz's father, a city ditchdigger, be fired; the landlord ordered the Czolgoszes out; and Los Angeles police kept Czolgosz's brother in custody during President Roosevelt's visit. From Fifth Avenue to Main Street, people said: "Down with anarchists!"[38]

While citizens and local authorities were thus dealing with anarchists, Senator Hawley offered $1,000 for a shot at an anarchist. President Roosevelt called Czolgosz's crime "a crime against a free government, a thousand times worse than any murder of a private individual could be." Roosevelt declared "war with relentless efficiency not only against anarchists, but against all active and passive sympathizers with anarchists," the enemies of progress, the deadly enemies of liberty.[39]

The national government and the states considered anti-anarchist measures.[40]

• *Exclude* was heard oftenest. Anarchists, foul, must be foreigners. Schwab's saloon attracted tourists like an exhibit from abroad. The Haymarket anarchists were nearly all Germans, afraid to do in Germany what they did here; yet they spat on a fairer trial than they would have gotten there. Though born in the United States, Czolgosz was called a German Pole, as if double provenance would make him foreign twice and doubly guilty.[41] Anti-anarchists stumbled over the names of Bakunin, Kropotkin, Vaillant, Ravachol, and Bresci, and trembled when thinking of the depravity these names signified, and shook when remembering that Bresci went from America to Italy to kill the king. And how do you pronounce that? BRESS-see, BRESS-she, BRESS-CHEE, or Bress-KEE? Some maniac with a name so foreign it could not be pronounced killed President Garfield, and who could say *Czolgosz* with a straight tongue? The loudest voices of terror were Goldman and Most, a Russian and a German, though at least you could pronounce their names. About Most, what struck you first and stayed with you longest were his "strong German features"; it served him right to be denied citizenship. Anarchists came from abroad, hence could and should be kept abroad.

• *Banish* was voiced nearly as often. Anarchists, whether citizens or not, should be deported or preferably, as Senator Hoar proposed, exiled to a Pacific island. Hoar realized that every civilized country would want to banish anarchists; uninhabited islands, or ones inhabited by savages, were the only places to put them. Serve them right if they were turned loose among headhunters.

• *Control* was the purpose of legislation spelling out what anarchists were not allowed to do, such as advocate violence and urge revolution. Assaults on federal officials would become federal offenses or treason. Guards for the president would deter assaults. Legislation would also ban meetings, suppress publications, and provide punishments cruel enough to teach a lesson and discourage wrongdoing. New York, New Jersey, and Wisconsin enacted criminal-anarchy laws; and Congress passed an anarchist-exclusion law, signed with glee by President Roosevelt. America would now be straight, clean, and white—like his teeth.

Under the new law, British anarchist John Turner was sent to Ellis Island and locked in a six-by-nine-foot cage, to await expulsion to Britain for possession of Most's "Free Society," for being

scheduled to appear with Most at a memorial to the Haymarket
anarchists, and for announcing he would speak on "The Legal
Murder of 1887."[42]

Unlike Turner, Most had no Britain to return to and nowhere
else to go; so he stayed in America and made his last stand.

THE LAST STAND

"If *Freiheit* fails," Most said, "the Cause is lost." Anti-anarchist
furor scared off 1,000 subscribers. Debts jumped to $700. When
he sought subscribers and solicited contributions, apathy, apathy,
and more apathy met his requests. And if he overcame apathy, he
faced hostility.

"I'll continue, no matter what!"[43]

He changed *Freiheit* from a party organ, designed to inform and
inspire the faithful, to a propaganda sheet, intended to reunite old
comrades, gain new, and win a hearing among the skeptical, apa-
thetic, and hostile. He turned a *Freiheit* big, awkward, and printed
in Gothic script into a *Freiheit* easy to hold, carry, and read. Latin
typography replaced Gothic, and headlines and illustrations increased in size and number. "Welcome, reader," the new *Freiheit*
seemed to say, "come in and make yourself at home."

Content too must appeal, he decided. "Catch attention, hold it,
and compel the reader to say *yes*." Since great authors catch attention and compel assent, *Freiheit* serialized Bakunin, Kropotkin,
and others. But the majority of articles got attention and won assent
on their own merits, through urgency and verve.

Some articles read like dispatches phrased in hyperboles, imperatives, and exclamations. "Comrades!" an article might begin.
"Watch out! You are in peril!" Imperatives gained immediacy in
the second person: "you will"—"you should"—"you need"—"you
must." You were ordered to stop, look, listen, read, hear, see,
know, and act—as if addressed face to face. You were told to
expect an onslaught from plutocrats and their bloodhounds:
"Workers, protect yourselves!"—"Brothers, on guard!"—"Comrades, to arms!" Urgency imparted a vigor absent from such prosaic rivals as *Sozialdemokrat* and *Autonomie*.

Freiheit's verve, Max Nettlau said, merited preservation in an-

thologies.[44] The Vienna *Arbeiterzeitung* praised "strong and original invective."[45] Sarcasm, a favorite, enlivened many an article,
such as the description of how the wind of humbug took people's
breath away. Figures of speech "punched enemies in the nose with
an iron fist," and wasn't the rebirth of Social Democracy a mis-
carriage? Terence Powderly was a simpleton, Samuel Gompers a
rowdy, Daniel De Leon a lickspittle, and William McKinley an ass.
Repetition of the name added power to this name-calling, in slogans such as "Down with the scoundrel!" repeated fifteen times in
an attack on Theodore Roosevelt. Atheism did not blind to the
strength of biblical allusions: errant comrades "worshipped the
golden calf of Social Democracy." The dark hint, suggesting something sensational, left details and conclusion to the reader's imagination; innuendoes about Peukert's money insinuated that Peukert
was a spy. Bold, vigorous, trenchant, witty, these sources of verve
prompted Dieter Kühn (who wished many radicals had written less)
to wish that Most had written more.[46]

Although style won praise, it earned a pittance. *Freiheit* carried
few advertisements, and Most charged comrades little for notices
of rooms to rent, things for sale, help wanted, or services offered.
"I'm no capitalist!" Loss of subscriptions, after Haymarket, forced
reduction from eight to four pages, without reduction in price:
Freiheit cost a nickel in the era of the penny press. He gave all he
had of time and money, while his wife wondered whether they
could afford all that. Was it worth his sleeping so little and burst-
ing out of sleep so much, shouting, "Money! There must be more
money!"? He edited and wrote without salary; and she, able editor
and skillful writer, worked gratis.[47] To save *Freiheit* he produced
plays and lectured.

He created the Free Stage of New York, after troupes in Paris,
Berlin, and Vienna.[48] Thirty gifted and enthusiastic amateurs, with
him their star, in New York's Thalia Theater and on tour per-
formed Hauptmann's *Weavers* and *Florian Geyer,* Ibsen's *Pillars
of Society*, Sudermann's *Honor* and *Sodom's End*, and the anonymous *Skinning of the Robber Knight*. He changed, deleted, and
inserted dialogue; edited, rearranged, and added scenes; and thereby
made these anticapitalist polemics more anticapitalist, because he
believed the stage the ultimate propaganda, stronger than the press

and more influential than the platform. He also appeared in *The Strike*, a pro-labor play by another troupe, in the Windsor Theatre on the Bowery. Producing, directing, and acting realized in middle age his youthful dream; and audiences and critics, even reviewers for the hostile press, sweetened it: they complimented the productions, praised the directing, and applauded his acting.

Plays raised money; the platform raised more. When not lecturing in New York City or environs, he was on tour. Through the 1890s he toured the Northeast and Middle West. In 1899-1900 he gave over 200 speeches across the country and up and down the West Coast. Every year thereafter he took to the road in the Northeast and Middle West. He solicited subscribers everywhere, and always the hat passed "for our brave comrade and his bully newspaper."

So he sustained *Freiheit* and, his "pride and joy," it sustained him. It "has readers in every state and nearly all the territories," he said. "It finds its way to England, France, Belgium, Holland, Germany, Austria, and Switzerland, as well as Australia, Argentina, Brazil, and South Africa. It has friends in every zone of the earth, and its editor repels with proud defiance anything its enemies, whatever their stripe, say or do against him." Engels predicted that it would not last six months. It lasted thirty-one years, outliving Engels.

> A newspaper that has often vexed emperors and kings; a sheet that innumerable beadles have pursued, various governments banned, and many legislatures debated; an organ that has been attacked as much as any in any language; a journal that a hundred demagogues and envious persons have tried to slander and with competing publications drive out of business—in short, *Freiheit* (which has resisted and repelled every conceivable attack) will continue until its mission is accomplished: the making of the social revolution.[49]

In America, revolution could be kindled and might take fire in German because the majority of the radical Left were Germans. But with Germans a tenth of the population, revolution would sweep the country only if it spread in English and caught native speakers. The Socialist Labor party apprehended this fact in the 1880s. Abraham Cahan argued that immigrants could not make revolution; the SLP had to Americanize or die. Therefore he learned English and used it for the SLP, and English-language orators spoke at SLP rallies.[50] The SLP grew into the Socialist, an American, party. Similarly, John Mitchell joined English-speaking and foreign-language miners into the United Mine Workers.

Unfortunately (as Most saw it), the anarchist leader fluent in English and prestigious enough to influence Americans had been Albert Parsons—dead on the Haymarket gallows. His widow, trying to take his place and honor his memory, spoke in principal cities. "Albert Parsons' widow Lucy to speak" drew crowds, and Most appeared with her. But despite her pleas and his reinforcement, the crowds' curiosity did not become commitment.

Nevertheless, "We do what we can with what we have," Most said; "we make our best better."[51] He encouraged English-speaking comrades to organize Americans. To avoid quarrels, he instructed, enumerate no principles at first; let groups be "interest groups" that take up common concerns. Be flexible. Put aside formulas and phrases and slogans, stop bickering, and stand together until the movement grows to represent the proletariat of America; time enough later to expose disagreements, expound ideals, and settle differences. When British anarchists Charles W. Mowbray and John Turner toured, addressing workers in English, he appeared on the same platforms and with them asked, "Join the Cause." He also promoted multilingual rallies in New York City, Chicago, St. Louis, Buffalo, Milwaukee, and Pittsburgh, at which he spoke German, others English, Italian, and Yiddish. Then he tried English, but only a few times; he was laughed at. He and comrades distributed a million copies of a hundred books and pamphlets in English.

These measures to win a native-American following failed. Seldom were books and pamphlets paid for, and less often read, by the desired audience. Few Americans joined. Why should they? Why discuss with immigrants the issues immigrants called "of common concern"? Against capitalism for reasons not clear, immigrants talked of revolution and class struggle: Greek to American radicals. Even strikers in the bloody seventies did not recognize class struggle and disliked revolution; while American unions, a branch of capitalism, wanted nothing but a liberal share of capitalism's abundance. Anarchists, said Mr. Dooley, "What are they anny how but furriners an' what r-right have they to be holdin' tor-rchlight procissions in this land iv th' free an' home iv th' brave? Did ye iver see an American or an Irishman an arnychist? Naw, an' ye niver will."[52] Thus audiences for Mowbray, Turner, and Kropotkin, and at Most's rallies, were of the curious; and the enthusiasm of curiosity died when curiosity died. Grinning at linguistic blunders, audiences at Most's English speeches vanished like the Cheshire Cat, from front to back, and left in his mind their grins, their terrible grins. .

If few native Americans understood him and many hated him, the majority did not hear him: Americans at a rally of his, whether come to clap or scoff, grew rare. Meanwhile his immigrant audience diminished and changed. With expansion of German industry, emigration slowed. With the repeal of the Anti-Socialist Law and moderation of persecution, emigrants included fewer idealists and more opportunists; and some of the radicals, driven by the Law out of Germany, returned to Germany. More Germans in America, prospering, dropped radicalism and became solid citizens, regular bourgeoisie. Therefore Most's sphere of action narrowed, and his circle of influence constricted. Shouting "Hail, Anarchy!" in 1886 he boasted 10,000 for the Cause. In 1903 he confessed that twenty years' trying to sell Americans anarchism had failed.[53]

But, refusing to confess failure with the foreign-born, he would not acknowledge the difference between 1892 and 1905. In 1892, at the celebration of his release from Blackwell's Island, every seat in Cooper Union was taken; aisles were filled; and hundreds turned away disappointed. Forty policemen kept watch, with a hundred in reserve. In 1905, Cooper Union was too big.[54] Comrades trickled into Grand Street Hall, which, though smaller, was also too big; and halfhearted cheers echoed in a void of unfulfilled hopes. Eight policemen looked bored; two others played cards. Yet he blustered: "Our time will come . . . as surely as the sun rises." Another prophecy, after forty years of prophecies that failed.

Four months later, to mark the rebellion of Russians at Odessa, comrades met in Clinton Hall, the smallest on the East Side.[55] Announced as the "bright star in a galaxy of speakers," Most said:

"We will not [cough] back [cough] until every bloodhound of [cough] is killed and [cough] Czar is blown limb [cough]. . . ." His voice cracked. A spasm bent him double. He staggered off, on somebody's arm.

The next star in the galaxy, Henry Weinberg, Philadelphia cigarmaker, rose and asked contributions for the Russian comrades.

"Who will give $10.00?"

No answer.

"Who will give $8.00?"

No sound, not a stir. The audience stared at their shoes.

"Who will give $5.00?"

He could not catch an eye.

"Who will give $3.00?"

Some tiptoed out, hands on wallets.

"Who will give $1.00?"

A few dollars appeared.

"Let crowned as well as uncrowned Czars tremble."

Less than a year later, Most died. The movement, the largest and best-organized of American radical movements, his movement, was already dead.

NOTES

1. *Freiheit*, 25 July 1896.
2. Ibid., 27 August 1892.
3. Emma Goldman, *Living My Life*, p. 99; *see also* pp. 96-105, 109-110, 201. Carolyn Ashbaugh, *Lucy Parsons*, p. 185.
4. Caroline Lloyd, *Henry Demarest Lloyd* 1:243.
5. Goldman, *Living My Life*, pp. 157-58.
6. *Freiheit*, 19 September 1896.
7. Ibid., 1 August 1896.
8. Ibid., 5 September 1896.
9. *Freiheit*, 23 December 1882. *See also* A. Sartorius, *Der moderne Socialismus in den Vereinigten Staaten von Amerika*, pp. 198-99.
10. *New York Tribune*, 10 November 1896.
11. Abraham Cahan, *The Education of Abraham Cahan*, pp. 227-28, 235, 327.
12. Ibid., pp. 337-38.

13. Morris Hillquit, *History of Socialism in the United States*, pp. 230-35.

14. Reinhard Höhn, *Die vaterlandslosen Gesellen*, pp. 317-18.

15. Ibid., p. 345. *Freiheit*, 25 July 1896.

16. Hillquit, *History of Socialism*, pp. 236-52.

17. *Freiheit*, 5 September 1896. *See also* 12 June 1886.

18. Samuel Gompers, *Seventy Years of Life and Labor* 1:100-101.

19. Cahan, *Education*, pp. 330-37.

20. *Freiheit*, 14 May 1904.

21. Carl Sandburg, *Always the Young Strangers*, pp. 133-34.

22. Henry David, *The Haymarket Affair*, pp. 528-29. Of Altgeld's pardon the *Chicago Graphic* (15 July 1893) doubted "if any other official act in the history of any American state has met with so general condemnation from every class of citizens."

23. James Ford Rhodes, *History of the United States* 8:279-84. Gary defended himself in "The Chicago Anarchists of 1886" (p. 837): "Right-minded, thoughtful people" would "read what I have written," realize the menace, and recognize the wisdom of his decision.

24. 2 February 1900.

25. 12 November 1900.

26. 24 November 1887, p. 4.

27. *New York Times*, 19 December 1882, p. 8; 10 March 1883, p. 8; 18 April 1887, p. 1.

28. Assembled from the *New York Times*, 20 November 1887, p. 11; *Chicago Times-Herald*, 16 April 1894; *Indianapolis News*, 19 November 1904.

29. *New York Times*, 27 November 1887, p. 4.

30. Benjamin Tucker, "The Beast of Communism," *Liberty*, 27 March 1886. Most, "Eine Stinkbombe," *Freiheit*, 10 April 1886. *New York Sun*, 3 May 1886.

31. *Philadelphia Bulletin*, 16 October 1883.

32. 30 November 1887, p. 4.

33. Carl Schurz, "Murder as a Political Agency," p. 847.

34. George Woodcock and Ivan Avakumovic, *The Anarchist Prince*, p. 287.

35. Goldman, *Living My Life*, pp. 316-17.

36. 12 November 1900.

37. 10 September 1901.

38. Sidney Fine, "Anarchism and the Assassination of McKinley," pp. 785-88.

39. Theodore Roosevelt, "Annual Message, 1901"; *Letters* 3:142.

40. Fine, "Anarchism and McKinley," pp. 788-94.
41. Harry Thurston Peck, *Twenty Years of the Republic,* p. 655.
42. Fine, "Anarchism and McKinley," pp. 796-97.
43. *Freiheit,* 7 January 1899.
44. "John Most," p. 19.
45. 20 March 1906.
46. *Johann Most,* p. 125.
47. *Freiheit,* 12 June 1886.
48. J. C. Blankenagel, "Early Reception of Hauptmann's *Die Weber* in the United States," pp. 334-40.
49. *Freiheit,* 7 January 1899.
50. Cahan, *Education,* pp. 407-408.
51. *Freiheit,* 12 May 1900.
52. *Chicago Evening Post,* 9 June 1894.
53. Kühn, *Johann Most,* p. 172.
54. *New York Times,* 23 February 1905.
55. Ibid., 30 June 1905, p. 2. *Freiheit,* 8 July 1905.

14
PENALTY AND PUNISHMENT

1850: Karl Heinzen arrives in America. He and others reprint his "Murder Against Murder" often before he dies in 1880.

1901, September 17: The Virginia constitutional convention moves to strike the guarantee of free speech, because free speech led to the assassination of the President.

1901: William Randolph Hearst's New York *Journal*, after many anti-McKinley editorials and cartoons, publishes a ditty about stretching the dead McKinley in his bier. In 1902, Hearst is elected to the House of Representatives.

1901: With McKinley the assassinations that substantiated anarchist pretensions cease in the Western democracies. The anarchists' record is a catalogue of stabbings, poisonings, shootings, and bombings that shook corridors of power and knocked at gates of privilege. The era of the anarchist ends, and the catalogue closes.

1902: Lyman Abbott, editor of *Outlook*, asks whether partisan government and unfair law did not justify anarchist anger.

Old Heinzen, the firebrand, recommended murder against murder. I agreed, and got burned.

Most, *Freiheit*, May 3, 1902

The assassination of President McKinley . . . was the outcome of propaganda carried on by Johann Most.

Alfred Vizetelly, *The Anarchists*

I'm all right—as "all right" as one can be in Purgatory.

Most, from Blackwell's Island, February 21, 1903

OFFICIALS AND POLICE

In April of 1892, comrades packed Cooper Union to celebrate Most's release from Blackwell's Island. Forty policemen kept watch. Denouncing the system that sent him to prison, Most hailed anarchism and promised to fight to the end. The audience's breathing became a growl, angry glances flew at the police, and the growl deepened. Police fists tightened on truncheons, police hands crept toward revolvers. But Most finished, the storm passed, and the meeting dispersed. The New York *Times* called him "a very vicious blackguard"; the Island had not reformed him.[1] Agreeing, the police put him at the top of the list of troublemakers. There he was when Czolgosz shot McKinley.

The day of the shooting, *Freiheit* carried "Murder Against Murder," Heinzen's article of fifty years before, a defense of tyrannicide to secure the rights of the people. "Murder" was a favorite of Most's; he had reprinted it several times. "Let murder be our study," it said. "Murder the murderers! Save humanity by blood, iron, poison, and dynamite!" Fifty years old but true yet, Most said.[2]

Knowing the danger of such language, he cursed the coincidence that put "Murder" on the street the same day as the shooting. True, he had never heard of Czolgosz. Yet "in anti-anarchist furor I become a suspicious character of the first magnitude," Most said, recalling the fatal *Freiheit*.[3] Comrades saw danger, too. Sales and renewals of subscriptions fell. Subscribers took new postal boxes, or new lodgings, to avoid *Freiheit*; and hundreds of copies went undelivered. But the recall was too late. A policeman bought one of the few sold, and Most was arrested.

The charge covered five-and-a-half pages. (Pretexts could arrest him and be spun into a tissue of allegations.) At headquarters, chief of detectives Captain Titus waved *Freiheit* at reporters and said, "We can find a place for men who publish such articles as this."[4]

Asked why Most was permitted no visitors, nor to see reporters, nor to issue a statement, Titus said Most would not be allowed to play martyr for the inspiration and agitation of others of his ilk.

Titus himself brought Most to police-court the next morning, early. "Docket for the Court of Special Sessions," the magistrate ordered, and released Most on bail.

Next day, McKinley died. Police commanders called an alert against "anarchists."

Nine evenings later, Most spoke at Frick's Hall, in Corona, Long Island.[5] According to him, the 25 listeners were peaceful. According to police, the 500 were militant. His voice boomed beyond the hall (according to police), the cash register jangled a brisk business in liquor, cheers hailed the liquor's effect, and Captain Hardy of the 77th precinct decided: *Danger. Anarchist meeting. Explosive.* He and Sergeant Baker, with Detectives Shay, Brasby, Kelly, and McCarthy, decided not to wait for reinforcements.

"Police!"

About 200 jackals of anarchy fled (still according to police). The rest encircled Most. The lions of the law marched through them until the lions reached a knot around Most. Heads cracked, scalps bled, the knot loosened, and Hardy collared Most. Hardy's lions handcuffed him, William and Christian Frick, and Adolph Baukuck and took them to headquarters. Hardy brought along as evidence a red cloth which he claimed was a flag, twelve feet by eight and with hemmed edges; it had hung from a staff in the middle of the hall, and around it the jackals rallied. (Most said the "flag" was a rag nailed to the wall as a decoration, which Hardy ripped down to help trump up a case.) Hardy charged Most with suspicious behavior, the Fricks with violating excise laws and keeping a disorderly house, and Baukuck with being drunk and acting contrary to public morality.

Hardy and other police snapped at Most, pushed him around, and roughed him up. They emptied his pockets, hoping to find incriminating evidence, but the bulges were not bombs; they were balls for his sons. Disappointed, the police searched his mind, hoping to find a confession. Readily he said he was fifty-five, married, father of two boys, editor of *Freiheit*, and living at 375 Fifteenth, in Brooklyn. But he had done nothing wrong. His had been a peaceful speech to a peaceful audience on a peaceful occasion with peaceful consequences, until Hardy and his rowdies brought violence.

"Sullen and defiant," said the police; and they locked him up.

Policemen and policewomen came by and glared, but his wife and comrades were kept out.

After his cold and sleepless night, detectives and the district attorney inspected him with evil looks. At 9:00 A.M. they took him, unwashed, uncombed, without breakfast, upstairs to a room where thirty policemen sat in three rows of ten each.

"Men," said Hardy, "this is the anarchist. Take a good look at him. Remember him. If you ever see him in the precinct, nab him!"

Half an hour later, Hardy returned his comb, watch, and money, but not his *Freiheits* and a pamphlet. Potential evidence, they were being translated and studied. Then Hardy and the squad of the previous night pushed him into a wagon, climbed in beside him, and pulled the flag in after them. Wound on a staff, it projected to the front and from the rear and aroused curiosity along the road. Loafers shouted obscenities.

The ride over hill and dale, past forests, across fields, and through boscages (so he remembered) took them to the courthouse in Flushing.

The turnkey locked him in large bright room with a view. The amenities included newspapers. He read the official account of his arrest and fumed. An incendiary speech, an audience of 500 militants, bloody skulls, the flag in the center of the hall—every newspaper proclaimed the same bosh! The police must have concocted it and fed it to the press, to justify assaulting the meeting.

Agreeing the account was bosh, the magistrate cleared him.

A few months later, newspapers said a ruckus in New Irving Hall at 214 Broome, Manhattan, attracted Detectives Walsh, Baxter, and Sheehan to a farewell for Most.[6] In a crowd of 5,000 they

arrested him and William MacQueen for whipping the crowd to a
frenzy by shouting:
"To hell with laws, to hell with government, to hell with Amer-
ica: I am an Anarchist!"
The crowd encircled the detectives and their prisoners. The circle
tightened. The crowd's eyes flashed, feet stamped, mouths opened:
"Most goes to jail tomorrow. Don't take him away from us tonight!"
The detectives drew revolvers.
"We're anarchists," the crowd shrieked. "We're not afraid to die!
Shoot if you dare!"
Police reinforcements arrived and, bludgeoning savage elements,
scattered the crowd.
With Most and MacQueen the police brought along Michael
Mantell, 19, and locked them up for causing a riot. A grilling
brought from Most nothing but the assertion that everything and
everybody were peaceful except the police. He read the official
account and snorted, "A likely story! Five thousand riot and
threaten detectives to the point of gunplay, a riot patrol has to disperse them, and they arrest two men and boy for causing the whole
thing. A likely story indeed!"
But the story turned opinion against him, and the prosecution
cited the story in his hearings and trials.

HEARINGS AND TRIALS

The look on Magistrate Connorton's face "foretold nothing
good," Most said. Connorton read the charges: "unlawful assembly"
and "inciting to riot," in violation of the penal code, section 451.
Captain Hardy testified: "This anarchist came to Corona because
he could not get a hall in Manhattan or Brooklyn. If he can't raise
hell one place, he'll raise it another." Most's attorney Morris Hillquit argued that the police were hounding Most; he did no more
than speak a few benign words at a peaceful and lawful meeting
of the Freiheit Singing Society. District-Attorney O'Leary, saying
he had not had time to gather evidence, asked for a hearing two
days hence. Connorton complied, and fixed bail. "Excessive," Hillquit objected, "a reduction, please?" Refused. Unable to put up

$5,000, Most spent the two days in Queens County Jail in Long Island City.[7]

He came back, Hillquit returned, and witnesses reassembled four more times. Each time, he arrived when the grand jury was adjourning; and its members, passing in single file, stared and cringed "as if I were a wild animal." Each time, O'Leary asked for postponement, citing need to gather evidence; it was hard, he said, to translate and study the documents Most was arrested with. The first time, Hillquit objected. Overruled, said Connorton; a representative of the people deserved every privilege to represent the people. Connorton granted Hillquit's request to reduce bail, and two comrades came forward to post the $1,500.[8] O'Leary asked and Connorton granted that the court examine their credentials. Connorton postponed bail forty-eight hours, to give time for the examination. Hillquit objected that forty-eight hours would keep Most in jail until the next hearing. Connorton agreed, examined the credentials on the spot, and ruled them deficient. Back to jail went Most, four more times.

Prosecution and court (he decided) wanted to cause maximum trouble and inflict supreme hardship; they, scheming prosecution and crooked court, wanted to harrass and discourage witnesses who for each session had to travel from Manhattan and New Jersey and lose a day's wages besides; and they, filthy prosecution and foul court, wanted an opportunity to fabricate evidence and connive at police misconduct.

The fifth time, a magistrate named Healy replaced Connorton. Healy's was "a halfway human face," Most said. Hillquit requested that the hearing proceed. Sustained. O'Leary had evidence neither that Most's speech was inflammatory nor that Most said or did anything to cause riot or disorder. O'Leary's evidence was the flag and nothing else. Most was discharged in time to be tried for "Murder Against Murder."

In that matter he had appeared in the Centre-Street Police-Court, been ordered to the Court of Special Sessions, and posted $500. A nonchalant ruling; minimum bail. Then McKinley died. "Of an anarchist's bullet," newspapers screamed. "Hang anarchists!" When Most appeared in Special Sessions, the court called his case grave and directed him to retain counsel. He retained Hillquit.[9]

Losses in courts in four countries, added to nine years in prison, scared and weakened him. Especially Blackwell's Island had taken a toll. He was fifty-five but, gray and haggard, looked sixty-five and acted seventy-five, limping into court. He clutched the rail and trembled. Every muscle screamed, "We give up; take another step and—fall!"

Hillquit helped him to a seat. Across the room, prosecutor Moses Herrman cleared his throat, frowned over his glasses at Most and Hillquit, smiled at the three judges, and began *People* v. *Johann Most*.[10]

The press asked, "Is it necessary to wait until some criminal anarchist has shot someone, or thrown a bomb, before placing him safely behind bars?" Let us "define by law as criminal all advocacy of assassination as a political method, all participation in meetings in which violence is approved, and all expressions of satisfaction in deeds of violence already committed."[11]

Taking a similar position, Herrman argued violation of the penal code, section 675. Most published a newspaper "reproducing an article, headed in display type 'Murder vs. Murder,' " teaching "the doctrine of anarchy and declaring that all rulers are enemies of mankind who should be hunted and destroyed through blood and iron, poison and dynamite," making Most "guilty of a misdemeanor" even though "it be not shown that the publication of the article was followed by any overt act of physical injury to anyone."[12] Herrman sat down.

Hillquit rose. He was young, studious, vibrant, eager, tireless, sympathetic to Most, and enamored enough of liberal causes to take the case without fee. During Herrman's speech he had made careful and copious notes, leaning over now and again to talk with Most in whispers. He argued:

- "Murder," directed at monarchs, was not meant for democratic leaders.

- Its author and the issues and people that inspired him were dead, long dead.

- It had been reprinted countless times, several by Most himself, without notice by either officials or police.

- Freedom of the press protected Most, absolutely.

- Section 675 was at best vague, often general, and sometimes meaningless; and it mentioned neither anarchists nor agitation. As courts had no right to create and punish crimes not defined by statute or common law, so this court had no right to create a misdemeanor and punish Most as if it had derived a definition from the generalities of section 675.

Hillquit buttressed arguments with an "array of authorities." The judges gave him "maximum praise 'for the able manner in which he conducted the defense and for his able brief' and gave the defendant the maximum penalty allowed by law—imprisonment for one year in the Penitentiary at Blackwell's Island."[13]

Justice Hinsdale wrote the opinion, Justices Holbrook and Wyatt concurring.[14]

- Section 675, deliberately vague, covered crimes incapable of specification; 675 was the flexible section.

- Anarchist crime, though new and novel to the law, was crime nonetheless; anarchists taught destruction and murder.

- Laws on slander and libel laid down and the death of the president confirmed that words can constitute crime; the words of Emma Goldman had inspired the assassin.

- Radicals who teach anarchism must be punished, whether or not the teaching caused crime; one who believes in violence is guilty of actual or potential effects of that belief. "The murder of the President" illustrated "the enormity of the crime of the defendant in teaching his diabolical doctrines."

- Prosecution under section 675 no more destroyed freedom of the press than the law of libel destroyed it.

• "Murder Against Murder" and Most's terrorism were alien to
this country. It would be well if it "could be said truthfully, that no
anarchist can breathe the free air of America."

Hillquit believed, "We had a complete defense in law," but "the
country was aroused against all anarchist agitators, and the courts
were fully responsive." The president, who had wanted to lead
roughriders to shoot strikers in 1886, said in his first annual message, "The man who advocates anarchy directly or indirectly, in
any shape or fashion, or the man who apologizes for anarchists
and their deeds, makes himself morally accessory to murder before
the fact." Hence Most "was convicted not so much because of the
fortuitous and ill-timed reprint of the hoary Heinzen article as for
his general anarchist propaganda."[15]

Most said, "What now? Appeal!"

Yet he knew the quagmires that lined the straits of appeal; experience had taught him the intricacies of law and complications
of courts. Contrary to popular belief, one did not appeal routinely;
a higher court must find for it. And finding did not postpone sentence; postponement took a separate decision. Furthermore, postponement did not spell release; bail had to be posted. Moreover,
bail (itself stiff) was but one of the costs that broke many who
appealed. Finally, appeals usually failed. Looking back in anger at
appeals rejected in four countries, he undertook this appeal with
pessimism. "Come the day when anarchy ends law and abolishes
courts!"[16]

Hence his surprise when Justice Charles F. MacLean, of the New
York Supreme Court's appellate division, granted stay pending appeal. Finding reasonable doubt, MacLean ruled that the prosecution proved only "that the defendant purloined an article, written
by another half a century ago, and published it as his own in a
paper professedly of some circulation, but of which is shown the
sale of but a single copy, that purchased by the policeman probably
for the purpose of prosecution." Moreover, prosecution under the
libel laws or section 675 was unfounded; "it is not shown that the
defendant's expression of borrowed sentiments has worked injury
to any individual by falsifying any fact, or to the public by disturbing or endangering the public peace." Thus MacLean riddled the

prosecution, and Hillquit saw "one ray of judicial enlightenment and courage in the whole litigation."[17]

MacLean postponed sentence and granted $1,500 bail. *Freiheit*'s "Send money, money, and more money" raised $1,500; and Most returned from the Island, free to raise more to pay for the appeal.

He established the "Workingmen's Defense Fund for the Freedom of the Press," and contributions came from across the country. His case was twice postponed, the fund grew, and he took heart: the fund was big enough that, if he lost in the appellate division, he could appeal to the New York Court of Appeals.[18]

In the appellate division, Hillquit stressed that the prosecution conceded the lack of connection between "Murder" and the assassination. Then he elaborated on the arguments he had presented to Special Sessions.

Robert Taylor, representing the district attorney, argued that conviction should be upheld because Most violated 675. Notice the title, "Murder Against Murder." How provocative, Taylor said. And content fulfilled title. Moreover, conviction did not infringe on freedoms of speech and press. The Constitution guaranteed them, but under law; the Constitution did not give the right to commit or encourage crime. Taylor pointed at Most: "Look at him. Look at his record. He is a dangerous agitator!"[19]

The court agreed.

Hillquit hurried to Albany, got a stay to keep Most off the Island, and won appeal to the New York Court of Appeals.

Most and comrades, not sharing Hillquit's hope in this court of last resort, prepared for Most's return to the Island. At the farewell rally, Most and William MacQueen shouted, "To hell with America!" They were arrested and held three days.[20]

"A bully story," thought journalistic punsters. "Let's make the Most of it." They splashed it over the newspapers.

Hillquit delivered a defense consisting of the same points as both before but longer and more elaborate than both before combined. Only, he could not deny Most's cursing America.

Taylor, grinning, offered no argument but trusted the competence of the court; the newspapers were more eloquent than anything he could say.

Justice Vann wrote the unanimous opinion. "Murder" pro-

pounded crime; criminals were ready to take such advice; and the
Constitution neither protected criminals nor sanctioned crime.[21]
Guilty.

Rising, Most upset his chair with a crash, shouting: "This is the
funeral day of the freedom of the American press," then collapsed
in a heap, sobbing. Officers yanked him erect and shoved him out.
His wife embraced and kissed him. The officers hustled him to
Blackwell's Island.

JAILS AND PRISONS

Most and MacQueen, arrested at the farewell rally, were roughed
up, shaken down, and thrown into the Essex Market jail. They
thirsted rather than drink from a putrid faucet over a greasy sink.
They lay on the bed of bare planks and shivered. Most slept fit-
fully, his back against the stone wall. At dawn he woke with his
back aching, joints grating, still shivering and too hoarse to talk.

At 9:00 A.M., detectives pushed them into a bare room and stood
them back to back at attention under a harsh lamp. Round and
round the detectives stalked, like dogs holding game at bay, growl-
ing insults and snarling questions.

"Oh, you want breakfast, you want coffee, you want brandy, do
you, bully boys? Well, suppose you sing for them. When's the next
rally, and where, and who's going to speak?

"Oh, you can't talk—you're hoarse, you've got a cold. You could
talk last night, though, couldn't you? And what did you say, besides
'To hell with America'? Eh?"

MacQueen especially they battered with the foulest of words and
lashed with the sharpest of tongues. Having played this game many
times, Most knew the object: provocation.

Failing to provoke and to extract information, the detectives
shoved them into a wagon, hauled them to Essex Market courthouse, and pushed them into a corral with others waiting a turn in
court. Passers-by peered in and hooted. "They round 'em up like
cattle, don't they, by golly!" An old woman pointed an umbrella
and cackled. A little boy stuck out his tongue and snickered. When
comrades and Helen Most approached, guards elbowed them away

and told them to get lost. Christian Heller, a teen-age comrade, ducked under a guard's arm, rattled the gate, and screamed he would "break Most out." A giant of a guard, brandishing a revolver, said Heller could "damn well break himself out," and pushed him in.

After three hours, Most and MacQueen went before the magistrate but heard only cryptic whispers between him and their attorney. Next they were locked in the adjoining room, perplexed. Then they were told that Heller had been let go with a warning; MacQueen could leave, comrades having posted bail; and Most, already convicted for publishing "Murder Against Murder," was to go to the Tombs and thence to the Island.[22]

He was greeted politely at the Tombs and shown to a clean bright cell. For improved conditions and changed treatment he could not account but enjoyed nonetheless. Although time and travail had damaged him (he was starting to wrinkle and stoop and lose his teeth), he remained in essence the Most of the last forty years. Eagerly he read books he had been meaning to read for months. Vigorously he wrote letters to comrades and copy for *Freiheit*. And when cells were opened between 2:00 and 4:00 P.M., he bounced everywhere and buttonholed everyone and talked and talked and talked.[23]

On the Island a barber shaved his face and cropped his hair, those shaggy objects of derision to people who hated the unconventional in dress and despised the radical in grooming. The barber swept up a pile of hair six inches deep, filled a bag, and said: "I can get a dollar a lock. The hair off this son of a bitch is worth more than this son of a bitch himself."[24]

To anarchist-haters like the barber, Most's face personified anarchism. Leering, the barber turned to the light the face twisted since adolescence into a wrinkled lurid malformed knot: newly exposed, reddened by rough soap and coarse towels, and cut here and there by the arrogant razor. Guards and barbers and prisoners pointed, sneered, and laughed, laughed, laughed. They had fastened on Most the way dogs fasten on a wounded dog.

Then they took him to his cell, six feet by eight, of iron and stone. Without a window, with a grating for a door, the cell sug-

gested a cage from which had flown the sweet bird of youth, leaving to an old man a year that might kill him.

Next morning, very much alive, he joined the hubbub.

> My day goes like this. At 6:00 the tocsin—general uproar,
> washing en masse and in a mad dance around the common trough.
> At 7:00 collective (march lockstep) to the assembly rooms (mess
> hall)—mass feeding of the beasts. Coffee and bread, with jelly,
> Sundays and Mondays; hash Tuesdays, Thursdays, and Saturdays;
> oatmeal and syrup Wednesdays and Fridays. Return to the cage
> in fifteen minutes. At 7:30 the parade of the excrement-buckets.
> Afterwards the march to the iron hammer. . . . At noon, feeding
> again; and sit huddled in a "closed society" until 1:00. Photo-
> graphed in this position from the bird's eye view we would look
> like a bowl of stewed dumplings, so closely we sit and so brightly
> our shaved scalps shine—even in winter. As much bread and
> water as you want; corned beef and beans Sundays; barley and
> mutton Tuesdays and Thursdays; barley soup and beef Mondays
> and Saturdays; corned beef and peas Wednesdays; fish, potatoes,
> and coffee Fridays. No knives, no forks: tear like a wild animal
> at the meat with hands and teeth (those who have teeth—what
> about me??). Then back to the smithy until 5:30. Again march to
> feeding—bread and coffee. Then the definitive march to the cage
> —lights out at 9:30—the end: the sleep of the just. Saturdays
> return to the cage at noon and stay until Monday morning, except
> for the marches to bathe, feed, and dump excrement.[25]

The goal of this penology, humiliation, was reached. Even a cold
humiliated, because when noses were wiped on sleeves soaked with
snot, where was dignity? Where was it in a shaved head? In marching in lockstep? In emptying and cleaning an excrement-bucket? In
taking a shower step by step on command?

"Strip!"

(One minute.)

"In!"

(One minute.)

"Out!"

(Ten seconds.)

"Wipe!"

(Thirty seconds.)

"Dress!"

(One minute.)

"Forward march!"

Where was dignity in toweling on the common towel thrown over a radiator to dry and used again and again without laundering? One syphilitic put it to his crotch and another used it on his face. It made the genteel puke on it, which might get it laundered in a week or two.

Where was dignity in sleeping on wire mesh without a mattress? Two horse blankets, issued when the prisoner arrived, stayed with him until he left, without cleaning. The straw pillow that crackled turned soon into a soggy lump, which he also kept until he left. Linen there was none.

Where was dignity in eating like animals herded into a pen? In being fed "mutton—a greasy mess suited for making soap"? "Beef —dog food! Corned beef—probably condemned rations from the Spanish-American War. Codfish—rotten wood that tastes like mold. Pea soup—alive with bugs. Barley, cabbage, and carrot dishes— seasoned and garnished with splinters, hair, thread, and mouse dung. Soups—prepared in rusty tin containers. Bread—sawdust mixed with cigar ash. Any prisoner can eat his fill, provided he has the stomach of a pig."

Years ago the prisoner could receive food from outside. But reforms restricted its entry now ("Unhealthy, you know, my good man, all this slop from outside"), and the prisoner could get only one package of food a month. This food had to be canned, to prevent spoilage; and the cans small, to minimize theft. Either the prisoner ate it at once, or carried it always, or hid it, or it was stolen.

Where was dignity when, from morning until night, Deputy-Warden MacManus prowled like Paul Pry—listening, looking, scolding, bullying? He elaborated the stool-pigeon system, hiring the evilest to betray the rest. Because terms were shortened on his recommendation, stool pigeons zealously watched and eagerly listened during work, and spied and eavesdropped evenings and weekends. A pigeon slinking barefoot down corridors and peeping into cells might discover tobacco, newspapers, pencils, knives, writing paper, or masturbation; run hotfoot to MacManus; win discharge three months early; and gloat over the three months added to the term of the one caught.

Wrongdoers could also expect ball and chain; flogging; fetters, manacles, and shackles; hanging by wrists or thumbs (for hours, toes able barely to touch the floor, by stretching); and blocking of the anus. Officials' delight and prisoners' terror was solitary confinement—its darkness, its slice of bread and pint of water a day, and its gift of rheumatism perhaps for life. Any infraction could bring two or three days there. Or the wrongdoer might get off with loss of light, loss of mail, loss of reading—any one or all together—for fifty days or more.

Where was dignity when smoking was prohibited? "I chew tobacco like a full-blooded Yankee," Most said. He spat into his excrement-bucket in his cell and into greasy rags at work.

Where was dignity when once every four weeks one letter could be written on one sheet of paper, in ten minutes, under the eye of a guard and subject to approval by the censor? To Most, infected with *cacoëthes scribendi*, this restriction was the hottest fire in the hell of Blackwell's Island. Nevertheless, his dispatches appeared regularly in *Freiheit*, signed Ahasuerus; he had not renounced talent at subterfuge or lost genius for smuggling.

So there was no dignity when, a few days before his release, officials crowded up to his cell and goggled.

"You think this is a zoo," he shouted.

He opened his excrement-bucket, turned his backside to them, lowered his trousers, and noisily relieved himself.

With that act of propaganda-by-the-deed he ended his term and closed "these sad 'Reminiscences and Reflections.' May the time soon come when such dungeons go the way of the Bastille!"

NOTES

1. *New York Times*, 21 April 1892, p. 1; *see also* 25 March 1894, p. 4. *Freiheit*, 30 April 1892.
2. *Freiheit*, 7 September 1901.
3. Ibid., 21 September 1901.
4. Ibid. *See also New York Times*, 13 September 1901, p. 1. *Volkszeitung* (New York), 14 September 1901.
5. *New York Times*, 23 September 1901, p. 1. *Freiheit*, 28 September and 3 October 1901. *Volkszeitung* (New York), 28 September 1901.
6. *Freiheit*, 10 May 1902. *New York Times*, 5 May 1902, p. 1.

7. *New York Times*, 24 September 1901, p. 2. *Freiheit*, 28 September 1901. *Volkszeitung* (New York), 28 September 1901.

8. *New York Times* 1901: 1 October, p. 10; 3 October, p. 14. *Freiheit*, 5 October 1901.

9. Court of Special Sessions, New York City, 36 (October 1901): 139. Morris Hillquit, *Loose Leaves from a Busy Life*, p. 125.

10. *New York Times*, 15 October 1901, p. 16. *Volkszeitung* (New York), 15 October 1901. *Freiheit*, 19 October 1901.

11. "Anarchism and the Law," pp. 2187-89.

12. Court of Special Sessions, New York City, 36 (October 1901): 139.

13. Hillquit, *Loose Leaves*, pp. 126-27.

14. Court of Special Sessions, New York City, 36 (October 1901): 140-45.

15. Hillquit, *Loose Leaves*, p. 127.

16. *Freiheit*, 19 October 1901.

17. Hillquit, *Loose Leaves*, pp. 127-28.

18. *Freiheit*, 18 January and 8 February 1902.

19. Ibid., 29 March 1902.

20. Ibid., 10 May 1902. *New York Times*, 5 May 1902, p. 1.

21. *New York Times*, 11 June 1902, p. 6. *Freiheit* 14 June 1902.

22. *Freiheit*, 10 May 1902.

23. Ibid., 28 June 1902.

24. Ibid., 25 April 1903.

25. Ibid., 8 November 1902. The rest of this chapter is assembled from Most, "Reminiscenzen und Reflexionen eines 'Ex-Convicts.' "

15

THE FINAL DAYS

1892: Among militia mustered to break the Homestead strike, a militiaman named W. L. Iams proposes, "Three cheers for the man who shot Frick!" Court-martialed and strung up by the thumbs, Iams still wants those cheers. A disciplinary barber cuts off half his hair and half his beard, and a disciplinary drummer drums him to dishonorable discharge.

1901: The state of New York destroys Czolgosz's corpse with quicklime and acid.

1901: Emma Goldman, in court again, remains the second woman in American history, first since Mary Surratt, to be tried for political crimes.

1906: Britain's Winston Churchill reads *The Jungle* and says, "The issue between capital and labor is far more clearly cut today [in America] than in other communities or in any other age."

1915: Joe Hill, of the Industrial Workers of the World, songwriter and agitator, dies before a firing squad at the Utah penitentiary.

1917: Masked men pull IWW organizer Frank Little out of bed, drag him to a railway trestle, and hang him, broken leg and all.

1917: Emma Goldman and Alexander Berkman, 2 of 3,000 arrested for violating the Espionage Act, begin two years in prison.

1919: Grant Hamilton cartoons a scowling Uncle Sam pushing a boat jammed with anarchists "back to where they came from." Above the crowds on the decks signs protrude: "Kill," "Destroy," and "Down with the government." Caption: "The alien will do anything for his fatherland except go back to it and he seems determined to do anything to the land of his adoption—his step-fatherland—except leave it."

1919: Goldman and Berkman sail on the USS *Buford*. The leaky "Red Ark" carries 249 communist and anarchist deportees to Finland and Russia. Thus, former pupils of the late Johann Most are (in Goldman's words) "cast out, pursued by the furies, and nowhere at home."

1927: Nicola Sacco and Bartolomeo Vanzetti fry, in Massachusetts, after giving American liberalism its *cause célèbre*. Judge Webster Thayer: "Did you see what I did with those anarchist bastards?"

Wherever the cause of revolution is to be advanced, there he will advance it. His propagandizing for anarchism, and his agitation for social revolution, will end only when his life ends.

Most, of himself, in *Acht Jahre hinter Schloss und Riegel*

About my own fate I am the sourest of pessimists.

Most, *Freiheit*, February 8, 1890

The death of Johann Joseph Most removes one of the picturesque figures of the day.

The New York *Tribune*, March 18, 1906

Most promised an anarchist earthquake, but in 1906 the San Francisco earthquake shook the country more than anarchists could shake it. Justus Schwab was dead; and his saloon, once center, symbol, and inspiration, was closed. Robert Reitzel was dead; and his

Arme Teufel, once second only to *Freiheit*, was defunct. Emma Goldman was an ex-convict; and her once vibrant (now dogged) hope for an anarchist future suffered harrassment, imprisonment again, and deportation. Alexander Berkman, released in 1906 after fourteen years behind bars, never again had three happy days in a row. Anti-anarchism made his life and Goldman's miserable; executed the Haymarket anarchists and Leon Czolgosz; found voice in Theodore Roosevelt and prompted action in Congress; hailed anti-anarchist legislation and applauded the pugnacity with which it was enforced; sent Most three times to prison and muffled his terrorism; harrassed, imprisoned, and deported hundreds besides Goldman and Berkman; and maligned and executed Sacco and Vanzetti. Never again the anarchist prosperity of 1878-1883 and 1890-1895. In 1906, on once-radical corners of the Lower East Side, Most climbed a soapbox twice as high and shouted twice as loud to attract half the crowd. Most, once eloquent, was intellectually disheveled: disorganized, discursive, disjointed, discombobulated. People more often jeered than applauded and left before he finished, chuckling about *that crank*. The era of the anarchist was over. Most's terrorism had failed. Success had run like mercury through his fingers, seen and touched but never held in arms that reached and hands that stretched too far.

Yet he refused to mark anarchism's demise and heed terrorism's death. Sixty years weakened and tired him but did not diminish his élan. "To anarchism belongs the future," he proclaimed to dwindling listeners. "For every minute not ours today, an eon shall be ours tomorrow."[1]

He began another agitation-tour, in Massachusetts, and got support, even met some fervor, in Fitchburg, Lawrence, Lynn, Lowell, and Boston.

Back in New York City, announcing the rest of his itinerary, he said: "Most is in action. Let comrades know and rejoice! Let the world hear and tremble!" He would be gone a month, with rallies and speeches in McKeesport, Pittsburgh, Philadelphia, Cincinnati, Chicago, Milwaukee, Detroit, Cleveland, and Buffalo. He expected to return with money in his pocket, subscriptions and pledges in his hand, and a revitalized movement at his back. "Look what I did in 1872 and 1873, you little-faiths, and take heart! Look what I did in 1882 and 1883, you capitalists, and despair!" And he planned to agitate in the West again soon, in a tour bigger than the one of 1899-1900.[2]

After successes in McKeesport and Pittsburgh he arrived in Philadelphia. Voltairine de Cleyre called a meeting to celebrate his birthday. He walked in one door, and police rushed in the other. Lieutenant Atkinson dragged de Cleyre from the platform. Comrades resisted but could not stand against truncheons. Atkinson told her and comrades to "go to hell" and Most to "get out of town." Atkinson's men took Most through a downpour to the train station and put him soaked and chilled on the train to Cincinnati.[3]

His clothes dried on his back, then were soaked again by sweat. Chilled by cold wind, he shivered to the door of Cincinnati comrades Adolph and Pepi Kraus, shook hands, begged forgiveness for exhaustion, and lay down on the sofa for his first rest in days.

His face reddened. His mouth opened in a rictus of agony. Adolph and Pepi touched his face, looked at each other, and said, "Hot."

"Leave me alone! Don't you know I'm expected at a meeting in Chicago? Let me go! I can't disappoint them. I must not!"

Breathing heavily, he lay with eyes closed. Then his breathing slowed and lightened.

He woke. His fever rose. A deep-red inflammation spread over his skin. He recited old speeches. Dr. Joseph Meitus diagnosed "St. Anthony's fire," malignant erysipelas. Frowning, Meitus administered an antitoxin, the last resort. Most complained because he could not continue his tour.

He called Adolph, took Adolph's hand, and with weird light in his eyes said, "The Cause grows stronger. The people are awakening; they are looking for something better."

He squeezed Adolph's hand. The effort was great, the pressure slight. "I love the Cause. I have given my life to it."

Comrades came, opened pocketbooks, and asked, "Does he want for medical aid? Does he need a nurse?"

Adolph blinked back tears. "No. I will care for him. I will spend my last cent. Thank you."

They prevailed on Adolph through Pepi to rest; and he slept, after four days at Most's side. Two comrades attended Most.

Mail brought offers of aid and aid itself, in notes and coin. Comrade Nicholas Klein began a subscription for Most's wife and children, who could not leave New York until they found money for tickets.

Most recited speeches given in Vienna, Mainz, Berlin, London, New York . . . in the German parliament . . . in St. Louis, Chicago, San Francisco, Brussels. . . . He feared he could not keep engagements. He screamed in fear, shouted with rage, and babbled out of stupor, one at a time and all at once.

He went blind. He spoke of the people, of hope for their liberation. He rubbed his face, as if to wipe away fever and lift shades. He called for his wife.

"Helen! If only Helen were here! She would set things right!"

Between Monday and Friday he went from stronger to weaker, weaker to stronger, in cycles.

Friday, Adolph whispered to Pepi that fresh underwear was needed.

"Hey, hey!" shouted Most. "You want everything, down to my skin—and I'm not even dead!"

His strongest voice in days.

Adolph and Pepi and comrades took hope. With high hearts they watched the night through. Soon (they said) Helen would be here, capable Helen. She would head him toward recovery.

In the morning, with twice the energy, he lamented breaking engagements. Those people left waiting! He could not be kept in bed. He silenced requests and slapped hands that would restrain him. He punched arms and contradicted pleas that would keep him from the Cause. He fumbled, blind yet, about the room, then dropped, wheezing, into a chair. His head sank. A deep breath. . . .

Pepi to Adolph and comrades: "Be quiet. Leave him alone. Sleep will do him good."

Later she made broth.

Holding a steaming bowl in one hand, she touched his with the other. "Here's a good hot broth, to make you strong."

His hand was cold, arm stiff.

She recoiled, spilled broth, and screamed.

Soon Helen was there. He had been brave, they told her. He had called for her.

She wanted to take the body back to New York. Fearing contagion, the authorities forbade it.

Hundreds gathered at the crematorium. One said, "I never met him, I never wanted to, but I want to say goodbye." Wreaths of smilax and bouquets of red flowers tied with red ribbons decorated the coffin. The choir sang "The Son of the People" and the "Marseillaise." Selections were read aloud from his works. Eulogies lauded an honest sincere man, a martyr, a hero. The choir sang "Goodbye." For days after, Pepi with a tear-stained face received flowers and condolences.

Helen carried the ashes back to New York, to flag-decked full-to-overflowing Grand Central Palace. Most's "Workingmen" boomed from thousands of throats, Chopin's "Funeral March" raised tears in thousands of eyes, and eight orators in four languages extolled "the last of the greats . . . an original . . . generous . . . stalwart . . . noble . . . courageous . . . a nonesuch . . . a beacon . . . our leader . . . what a loss!"

Our soul
Had *felt* him like the thunder's roll.

Jenkintown—Philadelphia—Glenside
March 1976—June 1979

NOTES

1. *Freiheit*, 17 February 1906.
2. Ibid., 3 March 1906.
3. Ibid., 17 March 1906. *New York Tribune*, 18 March 1906. The rest of this chapter is assembled chiefly from *Freiheit*, 31 March and 7 April 1906. *See also Cincinnati Enquirer*, 16, 17, 18, 21, 22 March 1906; *Cincinnati Post*, 16, 17, 20, 21 March 1906; *New York Tribune*, 19 March 1906.

APPENDIX A:_____
Chronology: Johann Most,
1846-1906_____

From the time he landed he was a storm centre. His campaign against the established order of things took him to different parts of the country, and there is hardly a city in the United States where he did not address his anarchistical followers.

The New York Times, of Most, March 18, 1906

1846, February 5: Born in Augsburg, Bavaria.

1848: Parents marry.

1856: Mother dies of cholera.

1858: Expelled from secondary school. Apprenticed to bookbinder named Weber.

1859: Operation mutilates his face.

1863: Beginning of 5-year *Wanderschaft* in Germany, Italy, Hungary, Switzerland, and Austria.

1868: In Zurich until autumn. Member of workers' association called Harmony. Friendly with Herman Greulich, the outstanding figure in the Swiss labor movement for the next fifty years, and learns labor agitation. Unfit for military service because of mutilated face. Joins labor movement in Vienna in October.

1869, May 30: Speech to a meeting of 10,000 workers gets him a month's close confinement and denunciation by newspapers as an impudent bookbinder.

1870, March 2: Arrested as one of the leaders of the December 13 demonstration against parliament. July 4-19: Convicted of high treason and sentenced to five years in prison at Suben. Composes

poetry, including *"Arbeitsmänner"* (Workingmen), which becomes a socialist anthem.

1871: Amnestied in February. Banished from Austria in May. Begins
career in Bavaria as a leader of Social Democracy. To Chemnitz,
Saxony. In a smashing success of a speech says workers will get
the 10-hour day when they fight for it. Becomes editor of the
Chemnitz *Freie Presse* in June. Police break up his speeches on
the Commune. Delegate to party congress in Dresden in August.
Leads strike in Chemnitz in autumn. Jailed in the "Red Tower"
in Chemnitz.

1872: Organizes and leads party congress at Mainz. Convicted of lese
majesty for speeches during celebration of Sedan in Chemnitz.

1873: Studies French in Saxon state prison at Zwickau and proves a
feckless linguist. Makes digest of Marx's *Capital*; first printing
sells out. Leaves prison in October. Marries Klara Hänsch.

1874: To parliament, and becomes editor of *Volksstimme* in Mainz, in
January. Prosecuted in April by the district attorney of Prussia,
Hermann Tessendorf, for speech on the Commune in March.
Begins 26-month term at Plötzensee in September.

1876: Editor of the Berlin *Freie Presse*. Essay in praise of Eugen Dühring prompts Engels's *Anti-Dühring*. Lectures in Berlin on solution to the social question, a definitive statement of his Social
Democratic position, published as pamphlet. Meets August
Reinsdorf.

1877: Reelected to parliament, one of eight Social Democratic deputies. Prevents publication of *Anti-Dühring* in *Vorwärts*, at party
congress in May. Attacks Theodor Mommsen with lectures "on
the social revolution and Caesarism in ancient Rome" in July
and August.

1878: Debates Adolph Stoecker at mass meeting to found Stoecker's
Christian Socialist party and hinders formation of the party, in
January. Leads leave-the-churches movement. July 30: Loses
seat in parliament. October 23: His Berlin *Freie Presse* suppressed under the Anti-Socialist Law. December 16: Released
after five months in Plötzensee. Expelled from Berlin. To
London.

1879, January 3: First issue of *Freiheit*, subtitled "An Organ of Social
Democracy." March 18: Speech to English, French, and German radicals, hailing unity of international socialism and urging
preparation for coming struggles. *Sozialdemokrat* appears in
October and angers him into turning left. Dines often with Vic-

tor Dave and August Reinsdorf (anarchists), Wilhelm Hasselmann (social revolutionary), and Éduard Vaillant (Blanquist
and Communard). They teach him what they believe. Meets
John Neve.

1880: European leftists read *Freiheit* and like Most's ideas; the more
radical the leftists, the more popular the ideas. Social Democrats
publicly divorce themselves of identification with him. He spoils
their Rohrschach congress in May. Reinsdorf's articles on anarchism appear in *Freiheit* in July. Continental followers organize
into cells. Social Democrats expel him from the party, at Wyden,
Switzerland, in August. Dave and associates arrested in Leipzig
in December; the Continental organization smashed.

1881: A black-bordered *Freiheit* commemorates death of Blanqui.
March 15: Most holds rally celebrating assassination of the
Czar. March 30: Arrested for article of March 19 in praise of the
assassination. March 31 and April 7: Arraigned in Bow-Street
Police-Court. May 25-26: Tried in Central Criminal Court.
June 18: Conviction appealed. June 29: Sentenced to sixteen
months at hard labor in Clerkenwell.

1882: *Freiheit* subtitled "An Organ of the Revolutionary Socialists."
Klara Hänsch Most dies. June 3: Last British issue of *Freiheit*.
October 25: Most released from Clerkenwell. December 2: Sails
from Liverpool for New York; arrives December 18. Speaks at
Cooper Union. Begins agitation-tour. The Chicago *Times* of December 25 says, "The king-killer is here for speeches and other
radical mischief."

1883: On tour; speeches in Baltimore, Boston, Buffalo, Chicago, Cincinnati, Cleveland, Detroit, Kansas City (Missouri), Louisville,
Milwaukee, Omaha, Philadelphia, Pittsburgh, St. Joseph (Missouri), St. Louis, and Washington, D.C. The Milwaukee *Sentinel*
of January 6: he "cries aloud for buckets of gore." Until 1895
he inspires and leads a growing German anarchist movement in
America. October 16: Pittsburgh Proclamation published.

1884: On tour; speeches in Buffalo, Chicago, Cincinnati, Cleveland,
Denver, Detroit, Indianapolis, Lawrence (Massachusetts), Milwaukee, Omaha, Philadelphia, Pittsburgh, St. Joseph (Missouri),
and St. Louis. February 16: Speaks at mass meeting in Irving
Hall, New York City, to commemorate Hermann Stellmacher
and others who killed Viennese policemen: "Murder is the killing of a human being, and a policeman is not a human being."
May 24: Debates Paul Grottkau in Chicago. August 2: An-

nounces he is an anarchist, in article in *Freiheit*: "To the Anarchists of the World." Takes job in munitions factory in Jersey City.

1885: Speaking at memorials for August Reinsdorf (February 7) and Julius Lieske (November 29) in New York City, he calls them martyrs to the great Revolution. July 4: *Freiheit* becomes the "International Organ of German-Speaking Anarchists." July 18: *The Science of Revolutionary Warfare* issued; price: ten cents. Weekly ads: "Every revolutionary should have a copy." December 12: *Science* is in third printing.

1886, March 27: Benjamin Tucker's "firebug article" in *Liberty*: Most's followers, not by Most's instigation but with Most's knowledge, burn property to collect insurance. April 23: In speech at Germania Garden, New York City, Most urges arming and brandishes a rifle; arrested May 11; tried May 27-30; sentenced June 2.

1887, April 1: Released from Blackwell's Island. April 4: Speech at Cooper Union to thousands celebrating his release. September 12: Rejected for American citizenship. Early November: John Bonfield, captain of Chicago police, travels to New York City and adjures arrest of Most. November 12: Most speaks on the execution of the Haymarket anarchists; arrested for it November 16. December 8: Sentenced to year on Blackwell's Island. On bail pending appeal, until 1891. *Freiheit's* circulation is 8,000.

1888: Testifies before the House Committee on Immigration; favors immigration. The Committee concludes: immigration threatens national security.

1889: Meets Emma Goldman.

1890, January 25: Arrested. January 27: Released from the Tombs, pending second appeal. On tour; speeches in Baltimore, Cincinnati, Cleveland, Philadelphia, Pittsburgh, and St. Louis. March 22: Speaks under red flags and red banners in Turner Hall, Cincinnati, to large enthusiastic audience tricked out in red shirts, red dresses, red carnations, and red ideas. June 8: The Cleveland *Plain Dealer* remarks on Most's little eyes and puffy cheeks. November 7: Newark police disperse the audience and in a closed carriage haul away the speakers: Most, Lucy Parsons, and Hugh O. Pentecost. December 29: The Baltimore *American*: "Most's loose tongue wagging all day Sunday."

1891, June 16: Begins second term on Blackwell's Island.

1892, April 20: Released. Leftists pay ten cents each, crowd Cooper
Union, and welcome him back in what the New York *Times* calls
"a monster mass meeting." August 27: Opposes Berkman's attempt to assassinate Henry Clay Frick; publishes "Reflections on
Assassination" in *Freiheit*. December 18: Emma Goldman horse-
whips him. *Freiheit*'s circulation is 4,300.

1893: Marries Helen Minkin.

1894: Produces, directs, and stars in Hauptmann's *Weavers*; house fills
nightly during week in Chicago. Speaks at Haymarket memorials. November 17: Addresses 500 cheering leftists in Cleveland
amid "red flags, vile tobacco, and lots of beer," says the *Plain
Dealer*.

1895, June 15: *Freiheit* changes from Gothic to Roman type. On tour
with Charles W. Mowbray and Lucy Parsons, Most speaks in
Baltimore, Buffalo, Chicago, Detroit, Fitchburg (Massachusetts),
Milwaukee, New Haven, Philadelphia, Pittsburgh, and Water-
bury (Connecticut).

1896: Produces and stars in repertory of anti-capitalist plays in New
York City's Thalia Theatre. On tour; speeches in Buffalo, Chicago, Cleveland, Detroit, Milwaukee, Philadelphia, and Pittsburgh. *Freiheit*'s circulation is 5,000.

1897: *Freiheit* reduces dimensions, increases pages, and becomes the
"International Organ of German-Speaking Communists." In fi-
nancial straits, Most goes to Buffalo to edit the *Arbeiterzeitung*.
Meets Kropotkin.

1898: Returns to New York City and calls Buffalo the asshole of the
world. Says war with Spain is war of, by, and for plutocracy, like
all wars.

1899: The biggest tour of his career lasts until spring of 1900; speeches
in Baltimore, Boston, Bridgeport (Connecticut), Buffalo, Chicago, Cincinnati, Cleveland, Denver, Detroit, Fitchburg (Massachusetts), Louisville, Meriden (Connecticut), Milwaukee, New
Bedford, New Haven, Omaha, Philadelphia, Pittsburgh, Portland (Oregon), Providence, St. Louis, San Francisco, Seattle, and
Washington, D.C. November 13: The *Cincinnatier Zeitung*:
"Most, since his last visit, has grown snow-white, but retains
physical robustness and mental vigor."

1901: Meets Kropotkin in April. Plays himself in *The Strike* in May
and June. September 6: Publishes "Murder Against Murder";
arrested for it September 12. September 16: Arraigned in Centre-
Street Police-Court; released on bail. September 23: Arraigned

in Flushing for speech on Long Island. October 14: Convicted in Court of Special Sessions, for "Murder." October 15: Taken to Blackwell's Island. October 29: Released pending appeal.

1902, April 11: New York Supreme Court's appellate division upholds the conviction. April 18: Stay granted pending appeal to New York State Court of Appeals. May 4: Arrested with William MacQueen for utterances that attribute to the United States a canine ancestry and for shouting: "To hell with America!"; released on bail. June 10: Conviction upheld. June 20: Sentenced to third term on Blackwell's Island.

1903, April 11: Comrades welcome his release two months early for good behavior.

1904, January 1: *Freiheit*'s Silver Jubilee celebrated in Bronx Casino. November 19: The Indianapolis *News* sees Most "wearing a broad-brimmed felt hat, with spectacles on the end of his prominent nose," and hears him call labor leaders "weak, ignorant, or open to purchase by the opposition."

1905, February 23: He and comrades celebrate assassination of Archduke Sergius. June 30: They rejoice at mutiny on the *Potemkin*. November 11: He and Lucy Parsons share the platform in the commemoration of Haymarket. *Freiheit*'s circulation is 3,500.

1906, March 17: Dies in Cincinnati. The Philadelphia *Inquirer* says he was "known throughout the world as an Anarchist leader, lecturer, and writer." April 1: Memorial in Grand Central Palace, New York City; eulogists include Lucy Parsons, Max Baginski, Abraham Isaak, and Emma Goldman. Death spares him arrest and deportation under the Espionage Act. Helen Most, Max Baginski, and Frank Thaumazo continue *Freiheit* until 1909.

APPENDIX B:_____
The Pittsburgh Proclamation_____

Comrades!

In the Declaration of Independence of the United States we read: "When a long Train of Abuses and Usurpations, pursuing invariably the same Object, evinces a Design to reduce them under absolute Despotism, it is their Right, it is their Duty, to throw off such Government, and to provide new Guards for their future Security."

Has the moment not arrived to heed the advice of Thomas Jefferson, the true founder of the American Republic? Has government not become oppression?

And is our government anything but a conspiracy of the ruling classes against the people—against you?

Comrades! Hear what we have to say. Read our manifesto [this Proclamation], written in your interest and for the welfare of your wives and children and toward the good of humanity and progress.

Our present society is founded upon the exploitation of the propertyless class by the propertied. This exploitation is such that the propertied (capitalists) buy the working force body and soul of the propertyless, for the price of the mere cost of existence (wages) and take for themselves, i.e., steal the amount of new values (products) which exceeds the price, whereby wages are made to represent the necessities instead of the earnings of the wage-laborer.

As the non-possessing classes are forced by their poverty to offer for sale to the propertied their working forces, and as our present production on a grand scale enforces technical development with immense rapidity, so that by the application of an always decreasing number of [the] human working force, an always increasing amount of products is created; so does the supply of working force increase constantly, while

From *Freiheit*, 27 December 1890, official English version.

the demand therefor decreases. This is the reason why the workers com-
pete more and more intensely in selling themselves, causing their wages
to sink, or at least on the average, never raising them above the margin
necessary for keeping intact their working ability.

Whilst by this process the propertyless are entirely debarred from
entering the ranks of the propertied, even by the most strenuous exer-
tions, the propertied, by means of the ever-increasing plundering of the
working class, are becoming richer day by day, without in any way
being themselves productive.

If now and then one of the propertyless class become rich it is not by
their own labor but from opportunities which they have to speculate
upon, and absorb the labor-product of others.

With the accumulation of individual wealth, the greed and power of
the propertied grows. They use all the means for competing among
themselves for the robbery of the people. In this struggle generally the
less-propertied (middle-class) are overcome, while the great capitalists,
par excellence, swell their wealth enormously, concentrate entire
branches of production as well as trade and intercommunication into
their hands and develop into monopolists. The increase of products,
accompanied by simultaneous decrease of the average income of the
working mass of the people, leads to so-called "business" and "commercial" crises, when the misery of the wage-workers is forced to the
extreme.

For illustration: the last census of the United States shows that after
deducting the cost of raw material, interest, rents, risks, etc., the propertied class have absorbed—i.e., stolen—more than five-eighths of all
products, leaving scarcely three-eighths to the producers. The propertied class, being scarcely one-tenth of our population, and in spite of
their luxury and extravagance, and unable to consume their enormous
"profits," and the producers, unable to consume more than they receive
—three-eighths—so-called "over-productions" must necessarily take
place. The terrible results of panics are well known.

The increasing eradication of working forces from the productive
process annually increases the percentage of the propertyless population, which becomes pauperized and is driven to "crime," vagabondage,
prostitution, suicide, starvation and general depravity. This system is
unjust, insane and murderous. It is therefore necessary to totally destroy
it with and by all means, and with the greatest energy on the part of
every one who suffers by it, and who does not want to be made culpable
for its continued existence by his inactivity.

Agitation for the purpose of organization; organization for the purpose of rebellion. In these few words the ways are marked which the workers must take if they want to be rid of their chains; as the economic condition is the same in all countries of so-called "civilization"; as the governments of all Monarchies and Republics work hand in hand for the purpose of opposing all movements of the thinking part of the workers; as finally the victory in the decisive combat of the proletarians against their oppressors can only be gained by the simultaneous struggle along the whole line of the bourgeois (capitalistic) society, so therefore the international fraternity of people as expressed in the International Working People's Association presents itself a self-evident necessity.

True order should take its place. This can only be achieved when all implements of labor, the soil and other premises of production, in short, capital produced by labor, is changed into societary property. Only by this presupposition is destroyed every possibility of the future spoilation of man by man. Only by common, undivided capital can all be enabled to enjoy in their fullness the fruits of the common toil. Only by the impossibility of accumulating individual (private) capital can everyone be compelled to work who makes a demand to live.

This order of things allows production to regulate itself according to the demand of the whole people, so that nobody need work more than a few hours a day, and that all nevertheless can satisfy their needs. Hereby time and opportunity are given for opening to the people the way to the highest possible civilization; the privileges of higher intelligence fall with the privileges of wealth and birth. To the achievement of such a system the political organizations of the capitalistic classes—be they Monarchies or Republics—form the barriers. These political structures (States), which are completely in the hands of the propertied, have no other purpose than the upholding of the present disorder of exploitation.

All laws are directed against the working people. In so far as the opposite appears to be the case, they [laws] serve on one hand to blind the worker, while on the other hand they are simply evaded. Even the school serves only the purpose of furnishing the offspring of the wealthy with those qualities necessary to uphold their class domination. The children of the poor get scarcely a formal elementary training, and this, too, is mainly directed to such branches as tend to producing prejudices, arrogance and servility; in short, want of sense. The Church finally seeks to make complete idiots out of the mass and to make them forego the paradise on earth by promising a fictitious heaven. The capitalistic press, on the other hand, takes care of the confusion of spirits in public life. All these institutions, far from aiding in the education of the masses, have for their object the keeping in ignorance of the people. They are all in the pay and under the direct control of the capitalistic classes. The workers can therefore expect no help from any capitalistic party in their struggle against the existing system. They must achieve their liberation by their own efforts. As in former times a privileged class never surrendered its tyranny, neither can it be expected that the capitalists of this age will give up their rulership without being forced to do it.

If there ever could have been any question on this point it should long ago have been dispelled by the brutalities which the bourgeoisie of all countries—in America as well as in Europe—constantly commits, as often as the proletariat anywhere energetically move to better their condition. It becomes, therefore, self-evident that the struggle of the proletariat with the bourgeoisie must have a violent, revolutionary character.

We could show by scores of illustrations that all attempts in the past to reform this monstrous system by peaceable means, such as the ballot, have been futile, and all such efforts in the future must necessarily be so, for the following reasons:

The political institutions of our time are the agencies of the propertied class; their mission is the upholding of the privileges of their masters; any reform in your own behalf would curtail these privileges. To this they will not and cannot consent, for it would be suicidal to themselves.

That they will not resign their privileges voluntarily we know; that they will not make any concessions to us we likewise know. Since we must then rely upon the kindness of our masters for whatever redress we have, and knowing that from them no good may be expected, there remains but one recourse—FORCE! Our forefathers have not only told us that against despots force is justifiable, because it is the only means, but they themselves have set the immemorial example.

By force our ancestors liberated themselves from political oppression, by force their children will have to liberate themselves from economic bondage. "It is, therefore, your right, it is your duty," says Jefferson— "to arm!"

What we would achieve is, therefore, plainly and simply:

First:—Destruction of the existing class rule, by all means, i.e., by energetic, relentless, revolutionary and international action.

Second:—Establishment of a free society based upon co-operative organization of production.

Third:—Free exchange of equivalent products by and between the productive organizations without commerce and profit-mongery.

Fourth:—Organization of education on a secular, scientific and equal basis for both sexes.

Fifth:—Equal rights for all without distinction to sex or race.

Sixth:—Regulation of all public affairs by free contracts between the autonomous (independent) communes and associations, resting on a federalistic basis.

Whoever agrees with this ideal let him grasp our outstretched brother hands!

Proletarians of all countries, unite!

Fellow-workmen, all we need for the achievement of this great end is ORGANIZATION and UNITY!

There exists now no great obstacle to that unity. The work of peaceful education and revolutionary conspiracy well can and ought to run in parallel lines.

The day has come for solidarity. Join our ranks! Let the drum beat defiantly the roll of battle: "Workmen of all countries unite! You have nothing to lose but your chains; you have a world to win!"

Tremble, oppressors of the world! Not far beyond your purblind sight there dawns the scarlet and sable lights of the JUDGMENT DAY!

BIBLIOGRAPHY

Adamiak, Richard. "Marx, Engels and Duehring." *Journal of the History of Ideas* 35 (1974): 98-112.

Adamic, Louis. *Dynamite: The Story of Class Violence in America.* Rev. ed. 1934. Reprint. Gloucester, Mass.: Peter Smith, 1963.

Adler, Georg. *Geschichte der ersten sozial politischen Arbeiterbewegung in Deutschland.* 1885. Reprint. Frankfurt/M: Sauer, 1966.

Amerika (St. Louis), 27 April 1883.

"Anarchism and the Law." *Independent* 53 (1901): 2187-89.

Arbeiterzeitung (Chicago), 1882-1887 *passim*; 12 November 1895; 12 November 1896; 12 November 1900; 12 November 1904.

Arbeiterzeitung (Vienna), 20 March 1906.

Arndt, Karl J. R., and Olson, May E. *German-American Newspapers and Periodicals, 1732-1955.* Heidelberg: Quelle, 1961.

Ash, Roberta. *Social Movements in America.* Chicago: Markham, 1972.

Ashbaugh, Carolyn. *Lucy Parsons: American Revolutionary.* Chicago: Illinois Labor Historical Society, 1976.

Baginski, Max. "John Most." *di freye geselshaft* (Yiddish) 2 (1911): 129-39.

———. "John Most." *Mother Earth* 1 (1906): 17-20.

Baltimore American, 29 December 1890.

Barnard, Harry. *Eagle Forgotten: The Life of John Peter Altgeld.* Indianapolis: Bobbs, 1938.

Baskette Court Case No. 593: *Regina v. Most.* London: stenographic record, 1881.

Bax, E. Belfort. *Reminiscences and Reflexions of a Mid- and Late Victorian.* New York: Seltzer, 1920.

Bebel, August. *Aus meinem Leben.* 3 vols. Berlin: Dietz, 1946.

———. *Briefwechsel mit Friedrich Engels.* Edited by Werner Blumenberg. The Hague: Mouton, 1965.

Bell, Daniel. "The Background and Development of Marxian Socialism in the United States." In *Socialism and American Life*. Edited by Donald Drew Egbert and Stow Persons. Princeton: Princeton University Press, 1952.

Belli, Joseph. *Die rote Feldpost*. Berlin: Dietz, 1922.

Berkman, Alexander. *Prison Memoirs of an Anarchist*. 1912. Reprint. New York: Schocken, 1960.

————. "Vorwort" (in Rocker, q. v.).

————. *Nowhere at Home: Letters from Exile* (see Drinnon, Richard and Anna Maria).

Bernstein, Eduard. *Die Geschichte der Berliner Arbeiterbewegung, erster Teil*. Berlin: Buchhandlung Vorwärts, 1907.

————. *Sozialdemokratische Lehrjahre*. Berlin: Bücherkreis, 1928.

Bers, Günther. *Wilhelm Hasselmann*. Cologne: Einhorn, 1973.

Bismarck, Otto von. *Politische Reden*. 1894. Reprint. Aalen: Scientia, 1970.

Blankenagel, J. C. "Early Reception of Hauptmann's *Die Weber* in the United States." *Modern Language Notes* 68 (1953): 334-40.

Blitz, Samuel. Letter to Frederic Trautmann, 5 June 1976.

Boston Globe, 30 March 1891.

Brandis, Kurt. *Die deutsche Sozialdemokratie bis zum Fall des Sozialistengesetzes*. Leipzig: C. L. Hirschfeld, 1931.

Braunthal, Julius. *Victor und Friedrich Adler*. Vienna: Volksbuchhandlung, 1965.

Browne, Waldo R. *Altgeld of Illinois*. New York: Huebsch, 1924.

Brügel, Ludwig. *Geschichte der österreichischen Sozialdemokratie*. 5 vols. Vienna: Volksbuchhandlung, 1922.

Buchanan, Joseph R. *The Story of a Labor Agitator*. New York: Outlook, 1903.

Buchstein, Frederick J. "The Anarchist Press in American Journalism." *Journalism History* 1 (1974): 43-45.

Buffalo Express, 15 November 1895.

Cahan, Abraham. *The Education of Abraham Cahan*. Translated by Leon Stein, Abraham P. Cohen, and Lynn Davison. Philadelphia: Jewish Publication Society, 1969.

Carlson, Andrew R. *Anarchism in Germany: The Early Movement*. Metuchen, N. J.: Scarecrow, 1972.

Carlyle, Thomas. "Chartism." In vol. 29 of *The Works of Thomas Carlyle*. Centenary Edition. 30 vols. London: Chapman and Hall, 1895.

"The Celebrated Chicago Anarchists' Case: Spies v. People in the Supe-

rior Court of Illinois" (from *Western Reporter*, X), Rochester,
    N. Y.: Lawyers' Co-operative, n. d. [1887?].
Chicago Daily News, 15 May 1886.
Chicago Evening Post, 9 June 1894.
Chicago Graphic, 15 July 1893.
Chicago Herald, 5 May 1886.
Chicago Inter Ocean, 5, 6, 8 May, 21 August 1886.
Chicago Times, 30 May 1883; 6, 7, 8 May 1886.
Chicago Times-Herald, 16 April 1894; 12 November 1900.
Chicago Tribune, 18 March 1906.
Cincinnati Enquirer, 30 April 1883; 23 March 1890; 16, 17, 18, 21, 22
    March 1906.
Cincinnati Post, 16, 17, 20, 21 March 1906.
Cleveland Plain Dealer, 8, 9 June 1890; 18 November 1894.
Cohen, Morris Raphael. *A Dreamer's Journey.* Boston: Beacon, 1949.
Cole, G. D. H. *A History of Socialist Thought: Marxism and Anarchism.*
    London: Macmillan, 1957.
Conrad, Joseph. *The Secret Agent: A Simple Tale.* 1907. Reprint. Lon-
    don: Dent, 1947.
Court of Special Sessions, New York City 36, October 1901.
Crankshaw, Edward. *The Fall of the House of Habsburg.* New York:
    Viking, 1963.
Cross, Ira B. *A History of the Labor Movement in California.* Berkeley
    and Los Angeles: University of California Press, 1935.
David, Henry. *The History of the Haymarket Affair.* 2d ed. New York:
    Russell, 1958.
Dawson, William Harbutt. *German Socialism and Ferdinand Lassalle.*
    London: Swan, 1888.
Denver Times, 21 May, 4 June 1884.
Derecheff, Ralph. "Anarchism in England" (in Dubois, q. v.).
Destler, Chester M. *American Radicalism, 1865-1901: Essays and Docu-
    ments.* 1946. Reprint. New York: Quadrangle Paperback, 1966.
Detroit Free Press, 27 May 1883.
Diamant, Alfred. "Johann Most: American Anarchist." *Indiana Quar-
    terly for Bookmen* 3 (1947): 71-83.
Dictionary of American Biography, s. v. "Most, Johann Joseph."
Drahn, Ernst. *Johann Most: Eine Bio-Bibliographie.* Berlin: Prager,
    1925.
Drinnon, Richard. *Rebel in Paradise: A Biography of Emma Goldman.*
    Chicago: University of Chicago Press, 1961.
————, and Drinnon, Anna Maria, eds. *Nowhere at Home: Letters*

from Exile of Emma Goldman and Alexander Berkman. New York: Schocken, 1975.

Dubois, Félix. *The Anarchist Peril.* Edited and translated by Ralph Derecheff. London: T. Fisher Unwin, 1894.

Dulles, Foster Rhea. *Labor in America.* 3rd ed. New York: Crowell, 1966.

Ely, Richard T. *The Labor Movement in America.* 1886. Reprint. New York: Arno, 1969.

Engels (see Marx).

Faust, Albert Bernhardt. *The German Element in the United States.* 2 vols. New York: Steuben Society, 1927.

Fine, Sidney. "Anarchism and the Assassination of McKinley." *American Historical Review* 60 (1955): 777-99.

Foner, Philip S., ed. *Autobiographies of the Haymarket Martyrs.* New York: Humanities Press, 1969.

Frank, Walter. *Hofprediger Adolf Stoecker.* Berlin: Hobbing, 1928.

Franklin Club (later the Liberty Association) of Cleveland. Records. Western Reserve Historical Society. Ms. 445.

Freie Presse (Berlin), 1876-1878 *passim.*

Freiheit (London 1879-1882; Schaffhausen, Switzerland, 1882; New York, N. Y., 1882-1897; Buffalo, N. Y., 1897-1898; New York, N.Y., 1898-1909).

Fricke, Dieter. *Die deutsche Arbeiterbewegung, 1869-1890.* Leipzig: Enzyklopädie Verlag, 1964.

Fried, Albert. *Socialism in America.* Garden City, N. Y.: Doubleday, 1970.

Gary, Joseph E. "The Chicago Anarchists of 1886: The Crime, the Trial, the Punishment." *Century* 45 (1893): 803-37.

Ginger, Ray. *Altgeld's America.* New York: Funk, 1958.

Goldman, Emma. "Johann Most." *American Mercury* 8, June 1926, pp. 158-66.

———. *Living My Life.* New York: Knopf, 1934.

———. *Nowhere at Home: Letters from Exile* (see Drinnon, Richard and Anna Maria).

Gompers, Samuel. *Seventy Years of Life and Labor.* 2 vols. New York: Dutton, 1925.

Harris, Frank. *The Bomb.* 1909. Reprint. Chicago: University of Chicago Press, 1963.

Havel, Hippolyte. "Anarchists: John Most—The Stormy Petrel." *Man!* 2 (January 1934): 5.

Heilmann, Ernst. *Geschichte der Arbeiterbewegung in Chemnitz und dem Erzgebirge.* Chemnitz: Sozialdemokratischer Verein, n. d. [1910?].

Hellfaier, Karl-Alexander. *Die deutsche Sozialdemokratie während des Sozialistengesetzes.* Berlin: Verlag der Wissenschaften, 1958.

Henderson, W. O. *The Life of Friedrich Engels.* 2 vols. London: Cass, 1976.

Herrick, Robert. *The Memoirs of an American Citizen.* 1905. Reprint. Edited by Daniel Aaron. Cambridge, Mass.: Harvard University Press, 1963.

Hillquit, Morris. *History of Socialism in the United States.* 5th ed. New York: Funk, 1910.

————. *Loose Leaves from a Busy Life.* New York: Macmillan, 1934.

Höhn, Reinhard, ed. *Die vaterlandslosen Gesellen: Der Sozialismus im Licht der Geheimberichte der preussischen Polizei.* Cologne: Westdeutscher Verlag, 1964.

Hofstadter, Richard, and Wallace, Michael. *American Violence: A Documentary History.* New York: Knopf, 1970.

Howe, Irving. *World of Our Fathers.* New York: Harcourt, 1976.

Huneker, James Gibbons. *Steeplejack.* 2 vols. New York: Scribner's, 1920.

Hunter, Robert. *Violence and the Labour Movement.* London: Routledge, 1916.

Indianapolis News, 19 November 1904.

Institut für Marxismus-Leninismus. *Geschichte der deutschen Arbeiterbewegung.* Vol. 1. Berlin: Dietz, 1966.

James, Henry. *The Princess Casamassima.* 1886. Reprint. New York: Scribners, 1908.

Joll, James. *The Anarchists.* Boston: Little, Brown, 1964.

Jones, Mary Harris. *Autobiography of Mother Jones.* Chicago: Kerr, 1925.

Kahan, Yosef. *di yiddish-anarkhistishe bavegung in amerika: historisher iberblik un perzenlikhe iberlebungen* (Yiddish). 1905. Jubilee Issue. Philadelphia: Radical Library Branch 273, Workmen's Circle, 1945.

Kautsky, Karl. *Aus der Früzeit des Marxismus: Engels Briefwechsel mit Kautsky.* Prague. Orbis, 1935.

————. *Erinnerungen und Erörterungen.* Edited by Benedikt Kautsky. The Hague: Mouton, 1960.

————. "Johann Most." *Gesellschaft: Internationale Revue für Sozialismus und Politik* 1 (1924): 545-64.

Kedward, Roderick. *The Anarchists: The Men Who Shocked an Era.*
London: BPC Unit 75, 1971.

Kitz, Frank. "Recollections and Reflections." *Freedom* (London) 26
(1912): 2, 10, 18, 26, 34, 42.

Kropotkin, Peter. *Memoirs of a Revolutionist.* Boston: Houghton, 1899.

Kühn, Dieter, ed. *Johann Most: Ein Sozialist in Deutschland.* Munich:
Hanser, 1974.

Künzel, Johann Heinrich. *Der erste Hochverratsprozess vor dem Reichs-
gericht.* Leipzig: Max Hesse, 1881.

Laidler, Harry W. *Social-Economic Movements.* New York: Crowell,
1945.

Landauer, Carl. *European Socialism.* Vol. 1. Berkeley and Los Angeles:
University of California Press, 1959.

Laqueur, Walter. *Guerrilla: A Historical and Critical Study.* Boston:
Little, Brown, 1976.

————. *The Guerrilla Reader: A Historical Anthology.* Philadelphia:
Temple University Press, 1977.

————. *Terrorism.* Boston: Little, Brown, 1977.

————. *The Terrorism Reader: A Historical Anthology.* Philadelphia:
Temple University Press, 1978.

Latouche, Peter. *Anarchy! An Authentic Exposition of the Methods of
Anarchists and the Aims of Anarchism.* London: Everett, 1908.

Lens, Sidney. *The Labor Wars.* Garden City, N. Y.: Doubleday, 1976.

————. *Radicalism in America.* New York: Crowell, 1966.

Liberty (Boston), 27 March 1886.

Lichtheim, George. *A Short History of Socialism.* New York: Praeger,
1970.

Lidtke, Vernon L. *The Outlawed Party: Social Democracy in Germany,
1878-1890.* Princeton: Princeton University Press, 1966.

Liebknecht, Wilhelm. *Briefwechsel mit deutschen Sozialdemokraten.*
Edited by Georg Eckert. Assen: Van Gorcum, 1973.

————. *Briefwechsel mit Karl Marx und Friedrich Engels.* Edited by
Georg Eckert. The Hague: Mouton, 1963.

Linse, Ulrich. *Organisierter Anarchismus im deutschen Kaiserreich von
1871.* Berlin: Duncker, 1969.

Lloyd, Caroline. *Henry Demarest Lloyd, 1847-1903.* New York: Putnam's, 1912.

Lombroso, Cesare. "Illustrative Studies in Criminal Anthropology: The
Physiognomy of Anarchists." *Monist* 1 (1891): 336-42.

Louisville Courier-Journal, 10 January 1883.

Lum, Dyer D. *A Concise History of the Great Trial of the Chicago*

Anarchists in 1886. Chicago: Socialistic Publishing Co., n. d. [1886?].

Macartney, C. A. *The Habsburg Empire, 1790-1918.* New York: Macmillan, 1969.

Martin, James J. *Men Against the State: The Expositors of Individualist Anarchism in America, 1827-1908.* New York: Libertarian Book Club, 1957.

Marx, Karl, and Engels, Friedrich. *Werke.* Edited by the Institut für Marxismus-Leninismus. Vols. 34-36. Berlin: Dietz, 1966.

Mayer, Gustav. *Friedrich Engels.* Translated by Gilbert and Helen Highet. New York: Knopf, 1936.

Mehring, Franz. *Die deutsche Socialdemokratie: Ihre Geschichte und ihre Lehre.* 3rd ed. Bremen: Schunemanns Verlag, 1879.

———. *Geschichte der Deutschen Sozialdemokratie.* 11th ed. 4 vols. Stuttgart: Dietz, 1921.

Miller, Martin A. *Kropotkin.* Chicago: University of Chicago Press, 1976.

Milwaukee Daily News, 11 November 1895.

Milwaukee Sentinel, 3, 4, 6, 8 January 1883; 27 May 1884.

Morris, William. *Letters.* Edited by Philip Henderson. London: Longmans, 1950.

Most, Johann. *Acht Jahre hinter Schloss und Riegel: Skizzen aus dem Leben Johann Mosts von Anonymus Veritas.* 2d ed. New York: Johann Most, 1887.

———, and Grottkau, Paul. *Anarchismus oder Communismus?* Chicago: Central-Comite der Chicagoer Gruppen der I.A.A., 1884.

———. *August Reinsdorf und die Propaganda der That.* New York: Selbstverlage des Verfassers, 1885.

———. *Die Bastille am Plötzensee: Blätter aus meinem gefängniss Tagebuch.* 2d ed. Braunschweig: Bracke, 1876.

———. *Betrachtungen über den Normal-Arbeitstag: Ein ernstes Wort an die Arbeiter von Chemnitz und Umgebung.* Chemnitz: Selbstverlag des Verfassers, 1871.

———. *Freiheit* (London, 1879-1882; Schaffhausen, Switzerland, 1882; New York, N. Y., 1882-1897; Buffalo, N. Y., 1897-1898; New York, N. Y., 1898-1909).

———. "Freiheit." *Freiheit* 1896: July 18, 25, Aug. 1, 6, 15, 29, Sept. 5, 19.

———. *Zum Genossenschaftswesen.* 2d ed. Dresden: Klemichs Verlag, 1877.

———. *Internationale Bibliothek.* New York: Müller, 1883-1890. "An

das Proletariat," 1883; "Die Gottespest und die Religionsseuche,"
1883; "Die Freie Gesellschaft," 1887; "Die Eigentumsbestie,"
1887; "Die Hölle von Blackwells Island," 1887; "Zwischen Galgen und Zuchthaus," 1887; "Die Anarchie," 1888; "Der Narrenthurm," 1888; "Vive la Commune," 1888; "Der Stimmkasten,"
1888; "Der kommunistische Anarchismus," 1889; "Unsere Stellung in der Arbeiterbewegung," 1890.

————. *Kapital und Arbeit: "Das Kapital" in einer handlichen Zusammenfassung.* 1876. Reprint. Edited by Hans Magnus Enzensberger. Frankfurt/M: Suhrkamp, 1972.

————. *Der Kleinbürger und die Socialdemokratie.* Augsburg: Endres,
1876.

————. "Kunst und Wissenschaft der Gegenwart." *Oesterreichischer
Arbeiter-Kalender.* Vienna: Schwarzinger, 1878.

————. *Die Lösung der socialen Frage: Ein Vortrag, gehalten vor Berliner Arbeitern.* Berlin: Allgemeinen deutschen Associations-
Buchdruckerei, 1876.

————. *Memoiren.* 4 vols. New York: Johann Most, 1903 (I, II), 1905
(III), 1907 (IV).

————. *Offener Brief an die Wähler des 5. Berliner Reichstagswahlkreis.* London: Johann Most, n. d.

————. *Die Pariser Commune vor den Berliner Gerichten.* Braunschweig: Bracke, 1875.

————. *Proletarier-Liederbuch.* Edited by Gustav Geilhof. Chemnitz:
Genossenschafts Buchdruckerei, 1875.

————. "Reminiscenzen und Reflexionen eines 'Ex-Convicts.' " *Freiheit*
1903: April 25, May 2, 9, 16, 23, 29.

————. *Revolutionaere Kriegswissenschaft: Ein Handbuchlein zur Anleitung betreffend Gebrauches und Herstellung von Nitro-Glyzerin, Dynamit, Schiessbaumwolle, Knallquecksilber, Bomben,
Brandsaetzen, Giften u. s. w.* 3rd ed. New York: Johann Most,
1885.

————. "Die Scheune." *Oesterreichischer Arbeiter-Kalender.* Vienna:
Klinger, 1877.

————. *Die socialen Bewegungen im alten Rom und der Cäsarismus.*
Allgemeinen deutschen Associations-Buchdruckerei, 1878.

————. *Sturmvögel: Sammlung von Gedichten.* New York: Johann
Most, 1888.

————. *"Taktik" contra "Freiheit."* London: Freiheit, n. d. [1880?].

————. "Utopien." *Oesterreichischer Arbeiter-Kalender.* Vienna:
Klinger, 1876.

————. *Why I Am a Communist.* New York: Twentieth Century, 1892.

Muñoz, V. "Una cronologia de Johann Most." *Reconstruir: Revista Libertaria* (Buenos Aires) 55 (July/August 1968): 34-40.

Neidle, Cecyle. "Johann Most." In *Great Immigrants* by Cecyle Neidle. New York: Twayne, 1973.

Nettlau, Max. *Geschichte der Anarchie.* Vol. 3: *Anarchisten und Sozialrevolutionäre.* 1931. Reprint. Glashütten im Taunus: Auvermann, 1972.

————. "John Most." *Freedom* (London) 20 (1906): 9-10, 13-14, 18-19.

New York Herald, 18, 19 March 1906.

New York Sun, 3 May 1886.

New York Times, 1882-1906.

New York Tribune, 9 May, 13 October, 10 November 1896; 26 May, 2 June 1901; 18, 19 March 1906.

New York World, 24 April 1886; 13 November 1887.

Nold, Carl. "Fifty Years Ago." *Man!* 2 (January 1934): 5.

Nomad, Max. "The Preacher: Johann Most, Terrorist of the Word." In *Apostles of the Revolution* by Max Nomad. Boston: Little, Brown, 1939.

Oberholtzer, Ellis Paxson. *A History of the United States.* Vol. 4. New York: Macmillan, 1931.

Osterroth, Franz. *Chronik der deutschen Sozialdemokratie.* Hannover: Dietz, 1963.

Pack, Wolfgang. *Das parliamentarische Ringen um das Sozialistengesetz Bismarcks.* Düsseldorf: Droste, 1961.

Parry, Albert. *Terrorism: From Robespierre to Arafat.* New York: Vanguard, 1976.

Parsons, A. R. *Anarchism: Its Philosophy and Scientific Basis.* Chicago: Mrs. A. R. Parsons, 1887.

Peck, Harry Thurston. *Twenty Years of the Republic, 1885-1905.* New York: Dodd, 1926.

People v. Most 171 N. Y. 423 (1902).

————. 71 App. Div. N. Y. 160 (1902).

————. 16 N.Y. Crim Reports (1903).

Perlman, Selig. "Upheaval and Reorganization." In *History of Labor in the United States.* Edited by John R. Commons. Vol. 2. New York: Macmillan, 1921.

Peukert, Josef. *Erinnerungen.* Berlin: Verlag des sozialistischen Bundes, 1913.

Philadelphia Bulletin, 16 October 1883.

Philadelphia Inquirer, 18 March 1906.

Pinson, Koppel S. *Modern Germany: Its History and Civilization.* New York: Macmillan, 1966.

Pittsburgh Commercial Gazette, 13, 15, 16, 17 October 1883.

Pittsburgh Post. 19 November 1894; 16 November 1895.

Portland (Ore.) *Evening Telegram,* 1 February 1900.

Powderly, Terence V. "The Army of the Discontented." *North American Review,* April 1885, pp. 369-77.

————. *The Path I Trod.* Edited by Harry J. Carman. New York: Columbia University Press, 1940.

————. *Thirty Years of Labor.* 1890. Reprint. New York: Kelley, 1967.

Pratt, Norma Fain. *Morris Hillquit: A Political History of an American Jewish Socialist.* Westport, Conn., and London, England: Greenwood Press, 1979.

Protokoll des Kongresses der deutschen Sozialdemokratie. Zurich: n. p., 1880.

Quint, Howard H. *The Forging of American Socialism.* Columbia: University of South Carolina Press, 1953.

Rayback, Joseph G. *A History of American Labor.* New York: Free Press, 1966.

Reichert, William O. *Partisans of Freedom: A Study in American Anarchism.* Bowling Green, Ohio: Popular Press, 1976.

Rhodes, James Ford. *History of the United States.* Vol. 8. New York: Macmillan, 1920.

Rocker, Rudolf. *Johann Most: Das Leben eines Rebellen.* Berlin: "Der Syndikalist," Fritz Kater, 1924.

Roosevelt, Theodore. *Autobiography.* New York: Macmillan, 1914.

————. *Letters.* Vol. 3. Edited by Elting E. Morison. Cambridge, Mass.: Harvard University Press, 1951.

Roth, Guenther. *The Social Democrats in Imperial Germany.* Totowa, N. J.: Bedminster, 1963.

Runkle, Gerald. *Anarchism Old and New.* New York: Delacorte, 1972.

Russell, Bertrand. *German Social Democracy.* 1896. Reprint. New York: Simon & Schuster, 1966.

————. *Proposed Roads to Freedom: Socialism, Anarchism, Syndicalism.* New York: Holt, 1919.

St. Joseph (Mo.) *Gazette,* 15 May 1883.

St. Louis Post-Dispatch, 5 May 1883.

St. Louis Republican, 5 May 1883; 28 December 1904; 18 March 1906.

Sandburg, Carl. *Always the Young Strangers.* New York: Harcourt, 1952.

San Francisco Post, 12 January 1900.

Sartorius, A. (Freiherr von Waltershausen). *Der moderne Socialismus in den Vereinigten Staaten von Amerika.* Berlin: Bahr, 1890.

Scheu, Andreas. *Umsturzkeime: Erlebnisse eines Kampfers.* 3 vols. Vienna: Volksbuchhandlung, 1923.

Scheu, Heinrich, ed. *Der Wiener Hochverratsprozess.* Vienna: Volksbuchhandlung, 1870.

Schneidt, Karl. "Vom jungen Anarchismus." *Die Kritik* (Berlin) 3 (1896): 583-92, 621-32, 665-77, 717-21, 767-76.

Schröder, Wilhelm, ed. *Handbuch der sozialdemokratischen Parteitage.* 1910. Reprint. Leipzig: Zentralantiquariat, 1971.

Schurz, Carl. "Murder as a Political Agency." *Harper's Weekly* 41 (1897): 847.

Seattle Daily Times, 28 January, 3 February 1900.

Shannon, Fred A. *Centennial Years: America from the Late 1870s to the Early 1890s.* Garden City, N. Y.: Doubleday, 1967.

Sombart, Werner, *Socialism and the Social Movement.* Translated by M. Epstein. London: Dent, 1909.

Sozialdemokrat (Zurich), 1879-1881 *passim*.

Spies, August. *Autobiography; His Speech in Court, and General Notes.* . . . Chicago: Nina van Zandt, 1887.

Staatsarchiv Potsdam. Rep. 30. Berlin C Polizeipräsidium. No. 8720, 8721, 9892.

Steinberg, Hans-Josef. *Sozialismus und deutsche Sozialdemokratie.* Hannover: Verlag für Literatur und Zeitgeschehen, 1967.

Steiner, Herbert. *Die Arbeiterbewegung Österreichs, 1867-1889.* Vienna: Europa, 1964.

Stern, Leo. *Der Kampf der deutschen Sozialdemokratie in der Zeit des Sozialistengesetzes.* 2 vols. Berlin: Rütten and Loening, 1956.

Strauss, Rudolf, and Finsterbusch, Kurt. *Die Chemnitzer Arbeiterbewegung unter dem Sozialistengesetz.* Berlin: Tribüne, 1954.

Symes, Lillian, and Clement, Travers. *Rebel America.* New York: Harper, 1934.

Tageblatt (Vienna), 6 July 1870.

Tannenbaum, Edward R. *1900: The Generation Before the Great War.* New York: Anchor Press/Doubleday, 1976.

Tarbell, Ida M. *The Nationalizing of American Business.* New York: Macmillan, 1936.

Taylor, A. J. P. *The Habsburg Monarchy, 1809-1918: A History of the Austrian Empire and Austria-Hungary*. New York: Harper, 1965.

Tilley, W. H. *The Background of The Princess Casamassima*. Gainesville: University of Florida Press, 1961.

Times (London), 1, 8 April, 6 May 1881; 8, 18 May, 6 June 1882.

Trilling, Lionel. "The Princess Casamassima." In *The Liberal Imagination* by Lionel Trilling. New York: Macmillan, 1948.

Truth (San Francisco), 1882-1884 *passim*.

Tuchman, Barbara W. *The Proud Tower: A Portrait of the World Before the War*. New York: Macmillan, 1966.

Tucker, Benjamin. *Instead of a Book*. 1897. Reprint. New York: Hastings, 1969.

U. S. Bureau of the Census. *Historical Statistics*. Washington: Government Printing Office, 1975.

Vizetelley, Ernest Alfred. *The Anarchists*. London: John Lane, 1921.

Volkszeitung (New York), 24 May 1886; 31 August, 8 September 1897; 14, 28 September, 15 October 1901.

Vorbote (Chicago), 21, 28 May, 25 June, 2 July 1884; 25 February 1885.

Ware, Norman J. *The Labor Movement in the United States, 1860-1895*. 1929. Reprint. Gloucester, Mass.: Peter Smith, 1959.

Washington Evening Star, 18, 21 April 1883.

Washington Post, 19 April 1883.

Weckerle, Eduard. *Hermann Greulich*. Zurich: Gutenberg, 1947.

Weidner, Albert. *Aus den Tiefen der Berliner Arbeiterbewegung*. Berlin: Seemann, 1905.

Weinstein, Gregory. *The Ardent Eighties*. New York: International Press, 1928.

Woodcock, George. *Anarchism: A History of Libertarian Ideas and Movements*. New York: World, 1962.

————, and Avakumovic, Ivan. *The Anarchist Prince: A Biographical Study of Peter Kropotkin*. London: Boardman, 1950.

Young, Art. *On My Way*. New York: Liveright, 1928.

Zeitung (Cincinnati), 13 November 1899.

Zenker, E. V. *Anarchism*. New York: Putnam's, 1897.

INDEX

ABOUT THE AUTHOR

Frederic Trautmann is Assistant Professor of Speech at Temple University in Philadelphia. His many articles have appeared in journals such as *The New England Quarterly* and *Pennsylvania History.*

Recent Titles in
Contributions in Political Science
Series Editor: Bernard K. Johnpoll

Unequal Americans: Practices and Politics of Intergroup Relations
John Slawson

The Constitution of Silence: Essays on Generational Themes
Marvin Rintala

International Conflict in an American City: Boston's Irish, Italians,
and Jews, 1935-1944.
John F. Stack, Jr.

The Fall and Rise of the Pentagon: American Defense Policies in the
1970s
Lawrence J. Korb

Calling a Truce to Terror: The American Response to International
Terrorism
Ernest Evans

Spain in the Twentieth Century World: Essays on Spanish Diplomacy,
1898-1978
James W. Cortada

From Rationality to Liberation: The Evolution of Feminist Ideology
Judith A. Sabrosky

Truman's Crises: A Political Biography of Harry S. Truman
Harold F. Gosnell

"Bigotry!": Ethnic, Machine, and Sexual Politics in a Senatorial
Election
Maria J. Falco

Furious Fancies: American Political Thought in the Post-Liberal Era
Philip Abbott

Politicians, Judges, and the People: A Study in Citizens' Participation
Charles H. Sheldon and Frank P. Weaver

The European Parliament: The Three-Decade Search for a United
Europe
Paula Scalingi

Presidential Primaries: Road to the White House
James W. Davis